THE
LITTLE BOOK OF
READING FC

THE
LITTLE BOOK OF
READING FC

ALAN SEDUNARY

breedon **books**
PUBLISHING

First published in Great Britain in 2008 by
The Breedon Books Publishing Company Limited
Breedon House, 3 The Parker Centre,
Derby, DE21 4SZ.

A catalogue record for this book is available from the British Library.

ISBN 978-1-85983-658-3

Printed and bound by TJ International Ltd, Padstow, Cornwall.

CONTENTS

ACKNOWLEDGEMENTS

No publication of this nature could ever be the sole effort of just one person and so many people, too many to mention, have contributed, often unknowingly, to this book. However, the contribution of some cannot go without acknowledgement or thanks. These include:

Nigel 'Strap' Meek and his *Ultimate Reading FC Database* for the numerous unusual and increasingly bizarre facts and figures that feature throughout this book.

David Downs for his proofreading skills that combine an unrivalled knowledge of all things Reading-related with a position as head of the grammar police! With his help there are fewer mistakes in the final draft than there would have been.

The sports editors of the *Reading Chronicle* and *Reading Evening Post* for the consistently high standard of coverage of all aspects of Reading FC that has been a constant source of facts and stories included in this book. In addition, their support for previous publications has been much appreciated.

The numerous editors of the Reading matchday programme for encouraging, or at least putting up with, some of my increasingly strange articles, the facts from many of which have made their way into this book.

The late Peter Baxter, an inspiration for all interested in the statistical side of Reading Football Club, whose meticulous records remain in constant use to this day.

And finally to my wife Sonia for her support, despite the fact that her interest in football can be gauged by the knowledge that the last game she attended was in 1988; mind you, it was the Simod Cup Final!

INTRODUCTION

With 137 years of history to its credit, Reading Football Club has been involved in a wealth of unusual, strange and downright bizarre events, many of which are featured in the following pages.

Reading may not be able to boast the rich European heritage of, say, Liverpool but they have had their moments. *The Little Book of Reading FC* reveals how Reading have beaten European Champion nations plus two World Cup-winning countries, as well as notching up a 5–0 away win over AC Milan which led to the Berkshire Club being described as the finest foreign team seen in Italy. On the other hand, the book lists a series of Club 'bests' that even includes Reading's six best defeats. Similarly, Reading may not have fielded teams of world-famous players Manchester United or Chelsea have, but they can boast names ranging from three Olympic Gold medallists, to a Premier League star once described as half-man, half-goose and a player who was named man of the match in a game in which he never even played.

Alongside the footballing greats who have played for Reading, world famous names such as **George Best** and **Matt Busby**, or those who are only revered within the borders of Berkshire, the book also includes a host of well-known names who, although not normally connected with football, have featured in Reading's colourful history. Consequently, 'personalities' ranging from Oscar Wilde to Ernie Wise, Phil Collins to Joe Louis and Keira Knightley to the Kray Twins all have their links with Reading Football Club revealed.

These famous names find themselves alongside tales of goalscoring nuns, football-hating horses, some very strange injuries, the record scorer whose transfer fee was 32 years late in payment and the Reading player whose sending off resulted in suspension – for the referee. Also revealed are world records set at the Club's various grounds, which involve Guinness and Latvia, although, admittedly, not for the same record. And, talking of records, there is a special, if slightly bizarre, tribute to Reading's 2005–06 record-breaking Championship-winning squad.

Although Reading may have lost their Premier League status for the time being (you will need to read the book to find out why Wrexham's demotion to the Conference last season 'guaranteed' Reading an immediate return to the top flight!) the Club is still in a stronger position than at almost any time in its long history. That is emphasised by my 'career' as a contributor to the Club programme. My first article appeared 36 years ago for a Fourth Division game against Exeter City that attracted 4,138 fans. The last article I wrote before this book was completed in the summer was against Tottenham Hotspur, a game that attracted almost exactly 20,000 more fans than that game against Exeter.

Over the years Reading fans have endured more low spots than national successes, but that has made the triumphs all the more sweet. It has also enabled the Club's supporters to develop a self-depreciating sense of humour that has stood them in good stead. Hopefully, some of the stories within *The Little Book of Reading FC* will keep them, and all fans interested in football's more unusual tales, smiling until the next success on the pitch comes along.

Alan Sedunary

August 2008

ONE – A QUESTION OF SPORT

When Reading Football Club became a limited company in August 1897, part of the constitution stipulated, rather obviously, that 'The primary business of Reading Football Club is the holding of football matches'. It then went on to allow 'cricket, tennis, bicycle or running' plus 'gymnastics, bowling, golf, croquet, athletics or any other sports or pastimes which the directors might promote.' Over the years the directors have used those extended powers to their fullest with a wide range of sports, popular or obscure, being staged at the Club's grounds.

A GAME FOR ROUGH GIRLS *
(* From a quote by Reading's most famous resident Oscar Wilde – 'Football is all very well as a game for rough girls but it is hardly suitable for delicate boys.')

Almost immediately after Reading's constitution was drafted, the Club's Victorian directors were approached to stage that most controversial of sports at that time, ladies' football. The wonderfully named Nettie Honeyball, secretary of the British Ladies' Football Club, contacted the board to see if they could stage a match at Elm Park. Ladies' football, as it was called in those Victorian days, was frowned upon by the footballing establishment and the directors advised Nettie that there were no dates available, although they did find time to stage a game between the board of directors and the local press.

MIXED MESSAGE
It took over 20 years and a world war for women to finally play at Elm Park, and even then the game was a highly unofficial match, the FA Council having banned 'ladies' teams' back in 1902. This game, played in September 1917, was even more unusual as it was a mixed game between the nurses of Bearwood Hospital and convalescing Canadian soldiers. In probably the strangest match ever staged in Reading, the men's physical advantage was offset by the fact that they had to play with their hands tied behind their backs. This clearly evened out any such advantage the soldiers may have had because the nurses won 8–5, with Miss Barrell earning the 'Man' of the Match award, thanks to a hat-trick. Even without their hands tied behind their backs it was unlikely that the men would have misbehaved since the game was refereed by Colonel Mayus, the director of bayonet fighting and physical training. Despite atrocious weather, the game raised £161 for war charities, far more than several all-male games staged around the same time.

GIRLS ALLOWED
By the early 1920s ladies' football was proving to be a big draw, with the famous Dick Kerr's Ladies once drawing 60,000 to Everton's Goodison Park. In late 1921

this most famous of ladies' teams approached Reading to play a fixture at Elm Park but, despite the attraction of the team, their financial demands were too high and Reading had to decline the offer. However, this inspired the formation of a team in Reading for the specific purpose of raising funds for popular centre forward **Joe Bailey**'s testimonial. On Good Friday 1921 a crowd of 9,000, well above Elm Park's average for Reading's League games, saw the Reading Ladies beat their Swindon counterparts 7–0. Many of the ladies' sides of that era were 'works teams', even Harrods had their own ladies' football XI, and most of the Reading team worked for the town's main employer, Huntley and Palmers. As with the mixed game in 1917, this match raised considerably more than Joe's official benefit game, swelling the fund by £362. A rematch in Swindon again saw Reading win, this time 5–0, and a third game was staged on 16 May as part of Reading Football Club's annual fête in nearby Prospect Park. This game attracted a huge crowd, estimated at 20,000, and it proved difficult to clear the pitch. In the end the game went ahead on a small sized pitch, but this did not affect the Reading team who completed a hat-trick of victories with a goal described, slightly patronisingly by the *Berkshire Chronicle*, as 'a humorous affair, the Reading centre forward bustling the Swindon goalkeeper into the net, ball and all, from a well-placed corner.'

The FA soon imposed a ban on women's football on Club grounds, and it was another 50 years before they relented. Several teams were formed in affiliation with League Clubs and in October 1970 Reading joined the growing list. Formed by Ann Bell, wife of Reading forward Terry, and centre half **Stuart Morgan**'s fiancée Jan Stockdale, the team played a practice match against another fledgling offshoot of the football Club, the Supporters' Club team. Unlike the mixed game of 1917, there was no need to protect the ladies from their male opponents; with Club hard-man Morgan refereeing the match no one was ever going to step out of line! As it was, an honourable draw resulted, with Ann Bell proving the star by scoring both her team's goals. Later in the month Reading Ladies played their first official game, losing 5–1 to QPR but raising over £100 for Dr Barnardo's Homes. Gradually, the players' wives withdrew and the Club grew to be one of the leading women's teams in the South. They did hit the headlines in 1992 when it was revealed that their star striker, Martine Hewitt, had celebrated being the Women's Southern League top scorer with 50 goals by having a sex-change operation and becoming Paul Hewitt.

LADIES FIRST

The FA's gradual acceptance of women's football saw international matches begin to take place, and on 9 November 1973 Elm Park staged the very first women's international football match on a League ground. England beat their Dutch opponents 1–0, the winner being a powerful long-range shot by a cousin of Manchester United's Pat Crerrand, who had previously been a novice nun. Some 10 years later Elm Park was host to a UEFA match against the Republic of Ireland and, again, England were the winners, scoring six goals without reply.

STICKY WICKET

Traditionally, footballers played cricket in the summer until the two seasons overlapped to such an extent that it was no longer possible. In 1921 Reading went one step further, renting Elm Park to the Seven Bridges Cricket Club for the summer. This proved to be a short-lived arrangement, but through the years the players have formed ad-hoc teams to play charity matches, and in the mid-1930s this led to the unusual sight of a team of footballers playing cricket at the town's greyhound stadium.

GUNNERS OUTGUNNED

Another cricket match, in August 1947, provided Reading with something of a sporting rarity for the Club, as they beat Arsenal. Scoring 175 all out, thanks to 77 from their manager, former Hampshire cricketer and Arsenal forward **Ted Drake**, Reading bowled out the Gunners for 107. The damage was done by winger **Freddy Fisher**, with 3–34, and another former Arsenal player, **Les Henley**, who took the other seven wickets for 44 runs.

THE ROYAL CRICKETERS

In the days when the two sports had defined seasons, Reading had several top-class cricketers and the following 'XI' excelled at both sports:

Shaka Hislop: One of Reading's greatest goalkeepers, Shaka played in the same school cricket team in Trinidad as West Indies cricket captain Brian Lara.

Martin Booty: He chose an apprenticeship at Coventry City over a groundstaff place with Leicestershire Cricket Club, and subsequently spent three years with Reading at the end of the last millennium.

Len Vallard: Len once scored five sixes and a four in one over, leading to him being named *Reading Evening Post* Cricketer of the Month for May 1974, some 12 years after he had enjoyed a four-year spell at Elm Park.

Joe North: On the playing staff at Lords, Joe later became a minor League umpire. He had insisted that he be allowed to continue his cricketing role before he agreed to sign for Reading in 1922.

Albert Hayhurst: His seven appearances for Warwickshire in 1934 as a medium-fast bowler are overshadowed by the 220 League games he played for Reading up to 1939.

Gordon Brice: A great defender, Gordon once made 148 consecutive appearances for Reading before he took 72 wickets for Northamptonshire as a medium-fast bowler.

Dennis Watkin: A goalscoring winger who also replaced the injured Harold Larwood at Northamptonshire, his best figures being 6–48.

Tom Dollery: Tom is the captain and undoubted star of this fictional Reading team, even though he only played one League game for his home-town Club in 1936, before concentrating on his cricketing career. Tom scored over 24,000 runs for Warwickshire, including 50 centuries. He won four test caps and in 1949–50 became the first professional to captain his team to the County Championship title when Warwickshire won the trophy.

Ron Tindall: Rob controversially chose cricket over Reading and, as a result, never played football for the Club after Easter. As a cricketer he took over 150 wickets and averaged 25 runs for Surrey.

Fred Gamble: Fred quit Reading after one season in 1933–34 to become another Surrey cricketer who, as a medium-paced bowler, took 40 wickets in 1934.

Horace Fielding: Scored consecutive centuries in local cricket, winning a bat as the local Cricketer of the Week. He also scored regularly for Reading, leaving Elm Park in 1937 with 42 goals in 152 games.

This team would be managed by Ted Drake, who played 15 games for Hampshire over a six-year period, while appearing for Southampton and then Arsenal in the winter.

FUNNY-SHAPED BALLS

The Madejski Stadium has been a regular venue for rugby union with first Richmond and now London Irish as tenants. However, it is over 80 years since Elm Park staged its first rugby match. On 24 January 1922 Berkshire Wanderers played, coincidentally, Richmond at Elm Park. Despite the fact that torrential rain kept the Wednesday afternoon crowd down, the event was such a success that the Wanderers approached the football Club to play regularly at Elm Park. Although the board turned down this suggestion, they did allow them to play a game against Thames Valley in aid of charity the following year. As well as Clubs using Reading's grounds, the Tetley Cup staged a double-header at the Madejski Stadium, as London Irish and Northampton plus Bristol and Wasps faced each other on 8 April 2000, in Rugby Union's Cup semi-finals. The event was such a success that it was intended to be repeated the following season, but with The Exiles semi-finalists again, and by then tenants at the Madejski Stadium, the idea had to be abandoned.

KIWI KINGS

A less regular feature has been the other oval-shaped code, Rugby League. In March 1981 Reading looked into the possibility of running their own Rugby League team after Fulham had attempted to launch the sport in the South. In the end the directors again decided to stick with the round ball, being put off by the estimated launch costs of £300,000, and so fans of the northern-based sport had to wait until 2 November 2000 to see it in Reading. It was worth the wait as the

Madejski Stadium hosted a Rugby League World Cup fixture between the mighty New Zealand and the somewhat less impressive Cook Islands. This one-sided affair saw the Kiwis win 84–10, a then record score, on their way to the final.

THE YANKS ARE COMING

The third code using an oval ball, American Football, became popular in Britain through Channel Four's coverage in the 1990s, but some 50 years earlier 'Gridiron' was already popular in Reading. During World War Two Elm Park was the centre of all forms of activities, thanks in the main to Club manager Joe Edelston, who strived to make full use of the ground's facilities to boost the town's morale. Along with director Jimmy Carter, he approached local American bases with an offer to stage American Football at Elm Park.

On 17 October 1943 Reading saw its first game of 'Gridiron' as Red Tornadoes beat Gremlins 14–0 in front of a crowd of over 6,000. Played on a Sunday, no admission charge could be made but a collection raised £137 for the British War Orphans Funds. Over the next few weeks a series of games were played, featuring exotically named teams such as Sky Train and Screaming Eagles, but the experiment was never repeated.

DIAMOND DAYS

There was no repeat for another of America's national sports either. On Good Friday 1918 Elm Park staged its first full international, not for football but baseball. With the ground marked out with the familiar diamond, two teams representing the United States and Canada played each other for national honour. The Stars and Stripes and the Union Jack were flown from the Club flagpoles, national anthems were played and the Club even produced a programme explaining the rules. Even so most fans present were totally bemused, many not even knowing who had won, a fact that also failed to make the reports in the local press. This is slightly surprising, because three years earlier convalescing Canadian soldiers from the nearby Bearwood Hospital had staged two baseball games at Elm Park. The lack of understanding of the rules probably contributed to the poor attendance for the event, which only saw £13.4.6d raised for charity. With that confusion still in their minds it might have been the reason that the board refused a request from the Monarch Baseball Club to use Elm Park in the summer of 1950. Strangely, it was 85 years after that first international that Reading finally staged a full football international, hosting the Australia versus Jamaica soccer friendly on 7 September 2003.

THE NOBLE ART

Over the years Reading staged several boxing tournaments at Elm Park, but by far the most famous fighter to appear at the Club's old ground was the legendary World Heavyweight Champion Joe Louis. The main feature of a three-hour programme staged on 7 August 1943 was a three-round exhibition bout between the 'Brown

Bomber' and Ezra 'Tommy' Thompson. Wartime security meant that the fight was announced as being staged at 'a stadium in the Home Counties' but, despite these less than specific directions, the visit of Louis attracted a large crowd.

──────────── BEST OF THE REST ────────────

GOING TO THE DOGS

Other sports staged at the multi-purpose Elm Park included whippet racing, which was a regular feature during the summer of 1909, raising vital funds for cash-strapped Reading. Three years later Elm Park was hired by the Central Whippet Club, who paid 10/- to use the ground for a meeting. However, 20 years later the directors drew the line at agreeing to a full-blown greyhound track being installed at the confined ground, and the matter came to a definite conclusion almost immediately when the FA refused permission for a dog-racing syndicate to buy Elm Park. Soon, a purpose-built greyhound stadium was erected in the Oxford Road area of the town, and to prove that there was no ill feelings from the greyhound racing fraternity the stadium held a series of meetings in 1932 to raise funds for the, again, cash-strapped football Club. Further proof of the good relationship between the football Club and the greyhound racing stadium came when Reading used the Oxford Road Stadium as their training ground during the summer of 1967.

ON YER BIKE!

Another sport that failed to receive approval from the board of directors was the approach by the World Midget Auto Racing Association to build a track for mini-car racing around the pitch. The Club also declined an offer to stage speedway at Elm Park shortly after World War Two. However, speedway did feature once at Elm Park, or at least speedway riders appeared. On 15 October 1973 a charity match was staged at Elm Park between the Reading Challenge Cup XI, a side chosen from local footballers, and a team of speedway riders. Not surprisingly, the footballers won 8–2, but there was no explanation why former Reading favourite **Douggie Webb** turned out for the riders, while Anders Michanek, destined to win the World Speedway Championship the following year, played for the footballers.

WHAT A RACKET

Another summer sport played at Elm Park was tennis, although this was also short-lived, the directors taking a dim view of West Reading Liberal Club leasing the ground in 1919 for £25 and then promptly sub-letting it to St George's Tennis Club for a profit.

JUMP TO IT

A virtually unique event for the times took place on 27 June 1908 when the Club was hired by Spencer Trickery & Co for their annual fête, the highlight of which was a parachuting descent. The 1922 Reading Football Club fête also featured a parachute jump.

ELM PARK'S STRANGEST SPORTS

In addition to many well-known sports, Elm Park staged a number of other competitions that could, at best, be described as obscure:

⊛ **Wrestling on Horseback** – featured as part of what was described as 'the greatest military display ever held in Reading', held on 1 May 1897 at the end of Elm Park's debut season. Although the admission charge of a shilling was higher than the cost of watching Reading play, it must have been worth it just to see this unique sport.

⊛ **Pushball** – a popular sport in the 1920s, this long-forgotten event first featured at Elm Park in May 1922 when the Licensed Victuallers took on the Reading Borough Police. The game involved two teams trying to push an 8ft ball and their opponents over a defined point, a kind of tug of war in reverse. The sport is so obscure that it is not even mentioned in the encyclopaedic *Oxford Companion to Sports and Games*, despite the fact that the book was edited by John Arlott, who was a Reading supporter in those days. Despite this glaring omission, pushball's popularity continued throughout the 1920s and in 1927 the *Daily Mail* sponsored a tournament at Elm Park as part of the Reading Sport Week.

⊛ **Five-a-side football** – nothing unusual in such a tournament being played at a football ground, except that that this particular one, staged as part of the annual Football Club fête in May 1919, required all the players to perform in sacks!

⊛ **Ham carving competition** – the award for the strangest 'sport' to be staged at Reading's or any other football ground, however, must surely be that organised by Reading player **John Boden** and featured at another Club fête back in 1908. That event was a ham carving competition – the only time, presumably, when the shout of 'He's sliced it' at a football ground would be a compliment rather than a criticism!

ALL-ROUNDERS

As well as displaying their skills on the football pitch, several Reading players have performed at other sports as well:

⊛ **Air Racing** – Hardly a sport normally associated with footballers, but Reading's flying vicar **Revd Albert Hurley** was not a typical player. Having already won his 'blue' for Oxford University at football, Albert, or 'AV' as he appeared in matchday programmes to denote his amateur status during his two-game spell for Reading in 1920–21, also took part in the first annual Varsity air race.

⊛ **Athletics** – Most footballers excelled at athletics at school, but popular 1980s full back **Steve Richardson** made it all the way to the English School's final for the 100m. The man who was Chairman of Reading during part of Steve's Elm Park career was no mean athlete himself. As a 16-year-old **Roger Smee** won the National Association of Boys' Clubs 880 yard final, while in 1983 one of his first acts as Chairman was to raise £2,500 towards the Club's youth team by competing in, and finishing, the New York Marathon. The late **Dean Horrix** was a natural athlete and at school he was a top javelin thrower, a talent that he transferred to the football pitch in the form of a prodigious throw in. A combination of football and athletics occurred in the 1991–92 season when bookmakers Ladbrokes sponsored a competition to find the League's fastest player. The final was held as part of the pre-match entertainment of the League Cup Final at Wembley, with **Michael Gilkes** qualifying for it. For the first 60 yards, the flying Reading winger led the field but was caught near the line, finally finishing third. Gilkes's time, in full football kit, was 11.62 seconds for the 100m, and although it was not good enough to win the event it was sufficient to beat former Reading loan player **Tony Witter** and pre-tournament favourite **Keith Curle**, another former Royal. The event was not held again, possibly because the lack of publicity led to Reading fans trying to place a bet on their favourite being asked if the event was for greyhounds!

DALEY TREAT

The greatest athlete to play for Reading was undoubtedly **Daley Thompson**. Two Olympic golds, a World Championship title, three Commonwealth Games triumphs, two European Championship wins plus four world records in the decathlon make Daley the greatest British athlete of all time. But after retiring from athletics he spent a month at Elm Park in August 1994, joining in Reading's pre-season training as part of a television documentary. He had not played organised football for 16 years, but within a minute of his Reading debut, as a substitute in a friendly at Leatherhead, he had scored his first goal. Daley made a second appearance in a prestigious friendly against Real Sociedad, and although he was only on the pitch for seven minutes his imposing physical presence was enough to unnerve the Spaniards' defence.

Another gold medalist with a Reading connection was sprinter George Saunders. A local schoolmaster, George was allowed to use the facilities at Elm Park in the early 1930s and was trained by the football Club's trainer Bill Clancy. Overcoming the disappointment of missing out on the 1932 Olympics through injury, George bounced back to win the Amateur Athletic Association sprint title, and in 1934 he was a member of the England relay team that won gold in the Empire Games. His exploits were such that he was featured in a set of Park Drive cigarette cards, alongside such other sporting greats as Dixie Dean and Fred Perry.

☙ **Ballroom Dancing** – Believe it or not, 'Competitive Ballroom Dance' is now recognized by the International Olympic Committee as a sport, although there are no plans for it to be included in the Games just yet. When it is, Reading's post-war centre half **Vic Niblett** can claim it as a second sport, since he and his wife were rated as 'gold medal' standard in this 'sport'. (If you think ballroom dancing is hardly worthy of the Olympics, consider that between 1912 and 1928 Olympic gold medals were awarded for painting, sculpture and architecture!)

⊛ **Baseball** – Reading full back **Paul Bodin** was a regular for Tavistock's baseball team in the 1990s.

⊛ **Basketball** – **Bryan Carnaby** was so determined to become a professional footballer that he wrote to all of the 92 League Clubs requesting a trial before getting his break with Reading in October 1971. He must have been even more determined to be a success at basketball since he was only 5ft 8in tall. Despite that, he became a full international and, surprisingly for someone who was born in Plymouth and brought up in London, his cap was won playing for South Africa.

⊛ **Bowls** – 1920s left winger **Jimmy Carr** never came close to representing his native Scotland at football, but at the age of 61 he finally received international recognition, representing his country in the 1954 Empire (now Commonwealth) Games in Vancouver at bowls. Carr was involved in one of football's stranger transfer deals when he was released from Reading in 1923. He put an advert in *The Athletic News* offering his playing services to any Club that would provide him with a business to run. Southampton presumably came up with an appropriate offer because Jimmy moved to The Dell as a result of his advert. Carr did not win a gold medal in Canada but neither did the participants in a bowls competition held at the Club's ground as part of the 1918 football Club fête. The winner of that bowls competition went home with a whole pig, while the runners-up won a chicken and a rabbit.

⊛ **Boxing** – A week before he signed for Reading in November 1969 **Stuart Morgan** had become the first West Ham player to be sent off since the war. He was involved in a fight with Arsenal's Ray Kennedy in a London Challenge Cup tie, which was appropriate because the tough central-defender had previously been Welsh Amateur Light Heavyweight Champion and had subsequently turned down the chance to fight for his country in order to concentrate on his footballing career.

⊛ **Darts** – Even in the affluent days of Premier League football, darts remains a popular pastime for footballers, as the Reading team were able to prove when they took part in a charity event in March 2008 to raise funds for Royal Families, the fundraising group organised by their wives and girlfriends. Not only did the event raise over £4,000 for local charities, but Reading winger **John 'The Hammer' Oster** notched up a memorable victory, beating the world's most successful darts player, 13 times World Champion Phil 'The Power' Taylor, by two games to one.

⊛ **Golf** – Most players try their hand at golf during and after their careers but few are as successful as **David Spence**. When Reading signed him in June 1920 from St Mirren they not only acquired a pacey winger, they also obtained the reigning Scottish Amateur Golf Champion. The Club obviously appreciated the benefits of golf because in January 1930 the directors decreed that players would spend their Monday afternoons on the local golf course, with the cost being bourne by the Club. One modern player who could do with regular time on the golf course is defender **Andre Bikey**. The Cameroonian giant claimed he had never played golf before but gamely agreed to take part in a charity golf day in March 2008 with his more experienced teammates. Having made it to the first green, Andre promptly placed his ball on a tee and tried to putt the ball with his driver!

⊛ **Greyhound Racing** – Modern Premier League players earn enough money to own racehorses, but earlier footballers were not always as well paid and so had to set their ownership targets lower. Small-but-brave keeper **Percy Whittaker** combined his time at Elm Park with owning a series of greyhounds, and when he retired from football in 1939 he became a trainer at the town's greyhound stadium. It is rumoured that he would even bring injured dogs into the Elm Park treatment room for attention from the Club physio! Another small-but-brave keeper with an interest in greyhound racing was **Steve Death**. However, when 'Deathie' retired in 1982 he turned his attention to a different sport, becoming a greenkeeper at Mapledurham Golf Club.

⊛ **Hurling** – Young Reading striker **Shane Long** only began concentrating on football after he had enjoyed a successful career in hurling. A regular in Tipperary's under-18 team, he twice played in the semi-finals of the All-Ireland Minors' Cup. These matches were played at Dublin's Croke Park, and when he received his second cap for the Irish football team, against Slovakia on 28 March 2007, he became the first person to play two different sports at the famous venue.

⊛ **Ice Hockey** – Reading's January 2008 transfer window signing, Czech Republic international **Marek Matejovsky**, chose football over a promising career in ice hockey.

⊛ **Judo** – Giant Dutchman **Elroy Khromheer**, a central-defender, faced a difficult career choice in 1992. He was in line for selection for Holland's Olympic Judo team but decided to withdraw and play in the Dutch under-21s side in the football tournament. Unfortunately, that proved to be the wrong decision because the Dutch football team failed to qualify, and so Elroy missed out on the Barcelona Olympics altogether. At least his football career led to him playing in Reading's opening game at the Madejski Stadium.

⊛ **Pigeon Racing** – Virtually every other Reading player in the 1930s seemed to be a pigeon fancier, and the likes of **Michael Doyle** and **Jack Rimmer** were regular trophy winners, while **George Horler** graduated to becoming a national judge in the sport. The football Club even staged a race of its own as part of their annual fête back in 1922.

⊛ **Quoits** – A member of the first Reading team to play in the FA Cup back in 1877 and Reading's first victory in the final of the Berks & Bucks Cup the following season, **Alf Richardson** was one of the best half backs in the country and later became a respected figure in the town. He also played for Huntley & Palmers Invoice Office football team, which gives an indication of the size of 'The Factory' back in those days. Football was not his only sport as he played cricket for Huntley & Palmers and he was once Chairman of the Reading Quoits Club.

⊛ **Rugby Union** – Several Reading players turned to the oval ball when they were no longer fit enough to play football, but **Keith Knight** had to make a career choice as a teenager. Although he won six under-18 England Schools caps at football, Keith was offered a contract with Rugby Union giants Moseley but eventually decided to join his home-town Club Cheltenham Town, before signing for Reading in 1988.

⊛ **Swimming** – Classy 1970s defender **Tommy Youlden** turned his back on a promising swimming career to sign for Arsenal as an apprentice, but not before he had represented London versus South Africa's swimmers.

⊛ **Ten-Pin Bowling** – Former Reading defender **Bill Livingston** was responsible for bringing the 'in' sport of the 1960s, ten-pin bowling, to the people of the town as manager of Reading's first bowling alleys.

⊛ **Tennis** – One of Reading's most popular players just after the war, winger **Wilf Chitty** later became a top scout for West Ham United, discovering stars such as Trevor Brooking, Harry Redknapp and Reading legend **Steve Death**. However, it could have turned out differently for Wilf as he was also a top-class tennis player who once gave three-times Wimbledon champion Fred Perry a close game. Another Reading player to excel at tennis was 1950s forward **Brian Bedford**, who became a tennis coach when his footballing days were over.

⊛ **Weightlifting** – Although only weighing in at 10st 6lb throughout Reading's initial League season, forward **George Broskom** still packed enough power to become the Yorkshire Weightlifting Champion in 1915.

The strangest sport entered into by a Reading player, however, must be that involving local youngster **Darren McCance**. In March 1992 he was a member of the team that won the town's annual Shrove Tuesday Pancake Race.

TWO – MISSING IN ACTION

Injuries and suspensions are common reasons for missing a game – or are they?

INSULT TO INJURY
Neil Smith's joy at scoring against Tranmere Rovers on 20 November 2001 was tempered by the fact that an excited **John Salako** jumped on his back during the goal celebrations, causing Neil to suffer a broken rib. To make matters worse, Neil had only just won back his first team place and only started one more game after he recovered from his broken rib. Neil was not the first, or last, to suffer celebratory injuries. Most famously, former Reading loanee **Steve Morrow** broke his arm when Tony Adams dropped him on the Wembley turf after the ex-Reading defender had scored the Arsenal winner in the 1993 League Cup Final.

LONG STRETCH
After a successful summer in 2007, during which he finished as top scorer for England as they reached the semi-final of the European under-21 Championship, and was named in the tournament's Select XI, **Leroy Lita** missed the start of the new season when he pulled a muscle in his hip by stretching in bed.

AWAY TRIP
Centre forward **Ken Price** was due to play at Cardiff on 1 March 1983 but was ruled out when he injured himself falling on the steps of the team coach. The story almost had a happy ending as his replacement, **Kerry Dixon**, himself rushed back from injury because of Price's late withdrawal, earned Reading a penalty in the first minute of the game at Ninian Park, but unfortunately the spot kick was not converted and Reading had to settle for a goalless draw.

WALTZING MAUTONE
Goalkeeper **Steve Mautone** took an international route to Reading. Born in Australia, Steve played in Italy before being spotted by West Ham playing against Malaysia. Reading then signed him after seeing him play in a friendly against South Korea and he was an instant success, saving a penalty on his debut against Ipswich. Unfortunately, he suffered a freak injury during the warm-up at the less cosmopolitan surroundings of Port Vale on 1 November 1997, an injury that resulted in four knee operations and an 18-month spell out of the game.

SHORT SIGHTED
Reading thought they had a bargain when they signed Southampton starlet **Wesley Maughan** for £4,000 in February 1962, but his early form was disappointing. The

cause became apparent when it was discovered that he had defective eyesight, after which the Club tried – unsuccessfully – to recover part of the transfer fee from Southampton.

WHO ATE ALL THE PIES?

Reading faced one of the biggest games in their, then, brief history on 28 March 1901 when they faced Spurs in an FA Cup third-round replay at White Hart Lane. Their task was made even tougher when an unnamed defender had to leave the pitch for a while after a heavy challenge because he had eaten a steak and kidney pie just before kick-off. Although Reading stayed in the competition a little longer than the pie stayed in the player, not surprisingly this handicapped Reading, and Spurs went on to win the tie 3–0 before going on to become the last non-League side to win the FA Cup. With today's influence of sports scientists and nutritionists such a situation is unlikely to occur nowadays, or is it? Although it did not appear to affect his performance, Reading midfielder **James Harper** admitted to feeling decidedly under the weather after eating an undercooked sausage in the full English fry-up he ate before the televised Premier League game against Derby on 7 October 2007.

PUPPY LOVE

Born in Germany, brought up in Berkshire and capped for Wales, Chelsea's **Darren Barnard** spent a month on loan at Elm Park in November 1994, when his substitute appearance at Portsmouth was Mark McGhee's last action before he resigned as Reading's manager. Prior to that Darren faced plenty of mickey-taking after he injured himself when he slipped on an 'accident' left on the floor by his new puppy. It proved to be not so funny for Darren as he was out injured for five months following this mishap.

'KEEPER CUT OUT

Reading's on-loan keeper **Chris Woods** missed out on an international cap when he slashed his finger with a knife when he was trying to cut a cord in his tracksuit bottoms.

KICKABOUT KO

Legendary centre forward **Tommy Lawton** was a powerful man and accidentally injured several players during his career. One such injury occurred at Elm Park on 18 September 1948 when a wayward shot hit Reading winger **Tony Alexander** full in the face and knocked him out cold. What made this injury unusual was that the future Reading player was only 13 years old at the time, and as a schoolboy spectator he was struck by the misplaced Lawton shot in the pre-match kickabout.

BROKEN DREAMS

Not all serious injuries result in an immediate absence, thanks to the bravery of the players involved. Right back **John Ridley** fractured his jaw in an FA Cup tie against Oldham on 13 January 1934, but after only the briefest spell of treatment he returned to finish the game. Similarly, Reading's great centre half of the 1920s, **Alf Messer**, once played almost the entire 90 minutes at Middlesbrough with a dislocated jaw. Both **Stuart Beavon** and loanee **Tony Witter** carried on playing in games in which they suffered broken legs, Witter actually winning the Man of the Match award against Wrexham on 5 March 1994 even though he played the final 38 minutes with his fracture.

CASUALTY LIST

More strange injuries and illnesses include **Fred Garratt**, whose appearances in 1922–23 were restricted to just two games due to 'a tendency to suffer from boils'. Two seasons later **Henry Higginbotham** was released by Reading after he was found to be suffering from sleeping sickness, while almost 70 years later former Royal **Colin Gordon** contracted blood poisoning while at Birmingham when he was accidentally (?) bitten by a Swansea player. Another embarrassing 'injury' was sustained by legendary Reading defender **Stan Wicks**, who, during a pre-season friendly at Elm Park in August 1948, collapsed from sunstroke.

TOOTHLESS CHALLENGE

One of the most unusual injuries occurred in Reading's home game against Exeter on 25 March 1922. After a heavy collision, the visitors' captain, Harry 'Jazzo' Kirk, swallowed his false teeth. Quick action by City's trainer saw him give the player a salt solution so he could regurgitate his dentures. It could be said, although it probably should not, that this *Enterprise* meant that *Captain Kirk's* team did not have to see their *Star Trek* off the pitch and enabled them to *Klingon* for a draw!

Another tough player was **Jimmy Sharp** who, in January 1898, had four teeth knocked out during a Southern League game against Eastleigh. As a reward for carrying on, despite the obvious pain, the directors subsequently awarded him £1 to pay for his dental treatment. Remembering his earlier bravery, the directors appointed Sharp as the Club's player-manager later that summer, but he was eventually replaced, mainly due to his apparent dislike for paperwork.

EXCUSES, EXCUSES

Not all absences are due to injury. When Reading met Luton in a top-of-the-table Third Division clash on 11 March 1970, a bumper crowd of almost 19,000 plus a rain-swept evening brought the notorious west Reading traffic to a standstill. As well as delaying many fans, the congestion also meant that goalkeeper **Steve Death** was late in arriving at Elm Park. Rather than play such a vital game without their star keeper, Reading elected to start the game with only 10 men, **Dennis Butler** going in goal. With no announcement to this effect, plus Death and Butler being of similar build and appearance, many fans did not notice the swap until the proper keeper entered the pitch after about 10 minutes, allowing Butler to resume his normal role at left back.

Unfortunately, this was not the last time that Reading's legendary keeper came close to missing the kick-off. In dispute over his new contract in August 1976, Steve initially refused to travel with the team to the first League game of the season at Gillingham. After the team coach had departed a local reporter, David Dibben, persuaded Steve to play, and he rushed the reluctant keeper to Priestfield just in time for him to play a blinder in the 2–2 draw. There was a less happy end to Steve's last absence. Another dispute, this time over a Club house, saw Steve refuse to play in the local derby with Swindon on 22 February 1982. This decision led to Steve leaving the Club after a then record 537 Reading appearances, and also saw him miss out on a League first. With Reading's reserve goalkeeper, **John Turner**, also out injured, they were forced to field youth team keeper **Colin Court** in what was to be his only first team appearance. Unfortunately for Court he was credited with an own-goal in that game, although so was Swindon's vastly more experienced keeper Jimmy Allen – surely the only time a League game has ended 1–1 with both goals scored by goalkeepers.

COSTLY CONGRATULATIONS

Another keeper who went missing was Southern League custodian **Rab Bernard**. Nicknamed 'Daft Rab' by the fans because of his bravery, he chose a big match to display another side to his nickname. Having knocked out Spurs in the previous round, Reading fans were hopeful that the Club could pull off another FA Cup shock when another First Division Club, Blackburn Rovers, were drawn to play at Elm Park on 22 February 1913. That hope seemed well placed when Reading dominated the opening play and **Joe Bailey** gave them a well-deserved lead. Unfortunately, that goal was also Reading's undoing. Their goalkeeper was so excited that he rushed out of his goal to congratulate his teammates. He was still out of his penalty area, shaking hands with his captain **Jack Smith**, when the game restarted, leaving Latham to lob Rovers' equaliser into 'Daft Rab's' unguarded net. Not surprisingly, this unsettled Reading and Rovers scored again to end the Southern League Club's Cup run.

UNLUCKY CHARM

Another Reading keeper who nearly did not make it on to the pitch was **Horace Ricketts**. Having made his League debut at the age of almost 36, Horace was one of the most superstitious players to appear for Reading. One of his foibles was that he always carried a 'lucky' rabbit's foot in his shorts, but before one game his teammates thought it would be fun to hide Horace's good luck charm in the rafters of the dressing room. The keeper was beside himself and flatly refused to take to the pitch, so in the end manager Ted Drake had to intervene to ensure the return of the talisman and enable his keeper to take his place between the posts.

WHERE'S JOHNNY?

Managerial intervention was necessary to resolve another prank that went wrong. One of the great characters in Reading's history, **Johnny Walker** was a skilful and crafty player as well as being an inspirational captain, whose cry of 'Steady' settled many a nerve on and off the pitch. That said, Johnny did not have the physique normally attributed to a professional sportsman, and he used his unathletic appearance to play a hoax at away games. Dressed in a distinctly 'non-designer' coat, affectionately known as 'The Camel', and with his false teeth out, Johnny would pretend to be a down-and-out Reading supporter without enough money to pay for a ticket. This performance regularly amused his teammates until one day at Wrexham when his performance was just a little too accurate. The officious doorman refused Johnny entry, even after he had revealed his true identity, and in the end a Club director had to be summoned to confirm that the apparent down-and-out was indeed Reading's captain!

A different **John Walker** tried to avoid playing for Reading for an unusual reason. The full back had spent six happy years playing for Swindon Town before World War One, and when he joined Reading he requested that he be dropped to the reserves rather than play against his old team at the County Ground. The directors, who picked the team in those days, refused to listen to John's request, but maybe they should have, as Reading lost the game 3–0. The following season he played his final game for Reading on 8 April 1922 and so missed out on both of that season's games against his beloved Swindon. His final game was played when he was 40 years and five months old, and although that makes him Reading's oldest League player, he was still good enough to bow out with a victory and a clean sheet.

WARTIME WORRIES

TRAVEL TROUBLES

During World War Two transport difficulties often meant that Clubs would arrive at away fixtures, and occasionally home games as well, without a full team. This would result in the depleted side borrowing players from their opponents or even asking for volunteers from the crowd. On one occasion this backfired when, on 2 December 1944, Reading lent 10-man Charlton Athletic their reserve centre forward **Bob Yates** and he promptly scored twice to give the visitors a 3–2 victory. There was no such generosity from Charlton a year earlier when half the Reading team were delayed on their journey to the Valley; although the fact that the missing group also had the Reading playing kit with them played a major factor in delaying the kick-off. As it was, the game was so late in getting under way that only 27 minutes' play was possible before the January light faded. These last-minute changes meant that fans did not always know exactly who they were watching – former Reading manager and secretary Roy Bentley once recalled the time he was delayed travelling from Bristol to Southampton to play for Rovers. He arrived at The Dell well after the game had started, just in time to hear a fan shout 'Bentley, you're useless' at his ringer!

One Southampton player who arrived late more than most was **John Bradley**. He spent a successful spell as a wartime guest at Elm Park, scoring 32 goals in 49 matches, but few of those were scored in the early part of the game. With players only receiving a £1.50 match fee, John would supplement his earnings by hitch-hiking to matches in order to save his travelling expenses, which had a poor effect on his punctuality. One can only hope that he gave up his hitch-hiking for one of his most important roles, since he was legendary Southampton manager Ted Bates's best man.

PRISONER OF WAR

World War One saw many absentees due to the hostilities, but **Max Seeburg**'s reason for missing part of Reading's 1914–15 Southern League season was one of the more unusual. Although he had lived in London since he was two, Max had been born in Leipzig and, as a German national, he was interred as soon as war was declared. The first foreign player to appear in the League when he played for Spurs, Max never held his brief imprisonment against the town and stayed in Reading, running a local pub and even operating one of the Elm Park turnstiles in the 1930s.

ON THIN ICE

Some players, however, had no excuse for missing a match. On 27 December 1892 Reading played the biggest match of their 21-year history when Burslem Port Vale became the first professional side to play in Reading. A record crowd paid £24.5.6d to watch the game, but they did not get a chance to see the Reading captain, **Frank Deane**. Despite the importance of the fixture, Deane came in for a lot of criticism when it became known that, rather than play for his Club, he had preferred to go ice skating instead.

IT'S NOT CRICKET

Another player to choose a different sport over playing for Reading was **Ron Tindall**. A skilful centre forward who scored regularly for Chelsea and West Ham, Ron cost a record transfer fee of £11,000 when he joined Reading in October 1962. However, Ron was also a regular for Surrey County Cricket Club and he had insisted on a clause in his contract that he would be able to play cricket. As a result he never played for Reading after Easter, even though they faced a battle against relegation the following season.

PASSPORT TO FAILURE

Jimmy Quinn was Reading's most capped player with 17 appearances for Northern Ireland, until **Kevin Doyle** overtook his total in 2008. However, that total was almost only 16. When the Irish squad arrived at Riga Airport for their game against Latvia in 1995 it was discovered that Jimmy had brought his wife Jackie's passport by mistake. It is rumoured that only the exchange of some of his teammates' duty free goods secured his entry into the country, although the squad only admit to providing an autographed ball to smooth Quinny's passage through passport control.

———— SEEING RED ————

FIRST OFF

Before World War Two dismissals were something of a rarity, so much so that during their first 19 seasons up to the war Reading had only three players dismissed in League fixtures. The first to go was **George Murray**, who was sent off at Exeter on 6 January 1923. Not only did George face a four-week suspension, in those days the ban meant he could not even attend training and received no pay during that time. To make matters worse, the game in which he was dismissed was Arthur Chadwick's last in charge of the Devon Club before he became manager at Reading. His new boss clearly remembered George's indiscretion because he only played one more game for Reading before he was transferred in the summer to, of all Clubs, Exeter. He clearly made a better impression as a Grecians player because, some 70 years later, the matchball for the Exeter versus Reading game was sponsored in his memory.

The only Reading player to be sent off at Elm Park before the war was a great Reading favourite, **Tommy Tait**, who was dismissed in 1934. Purchased partly thanks to a donation from the Supporters' Club, Tommy repaid their faith by scoring a hat-trick on his debut and so there was great sympathy when, after an hour of physical provocation from Millwall's centre half, Tommy took the date, Boxing Day, literally and laid out the offending defender. Tommy had the last laugh as a month later he scored the winner in Reading's fourth-round FA Cup tie against Millwall.

WHAT A RIOT

Some players have suffered far longer suspensions, though. A tough-tackling, hard-drinking Southern League full back at the turn of the 20th century, **Tommy Clinch** was appropriately known as 'Terrible Tommy'. A series of misdemeanours, on and off the pitch, culminated in a brutal game at Brentford on 1 February 1902. After the final whistle, Tommy kicked out at the home captain, Bob Stormont, who retaliated by throwing a punch at Clinch. After that, mayhem broke out as fans and other players joined in the general free-for-all. Eventually police and Brentford officials calmed the situation, but the Reading defender and a spectator were charged with causing a riot. Players from both sides were called to give evidence at the trial but, not surprisingly, they had conflicting views of the events and the judge dismissed the charge against Clinch, stating that the matter should be dealt with by the football authorities. This the FA certainly did, banning Clinch for six months.

A SHORT LIFE

Another Reading player to face a lengthy ban was Bulgarian goalkeeper **Borislav Mihailov**. Playing for Levski Sofia in the 1985 Bulgarian Cup Final against CSKA, 'Bobby' and most of the other players were involved in an almighty brawl at the end of the game. The Bulgarian FA were so appalled at the players' behaviour that they did not award the Cup or medals to either side and handed out life bans to several players, including Mihailov. The bans were soon lifted, however, allowing the goalkeeper to become the first Bulgarian to win 100 caps and be voted the best keeper in the 1994 World Cup before joining Reading the following year. After injury ended his career at Elm Park, Bobby returned to his home country and in a case of 'poacher turned gamekeeper' he is now the president of the Bulgarian FA. As a footnote to that Cup brawl, Levski were so ashamed of the incident that they tried to change the Club name to Vitosha Sofia, but the fans' protests forced a change back to Levski Sofia.

However, the 'honour' for the longest suspension imposed on a Reading player goes to **John 'Jock' Allan**. Signed from Bury in 1922, Jock was ever-present for Reading in his first season so it was something of a surprise when he was given a free transfer in the following summer. The reason soon became apparent. Along with nine other Bury players and officials, Allan had been involved in attempting to fix the result of a match between Bury and Coventry. Banned for life, Jock emigrated to the US, who were not members of FIFA, and so he was able to play for several top American Clubs. Eventually the FA relented and the ban was lifted in 1929, but Jock was 38 by then and his playing career was over.

FREE FIGHT

Not all sending offs ended in a suspension. Indeed, the first recorded dismissal of a Reading player, on 20 October 1894, never even came to the attention of the FA. An early Southern League game against Luton degenerated as Reading's amateurs took exception to the foul play of their professional opponents. Midway through the second half a fight broke out between Reading's **Tug Wilson** and the appropriately named 'Punch' McEwan. This was no case of 'handbags' – the two swapped punches for some time before the referee was left with no alternative but to send off both players. Even then the fight continued off the pitch and order was only resumed when a sergeant major and some other fans intervened, and the protagonists were finally separated. Despite all this the referee did not see fit to report the incident and so no suspensions were incurred.

One of the most controversial sendings-off in Reading's history came in an epic third-round FA Cup battle against Manchester United on 8 January 1927. With Reading dominating play, United were forced to resort to foul play and, with a weak referee, play became increasingly fractious. On the hour mark a terrible tackle by Frank Bennion left Reading winger **Jim Dougall** with a compound fracture of his leg. It was an injury that led to him spending six months in hospital and ended his career, yet the referee only saw fit to award a dropped ball. Justice was done when, from the bounce-up, Reading took the lead through **Frank Richardson**. As the players returned for the restart Reading's Irish international **Billy McConnell** clashed with United's captain Frank Barson and was sent off. To this day no one is quite sure why the Reading player was dismissed, and contemporary reports state that it might have been for a comment or possibly a gesture, but either way the FA simply censured McConnell and, pointedly, removed the official from taking charge of the resulting replay.

ON, OFF, ON

Clearly sending off Reading players is something referees should avoid, as Mr C.N. Wood found out to his cost on 20 December 1930. In charge of the Bury versus Reading game at Gigg Lane, Mr Wood sent Reading's **Len Featherby** off for what even the local press described as an innocuous challenge. The Reading players protested, but it took the intervention of the Bury captain, who sportingly argued on Featherby's behalf, until eventually the referee relented and called Len out of the dressing room and back on to the pitch to continue the match. Clearly the FA was not impressed, and as they could not suspend the Reading player as he had not, in fact, been dismissed, they removed Mr Wood from the League list.

Fifteen months later another player escaped dismissal in slightly different circumstances. **Billy Lane** had left Reading by the time of that game at Bury, and by 14 February 1932 he was with Brentford. Retaliating to a bad foul by a Torquay United player, Billy punched the offender. The referee sent him off as Billy was carried off the pitch to receive treatment. When he recovered, Billy sneaked back on to the pitch and played for a few minutes before the United players pointed out his return to the referee. Remarkably, the referee then changed his mind and allowed Lane to continue to the end of the match.

OFF, ON, OFF

If there was a prize for the strangest reason for a sending off it would probably go to **John Chapman**. A tough-tackling defender, John was affectionately known to the Reading fans as 'Chopper' and he regularly lived up to his nickname so was not unused to incurring the wrath of match officials. Playing in a League Cup tie at Colchester on 14 August 1968, Reading were two down and struggling when a Reading player went down injured. Reading manager Roy Bentley called Chapman over to the bench to relay tactical instructions to his defender when the incident was spotted by the referee. The official called Chapman back on to the pitch and then promptly sent him off for leaving the pitch without his permission. Needless to say, this heavy-handed treatment did not result in any suspension.

ALL OFF

In most cases dismissals involve just one player, occasionally two and very rarely three, but in May 1921 a game at Elm Park saw both teams sent off. A game against Southampton became very heated and some fierce tackles culminated in a terrible foul on Reading's **Harold Weston**. This sparked a minor pitch invasion but the restart saw no reduction in the ferocity of the challenges, so the referee sent all players to the dressing room to calm down. They eventually returned, minus the sinning Saint who perpetrated the Weston injury, to play out a 1–1 draw. The hostility the game produced was out of character, especially as the game was only a friendly; although, perhaps appropriately, the profits of £400 were passed to hospital charities.

TRIPLE RED

As mentioned above, three red cards in one game is very rare, so three for the same player must be virtually unique. Former Reading winger **Andy McLaren** achieved that 'distinction' while playing for Dundee at Clyde on 16 December 2006. Shown his second yellow of the game, a red card automatically followed, but as Andy left the pitch he threw a punch at another opposition player. He had left the pitch before the referee could show him another red so, after the game was over, the official summoned Andy to his dressing room to brandish the second card. Disgusted at this, Andy turned and kicked a hole in the dressing-room door, earning himself a third card, a substantial ban and a bill to repair the door.

It is not just players who can be sent off. In Reading's game against Norwich City in March 1949 the referee, Mr G. Clark, was asked to leave the field by City's captain, Low, as the official's white shirt was clashing with Norwich's kit. Although the official put on a dark jacket it did little to help the visitors' cause and they ended up losing 4–1. Another strange dismissal came during Reading's game at Madejski Stadium on 18 September 2001. With Reading pressing for a winner, a Cambridge United player kicked the ball out of play but, in his eagerness to return the ball to a Reading player, the Club mascot, Kingsley the Lion, stopped the ball before it had fully gone out of play. As a result the mascot was ordered from the playing area for this misdemeanour. That was not the last time Reading's cheeky mascot incurred the wrath of the match officials – in a televised Premier League game against Newcastle on 30 April 2007, Kingsley was asked to move away from the touchline as the assistant referee was confusing the 7ft mascot wearing a giant lion's head with the Reading forwards!

BOARD BANS

It was not only the FA who could suspend players – in the Southern League days Club directors were just as quick to hand out bans, sometimes for strange reasons. Winger **Jos Davies** had become Reading's first Welsh international when he was capped on 26 March 1900 but this must have gone to his head. After being described as 'rather selfish', he was suspended by the Club for two weeks. That was not the only time that Jos fell foul of his employers – while with Sheffield United he was suspended for lodging in a public house.

Another strange suspension was imposed on centre half **John Boden** in 1908 when the Club banned him for 'weak and rough play', surely a contradiction, but it might be explained by the fact that he was also accused of being drunk at the time. Perhaps the strangest reason for a Club suspension came in Reading's first League season. The 'victim' was **Bert Yarnell**, the scorer of Reading's first League goal at Elm Park, who was suspended and transfer listed for 'misconduct with a married woman that was the talk of the neighbourhood' – a reason that would hardly raise a tabloid eyebrow nowadays.

THE ULTIMATE PRICE

Sadly, some players made the ultimate sacrifice when their playing careers were cut short by tragically untimely deaths. World War Two saw Reading lose two players, although neither had yet established their playing careers, a fact that made their deaths even more poignant. **Dennis Gill** was a 16-year-old clerical assistant at Elm Park who played two wartime games on the left wing for Reading in 1940. He was subsequently called up and died in India in 1946.

THE UNKNOWN SOLDIER

Frank Ibbotson is probably the least known of all Reading players. He signed for the Club on 10 May 1939 but was called up weeks later and posted to Birkenhead. Frank never even attended a training session, let alone played for Reading; indeed it is quite possible that he never even visited Elm Park as the Club's offices were situated in the Arcade Chambers in the town centre at that time. As part of the D-Day invasion force, Frank was severely injured on the Normandy beaches and died of his injuries in July 1944, being buried in a nearby Allied war cemetery.

Another tragic death, albeit after his playing days were over, befell **Alf Bacon**. The scorer of a Club record six League goals in a game, against Stoke City on Good Friday 1931, Alf later lost the sight in one eye due to damage caused by a lace while he headed a ball. During the war, Alf was a special policeman in Derby and was on duty on the night of 27 July 1942 when a bomb exploded at the nearby Rolls Royce factory, knocking him off his bicycle with fatal consequences. In addition, **Joe Stephenson**, an England international and a World War Two guest from Leeds United played twice for Reading in 1941–42, before losing his life during the Burma campaign.

WAR WOUNDS

Other players suffered less serious injuries and winger **Wilf Chitty** even managed to sustain a war wound without leaving Reading when he was hit by shrapnel from a nearby bomb. Wartime guest **Bill Ratcliffe** suffered a shoulder injury and was taken prisoner of war in Italy, but he recovered in time to sign permanently for Reading at the age of 37 and carried on playing League football past his 40th birthday.

An even more remarkable recovery was made by local favourite **Johnny Sherwood**. A member of a family music hall mime act, Johnny was top scorer when he toured with the select amateur side Islington Corinthians. Visiting 15 different countries, Johnny was introduced to the King of Egypt but, according to rumour, the good looking Reading youngster made more of an impression with the young actresses when the tour reached Hollywood. Posted to the Far East during the war, Johnny was captured by the Japanese in 1942 and forced to work on the notorious Burma Railway for three and a half years. As the Allies advanced he was shipped to Japan but his vessel was torpedoed and he spent three days in shark-infested waters. He was then rescued but unfortunately it was by another Japanese ship. Just when he thought it could not get any worse he was taken to Nagasaki where he witnessed the dropping of the atom bomb. Despite these terrible ordeals, Johnny's natural fitness and personality saw him not only survive the war but return to Elm Park as a player. He topped the reserves scorers' chart in 1946–47 and also re-established the refreshment facilities at Elm Park, overcoming the problems caused by post-war rationing.

NOT SO GREAT WAR

During World War One Reading had no fewer than 41 players and former players 'with the colours', but unfortunately not all of them survived. **Joe Dickenson** was killed along with 40 other Grenadier Guards when a huge bomb exploded in their midst, while other Southern League players **Ben Butler, Freddie Wheatcroft, Ginger Mitchell** and **Herbert Slatter** also lost their lives. Wheatcroft was Reading's top scorer in 1908–09 and had won the Southern League title with Fulham and then twice at Swindon. Slatter was a local player, in fact he could not have been more local, residing at 77 Norfolk Road, directly opposite the Elm Park main stand. Former Reading favourite **Jimmy Comrie** was also killed in action and his name is commemorated on the Menin Gate at Ypres, along with the thousands of other war dead whose bodies were never found. The greatest footballing loss came in August 1916 when **Allen Foster** was killed during the Battle of the Somme. A wonderful player, he had been tipped as a future international and, as with the other losses, Reading staged games for the players' families even though the Club had withdrawn from regular football in 1916.

GAME OVER

Not all World War One tragedies took place on the battlefields. When Reading faced Arsenal at Highbury on 19 February 1916 the home side were a player short so they enlisted former star Bob Benson to make up the numbers. Benson had just completed a 14-hour shift in a munitions factory and had not played for some time. He collapsed during the game and was carried to the dressing room, where he died in the arms of the Arsenal trainer, the loyal Gunner being subsequently buried in his Arsenal shirt. As a result of this tragedy the FA ruled that wartime games would be restricted to 40 minutes each half.

Another player to succumb after a game against Reading was Frank Bedingfield. A great centre forward for Portsmouth, Bedingfield returned after missing three games through illness to bring his total to six goals against Reading that season with the winner in an FA Cup tie on 8 February 1902. He collapsed in the Elm Park dressing room and was subsequently diagnosed as suffering from tuberculosis. Such was his popularity in Portsmouth that a collection in the town raised over £400 to send him to South Africa to convalesce, but it was to no avail as he passed away two years later.

Another Reading-related death harks back to the Club's record defeat at Preston on 27 January 1894. Nick Ross played for the home Club, although he was suffering with a bad cold, and when Preston reached double figures he was allowed to leave the pitch, but the damage had been done. The awful winter weather he was exposed to during his time on the pitch turned the cold into pneumonia and, sadly, Ross was dead before the following Christmas.

The greatest tragedy to occur in a Reading game happened on 25 October 1879. Playing against the London Pilgrims, Reading's captain **Henry 'Harry' Rogers** complained of feeling unwell and laid by the pitch awaiting the arrival of a medicinal brandy. However, seeing that the Reading goal was under threat, Harry returned to the fray but collapsed after only 15 minutes play, suffering an epileptic fit. Although the 25-year-old was treated by two doctors from the crowd, he died where he fell. When his body was moved to his home town of Leamington a huge crowd gathered at the station to pay their last respects. In tribute to an outstanding player and man, the football Club cancelled all games up to Christmas, even withdrawing from the FA Cup as a mark of respect. Fortunately, no other Reading player has died on the pitch although only the prompt action of physio Glenn Turner prevented a tragedy at Swansea's Vetch Field on 22 February 1986, after a Reading player swallowed his own tongue. Eerily, that player was **Andy Rogers,** the only other player of that surname to play in Reading's first team.

After officiating at Elm Park in a reserve game against Millwall on 26 October 1920, the car carrying the two linesmen from the game crashed and Mr R. Walton was killed while his colleague Mr V.T. Brennan was seriously injured. This led to the Reading directors issuing a warning to the Club's players as to the dangers of travelling by car.

Finally, the Club suffered a great loss when a coach carrying 28 supporters back from a Simonds Brewery works outing to watch the Second Division game against Chelsea on 27 April 1929 crashed on the A4 at Hare Hatch and burst into flames. Seven fans perished in the blaze while 13 more were severely injured.

THREE – RECORD
BREAKING ROYALS

PERFECT START

In the autumn of 1985 the phrase 'Record Breaking Royals' became a regular feature in reports on Reading games. The season had started under the terrible twin shadows of the disasters at Bradford and Heysel, although it seemed at the time that Reading were hardly likely to be troubled by the restricted attendance figures imposed following those tragedies.

As it was, Reading set off at a sensational pace, and by 5 October they had won all 10 of their opening League games. A win in the home game against Bolton Wanderers would see Reading equal the record for a winning start to a League season, set by the great Spurs double-winning side of 1960–61. Strangely, another Club were after Spurs' record as Manchester United also won their first 10 games, but whereas United faltered at this point Reading did not, and the following week thousands of Royals supporters flooded down the M4 to Newport to see if Reading could break that long-standing record. Goals from **Stuart Beavon**, a former Spurs player, and **Kevin Bremner** secured the record-breaking 12th victory. The following week the run was extended to 13 straight League wins from the start of the season, a record that has rarely been challenged in the subsequent 23 years.

This flying start contributed to another League record as Reading became the fastest team to reach 50 points in a season, hitting the half-century in just 20 games.

GOALLESS GREATS

At 3.06pm on 24 March 1979 Rochdale's Bobby Hoy scored what proved to be the only goal of their Fourth Division game against Reading, a goal that also proved to be the last conceded by the Royals in the League for almost five months. In keeping a clean sheet for the remaining 11 games of that season, Reading not only clinched the Fourth Division Championship but they also set a new League record run without conceding a goal. That defensive record was extended by another 29 minutes at the start of the following season until Brentford netted at Elm Park on 18 August, ending a run of 1,103 minutes without conceding a goal. Even then the goal was not scored by an opposition player, the run-ending effort being an own-goal scored by full back **Stewart Henderson**, playing in his first game for 30 months due to an early season injury crisis.

Justifiably, **Steve Death** received much of the praise for that defensive record, but the same back four were present for all of those 1,103 minutes. In fact, between them, **Gary Peters**, **Martin Hicks**, **Paul Bennett** and **Mark White** missed just two games all season. In total, Maurice Evans used just 17 players all season with two of them playing only one game each, while nine of the squad played 39 or more League games that season.

One of the many remarkable aspects concerning that record run involved **George Shipley**. On loan from Southampton, the young midfield player made his Reading debut as a substitute in the game at Rochdale. As he did not come on until after the goal was scored and then played in all the remaining matches that season, his Reading career consisted of 12 games, during which time his team did not concede a goal.

By coincidence the British record for not conceding is held by **Chris Woods**, who had a five-game spell on loan with Reading in 1995. Nine years earlier he had gone 1,196 minutes with Glasgow Rangers without letting in a goal. Chris's success transferred to his international career as his 24 games for England saw him concede just eight goals and keep 19 clean sheets to be, statistically, England's best goalkeeper.

PREMIER HOT SHOTS

On 29 September 2007 Reading and Portsmouth set a new Premier League record with a goal feast that saw a total of 11 goals scored as Pompey won 7–4. Even more remarkable was the fact that even though Portsmouth's Benjani Mwaruwari scored a hat-trick those 11 goals were still scored by 12 different players!

The confusion started with Reading's first goal, originally credited to **Stephen Hunt** in the Sunday press, until action replays revealed that **Liam Rosenior's** shot had already crossed the line. In the second half deflected shots from Sean Davies and **Nicky Shorey** were originally credited to the two Englishmen, only to subsequently be awarded to the deflectors, **Ivar Ingimarsson** and Sol Campbell as own-goals by the Disputed Goals Panel.

Remarkably, Reading also featured in the second highest scoring Premier League game when, three months after they lost at Fratton Park, they lost 6–4 at Tottenham, having led the game on three occasions.

THE MAGNIFICENT SEVEN

Appointed the day before the 1997–98 transfer deadline, Reading's new manager, Tommy Burns, wasted no time in strengthening his new Club. By 5pm on 26 March 1998 he had signed an amazing seven new players, the most transferred to a League Club on one day. Five of the players were from Burns's native Scotland, with three coming from his former Club Newcastle. Falling into both categories were **Jimmy Crawford** and **Paddy Kelly**. Kelly was in Newcastle at 2.30pm and flew down to sign at Elm Park to beat the signing-on deadline with just minutes to spare. Other signings included **Jim McIntyre**, the most costly at £420,000, goalkeeper **Scott Howie** and **Stuart Gray**. The best known was **Robert Fleck**, who later that season had the unique experience of being presented with Norwich's Player of the Year trophy despite having left them for Reading several weeks earlier. The seven were completed by **Paul Brayson**, who came to Elm Park with the reputation of being 'the Michael Owen of the North East' but ended up with the disappointing goal tally of just one goal in 48 first team games. In all a sizeable £760,000 was spent that day, but none of the new recruits proved to be a complete success and not a penny was recouped in transfer fees when they left the Club. More importantly, 'the magnificent seven' were unable to prevent Reading from being relegated that season.

ELEVEN MINUS ONE EQUALS SEVEN

When Reading played Brighton at Elm Park on 11 November 1950 they stormed into an early lead and were three up after 30 minutes of play. Their progress looked to be hampered when, at that point, left back **Harry Kinsell** was carried off with a serious knee injury. With no substitutes in those days, Reading were reduced to 10 men, but far from slowing down they continued to attack and ended up winning 7–0, the biggest winning margin for a League Club reduced to 10 men at such a relatively early stage.

QUICK STARTS

The opening game of Reading's 2004–05 season could not have begun in a worse way: Brighton's Congo under-21 international Maheta Molango scored after just 13 seconds. This goal was the quickest ever scored in a game on the opening day of the season. In just over a minute Reading were level, but that was nothing compared to the visit of Manchester United for an FA Cup replay on 27 February 2007. After just five minutes and 41 seconds Heinze, Saha and Solskjaer had all scored to put United three up for the fastest start in first-class football. Despite this dramatic setback, Reading came within the width of the crossbar from forcing extra time in that game.

BLACKMAN V SENIOR

Widely regarded as the two best goalscorers ever to play for Reading, **Ron Blackman** and **Trevor Senior** enjoyed remarkably similar careers, albeit separated by over 30 years.

⊛ Both were born near the south coast, Blackman in Gosport and Senior in Dorchester, and were record-breaking goalscorers for their non-League home-town Clubs.

⊛ Before joining Reading, Ron had a trial with Portsmouth while Trevor played at Fratton Park for 18 months, scoring just two League goals, coincidentally both against Reading.

⊛ Blackman holds the Club record with 11 hat-tricks during his Reading career, while Senior scored Reading's fastest ever hat-trick when he hit three in four minutes against Stockport County on his League home debut on 3 September 1983.

⊛ They share the Club's main goalscoring records with Ron's 39 in 1951–52 being a season's best for League goals, while Trevor's 41 in 1983–84 is the record for all competitions. Similarly, they share the Reading career records as well, Blackman with 158 League goals and Senior with an overall total of 190.

⊛ Ron was the first Reading player to top the division's goalscorers with his 1951–52 Third Division South tally; Senior was the first to be the highest scorer in all four divisions, in 1983–84.

⊛ Both players scored a high proportion of their goals with their heads despite both being told, early in their careers, that this was the weakest part of their play.

⊛ Neither Ron nor Trevor enjoyed particularly happy spells away from Reading, and certainly the goals never flowed as regularly for them with other Clubs. However, both are still held in the highest esteem and have received standing ovations on their returns as guests at Reading games.

BUSY SEASON

Geoff Barker was a good, honest lower-League defender who was signed by Reading in February 1975 to boost their Fourth Division promotion chances. Not the sort of player to hold a League record then, but that is just what Geoff did. By the time Reading boss Charlie Hurley paid Darlington £5,000 for Geoff, he had already played 34 League games for the Quakers that season. He added another 16 for Reading to give him a record-breaking 50 League appearances in 1974–75. Strangely, Reading brought Geoff with the money they received from the sale of **Dick Habbin** to Rotherham, a transfer that allowed Habbin to make 48 League appearances in that same season.

ADIE GETS SHIRTY

Reading-born **Adie Williams** also set an unusual record when he played against Wrexham on 5 March 1994. A versatile player, Adie began his career as a winger, made his League debut at right back, developed into one of Reading's greatest centre-halves, and had spells in midfield and as a striker. Thirty minutes in goal at Fulham after **Steve Francis** was injured five weeks before the Wrexham game meant Adie had worn every shirt for Reading except the number 10. This fact was pointed out to Reading manager Mark McGhee by Club historian David Downs, so when Adie was selected to play in midfield he wore that 'missing' number-10 shirt in the Wrexham game to complete a unique set that, in the days of squad numbers, will never be matched.

YOUNG BOSS

Not satisfied with wearing every shirt, **Adrian Williams** played for Reading under 11 different managers, 13 if you count two sets of joint managers during his two spells with the Club. But one manager he did not play for was himself! Recovering from an injury, he formed part of the five man committee that took temporary charge of the team for their game against Wolverhampton Wanderers on 18 December 1994. At least he can claim a 100 per cent success rate as Reading won that game. At the time of that game Adie was aged 23 years and four months, making him the youngest League manager on record, even if it was for just a fifth of a game.

That game saw six managers in charge (Graham Taylor was the Wolves boss) but another game that season also saw a crowded dugout. Reading's game against Charlton Athletic was unique in that both sides had joint managers in charge, Jimmy Quinn and Mick Gooding, plus Steve Gritt and Alan Curbishley for the visitors. During that same season Reading's games against Grimsby, Oldham, Middlesbrough and Barnsley all saw three player-managers on the pitch at the same time.

YOUNGER CANADIAN

On 3 August 1973 **Bob Lenarduzzi** became the first Reading player for almost 50 years to be capped by his country in a full international when he played for Canada against Poland. At just 18 years three months old Bob became Canada's youngest ever international, but his youth did not stop England manager Sir Alf Ramsey contacting the Reading defender for comments on England's World Cup opponents. If that is true it did not do England any good because Poland held England to a 1–1 draw at Wembley to deny them a place in the 1974 finals. Although destined for a great future with Reading, Bob became homesick and returned to Canada, where he set more records.

As star player for his home team Vancouver Whitecaps, he played in the first and last ever North American Soccer League games, making a competition record 312 appearances. He went on to win 47 caps for Canada, playing in the 1984 World Cup Finals, and set two more unusual records in the qualifying games in 1976. On 24 September he was a member of the Canadian team that played the USA in the first World Cup Qualifier to be played on artificial grass, and in the return fixture in Seattle a month later he played in the first World Cup match staged indoors. Despite these many claims to fame, Bob's surname often caused a few problems, not least to the editor of Lincoln City's programme who spelt the youngster's name as 'Leonard Uzzi'!

HOME COMFORTS

On 8 April 1933 Reading lost 1–3 at Elm Park to Brentford. From then on until 15 January 1936, when they lost 2–1 to Queen's Park Rangers, they remained unbeaten at home in the League, a run of 55 games that set a League record which stood until the mid-1960s. Then Millwall extended it to 59 games, their run ending on 14 January 1967 when Queen's Park Rangers also beat them, that score also being 2–1.

The first two-and-a-half seasons of that run were under the managership of Joe Smith, the Reading boss having a strong claim to be the 'King' of Elm Park. His four seasons at Elm Park saw Reading lose just three home League games, by coincidence all against London Clubs. In that 55-match run Reading won a remarkable 16 consecutive games over a year from October 1931.Virtually 80 per cent of his games in charge ended in a home win, while Reading averaged a healthy three goals a game at Elm Park over those four seasons. Joe's complete League home record was:

Played	Won	Drew	Lost	Goals For	Goals Against
84	66	15	3	252	87

Joe can claim the best percentages for most home wins, fewest defeats and most goals scored, with only Charlie Hurley claiming the best defensive record, his early 1970s spell seeing an average of just 0.7 of a goal conceded in each home League game. Sadly, the 'worst' records of any manager at Elm Park all belong to Terry Bullivant's ill-fated 1997–98 spell that saw him win just 36.8 per cent and lose 42.1 per cent of his home games, scoring an average of 1.32 goals a game and conceding 1.42.

Although Joe's away record was also good, it was not quite strong enough for Reading to top the Third Division South and so clinch the one promotion place, finishing second, fourth, third and second in those four seasons.

HALFWAY TO PARADISE

Before the days of strikers, midfielders and defenders, teams consisted of five forwards, two full backs and three half backs, those half backs being mainly defensive in their duties. Therefore, half backs were not expected to score too many goals, and for many years the record number of goals scored by a non-forward in a League season stood at 14, netted by Spurs' Arthur Grimsdell, set in 1919–20. In 1951–52 that record came under pressure from Reading wing half **Jack Lewis**. With seven games of the season to go, Jack equalled Arthur's record, but he then hit a dry spell and was still stuck on 14 goals into the second half of the final game of the season, at home to Bournemouth. Then Reading were awarded a penalty. Jack was Reading's regular penalty taker and, according to fans behind the goal that the kick was taken, he told the visiting keeper, a colleague from his time with Bournemouth, exactly where he was going to place the kick. Despite this advantage the goalkeeper was unable to prevent Jack's spot kick from entering the net to give Reading a 5–0 win and Jack a new League record. At the end of the game a fan ran onto the pitch and handed Jack a bottle of champagne. This must have slightly annoyed Reading centre forward **Ron Blackman**, since he had scored the game's other four goals to take his season total to a Club-record 39.

SIMOD SUCCESS

One of the greatest days in Reading Football Club's history was 27 March 1988 as it saw the Club win the Simod Cup at Wembley and set two of the stadium's records. Reading's goals in their 4–1 win over Luton Town were scored by **Michael Gilkes, Stuart Beavon, Michael Tait** and **Neil Smillie** – the first time that a Club had four different scorers in a Wembley Final.

With four goals in that game and three in the 1995 play-off final, their only other appearance at Wembley, Reading have a Wembley goals-per-game average of three-and-a-half, better than any other Club.

In reaching the final of the Simod Cup, Reading beat Coventry City in the semi-final after a penalty shoot-out at Elm Park on 2 March 1988. The game's kick-off was delayed due to crowd congestion at the turnstiles and then went to extra time. As a result, the winning kick was scored by **Michael Gilkes** at 10.38pm, at the time the latest first-class goal scored in British football.

CUP OF WOE

One of the greatest mis-matches in FA Cup history occurred when the amateurs of Reading were drawn away to the mighty professionals of Preston North End. This meant that after completing a full day's work the Reading players had to make the arduous journey to Lancashire. Consequently, it is not surprising that Reading lost, their 18–0 defeat by Preston on 27 January 1894 remaining the heaviest Cup defeat suffered by any Club ever to play in the League. Unfortunately, Reading held a most unwanted 'double' as regards Cup defeats, since the 7–0 defeat by champions-elect Manchester City at Elm Park on 31 January 1968 was the highest home defeat suffered by any League Club in the FA Cup. Fortunately, Wycombe Wanderers' elevation to the Football League in 1993 removed that half of the record as the Buckinghamshire Club had been beaten 8–0 at home in the Cup back on 28 October 1899 – by Reading.

Reading can claim to be the joint oldest of all League Clubs to have entered the FA Cup as they played their first game as far back as 7 November 1877, the same season as Notts County. However, County could only draw with Sheffield and lost the replay, so in beating South Norwood 2–0 in that first game Reading also have the oldest FA Cup victory of any League Club. That shared starting season with Notts County has given rise to the fallacy that, as County won the Cup once in 1894, Reading have suffered more Cup defeats than any other League Club. However, County lost twice in both 1889–90 and 1891–92, due to replays following protests, to give them 121 defeats in the competition. On the other hand Reading scratched in 1879–80 and 1881–82 without being defeated, and although they did lose twice in 1891–92 due to more protests, they have 'only' lost 120 times in the FA Cup, thus giving this record to the Magpies.

OLD CARD

Another 'oldest record' belongs to stalwart Reading trainer, **Jimmy Wallbanks**. Initially signed as a centre half in 1938, he had a spell assisting managerial new boy Bill Shankly at Carlisle United before returning to Elm Park in 1953. From then until his death in 1979 he was a permanent and popular fixture at the Club, even having a spell as caretaker manager in 1971. But 'Wally' was best known as Reading's trainer and it was in this role that he set his record. Rushing on to treat a badly injured Reading player in a game at Hartlepool, Jimmy had not received the formal permission of the referee and the overzealous official promptly booked the trainer. That incident took place on 8 September 1973 when Jimmy was a month short of his 64th birthday, and so he became the oldest person to be cautioned in a League match.

GOALSCORING GOALIES

* On 31 August 1962 **Arthur Wilkie** injured his back in Reading's Third Division game against Halifax after just 12 minutes and had to be replaced in goal by defender **Maurice Evans**. Arthur was able to return for the second half but was not mobile enough to play in goal so he went on the wing, as was the norm in the days before substitutes were allowed. In his unusual position Arthur scored twice, slotting home a **Denis Allen** cross to make it 3–1 and then reinstating Reading's two-goal lead with a spectacular diving header to make the final score a 4–2 win and also set a League record for goals by a keeper. This proved to be no fluke as Arthur later had a run in the reserves as a forward and then became a regular scorer in local Sunday League football.

* Another two-goal keeper was former Reading trialist **Sam Bartram** who, during World War Two as a guest with York City, netted two penalties against Darlington. As Sam had spent his six-month trial at Elm Park as an outfield player, only switching to goalkeeping after he left Reading, his double can probably be put down to his Reading training!

* Most Reading fans had to double-check the scorer of their winner in a 2006–07 pre-season friendly at Bromley when the name **Adam Federici** was shown. A spate of injuries meant that the young Aussie keeper had returned to the pitch to play as a striker and promptly put his name on the score sheet. Although it is unusual for goalkeepers to get on the score sheet, it is not quite as rare as you might think as Adam was one of several Reading keepers to score for the Club.

* Despite his being the most recent goalscoring keeper, Federici cannot even claim the bragging rights among that season's Reading goalkeepers. In October 2003 **Graham Stack** scored a penalty in Arsenal's shoot-out win over Rotherham in the League Cup. What gives Graham the edge over Adam is that not only did he save the Rotherham kick that won the Gunners the tie, but all this took place on his first team debut.

* Way back in 1897 Reading played a friendly against the Reading Wednesday League and one of the scorers that day was keeper **Micky Cannon**. His goal

was not quite so much of a surprise, as Reading won that game 24–0! Also, not surprisingly, that scoreline remains a Club record to this day.

❂ Another friendly saw Reading go 6–0 up by half time against Parisien Athletique, the first foreign Club to play at Elm Park. Reading's eccentric goalkeeper **Alex Newbiggin** spent the second half playing as a forward and was rewarded with two goals. Alex once entered a lion's cage at Baker's Hippodrome for a 2s 6d bet, but despite this, or maybe because of it, he later became Club captain after the legendary England defender Herbert Smith stood down.

❂ **Rab Bernard** was another equally eccentric Reading keeper – he was not known as 'Daft Rab' for nothing – but he exceeded all his fellow scoring keepers by netting a hat-trick within 10 minutes during a friendly at Newbury just prior to World War One. Rab's trio was matched by 1970s Reading keeper **John Turner** who, while with Derby County, once scored a hat-trick for the Rams reserves after moving to the forward line following an injury. A far more important goal was scored by **Frank Parsons**, a well-travelled keeper who had a short spell at Elm Park in 1974. Nine years later, Frank was playing down the M4 for Slough, for whom he scored the winner in an FA Cup tie against Hampton.

POACHERS TURNED GOALKEEPERS

❂ Before the days of specialist substitute keepers on the bench, an injury to the custodian would see an outfield player take over the keeper's jersey, and some made a good job of it too. Reading players like **Maurice Evans** and **Denis Allen** were fine stand-in keepers, but no one can compare with **Trevor Senior**. Reading's record scorer was equally adept at the other end of the pitch since, in his four spells in goal for Reading, 'Super Trev' kept a clean sheet on each occasion. His final appearance in goal was also his last game for Reading and his unique, but effective, goalkeeping style inspired his teammates to fight back from 2–0 down to win 3–2. All of these displays followed a predictive April Fool's hoax pulled by Trevor and manager Ian Branfoot. On 1 April 1986, Branfoot appeared on the local radio station to announce that both Reading's goalkeepers were injured and that he was considering playing Senior in goal. The star striker then explained that he had played in goal at school and that he was willing to give it a go if required. If only the listeners had known then what they know now, there would not have been so many worried fans listening to that report!

❂ Equally effective at both ends of the pitch was another great goalscorer, **Jimmy Quinn**. Although he could not claim Senior's record for clean sheets, Quinn was on the winning side in both of the Reading games in which he ended up in goal.

❂ Other Reading players to try their hand between the sticks include Irish international **Billy McConnell**, who was so desperate to continue his playing days after a serious ankle injury curtailed his career as a full back that he played a few games in goal for the reserves in 1930.

⊛ A few years later the versatile **Fred Gregory** was Reading's regular emergency keeper, being described as 'a useful stand-in goalkeeper'. The same could not be said for **Fred Bartholomew**. An even more versatile player, 'Bart' played in all 11 playing positions during his 20-year playing career but only once in goal, manager Harry Matthews describing him as 'the worst goalie in the world'!

⊛ A former Reading player could also claim that unwanted title. Shortly after **Neil Webb** was signed by Brian Clough at Nottingham Forest, the young midfielder played for his new Club at West Ham. Forest's keeper was injured during the game and 'Webby' volunteered to take over the green jersey, explaining that he had been the goalkeeper for his primary school team. Unfortunately, he could not keep out the Hammers forwards and Forest lost 4–2. Clough was far from impressed with his stand-in keeper's display, so much so that he dropped Webb from his normal midfield role for the next game.

GOAL GETTERS
Some of Reading's players (other than goalkeepers!) have set impressive goalscoring records with other Clubs:

⊛ Reading manager in the early 1930s, **Joe Smith**, was one of the most prolific goalscorers of his day, and his 38 First Division goals in 1920–21 set the League record for the most goals scored prior to the 1925 change in the offside law that reduced the number of defenders required to keep a player on side from three to two. That total also remains the best haul for a Bolton player to this day.

⊛ After World War Two another prolific England goalscorer became Reading's manager, and **Ted Drake** holds the record for most goals in a top-flight game when he hit seven goals for Arsenal at Aston Villa on 14 December 1935. By coincidence, Villa's consolation goal in that game was scored by former Reading favourite **Jack Palethorpe**.

⊛ Another record breaker was **Peter Simpson** who, seven years before moving to Elm Park, hit a remarkable 46 League goals in 1930–31. Not only does that remain a record for a Crystal Palace player but it is also the highest total scored by a player with a London Club. In addition, his 154 League goals in six seasons is another Club record for Palace.

⊛ Across London, Reading players hold two records with Charlton Athletic – **Sam Bartram**'s 583 League appearances between 1934 and 1956 and **Ralph Allen**'s 32 goals in 1934–35 are both records at the Valley. But these players' efforts pale before the exploits of **Ted Harston**. Although he was a regular scorer for Reading and then Bristol City, Ted really hit form when he joined Mansfield Town in 1935. He hit a record six hat-tricks in a year and in 1936–37 he played 41 Third Division North games for the Stags, scoring 55 goals, a total that has only ever been beaten twice in League history. Despite that, Ted's 55-goal haul was not enough to make him that season's outright top scorer since his total was matched by Luton's Joe '10-goal' Payne.

❧ More Reading players have set Club goalscoring records with other sides. At the start of his League career **Bobby Hunt** netted a Club best 38 League goals for Colchester United in 1961–62. That total was helped by the fact that Bobby netted four times in a game twice that season, again a Colchester record.

❧ A prolific scorer wherever he played, **Frank Newton**'s best season was in 1931–32 when he netted a Fulham Club record of 43 goals.

❧ **David Crown** was not quite so prolific, but that changed when he moved to Cambridge United in 1985 and, in his first season, he hit a Club best of 24 League goals.

❧ Later to play for Reading in 1965–66, **Maurice Cook** wrote his name into the record books on 26 September 1960 when he put Fulham into the lead after nine minutes at Bristol Rovers, and so scored the first goal in the newly inaugurated League Cup competition. That early goal was not enough to win Fulham the match, Rovers progressing to become Reading's first League Cup opponents in the next round.

SUPER SUBS

Six years later, on 22 August 1966, **Douggie Webb** came on for **Ray Dean** in the tie at Watford and so became the League Cup's first substitute. Nineteen years later and a few miles away from Vicarage Road, another Webb was coming on as a substitute to set a record. Douggie's son and former Reading favourite **Neil Webb** made his England debut at Wembley on 9 September 1987 when he came on as substitute for Glen Hoddle during the friendly against West Germany. His 26 minutes on the pitch were enough to make him England's 1,000th player.

TRIPLE TOP

Kerry Dixon completed a unique hat-trick by finishing the top scorer in three different divisions over consecutive seasons. In 1982–83 he scored 26 goals in 35 Third Division games for Reading to top the Third Division scorers, at the time only the second Reading player, after **Ron Blackman** in 1951–52, to top his division's scorers. That tally earned him a move to Second Division Chelsea and in his first season at Stamford Bridge he topped the division's scorers with 32 goals to help them to win promotion back to the top flight. He completed his hat-trick in 1984–85 to finish the highest scorer in the First Division, jointly with Gary Lineker, a feat that earned him an England call-up. Unfortunately his first season as a top scorer only earned him relegation with Reading, making him one of only two players (Blackpool's Bob Hatton was the other) to top their division's scorers in a relegated team.

HIGH FIVE

On 24 February 1951 Reading beat Aldershot 7–1, the goals coming from **Ron Blackman** (2), **Les Henley** (2), **Maurice Edelston**, **Ken Bainbridge** and **Dennis Simpson**. This is thought to be the first time that all five forwards scored in a League game but is certainly not the last. Later that year, on Christmas Day, the same five players scored in Reading's 5–1 triumph to repeat the feat. Remarkably, the victims of Reading's second five-scoring forwards were, again, Aldershot.

READING PAY THE PENALTY

In the early 1980s, Portsmouth suffered a succession of missed penalties, but the problem was solved when current Reading assistant manager **Kevin Dillon** scored two spot kicks in the same game played on Easter Saturday 1983. Unfortunately, Kevin's conversions were against Reading and saw them drop points in the 2–2 draw that they could ill-afford to lose. At the end of the season those missed points proved vital, as Reading were relegated by just one point. 'Dill' subsequently wrote his name in the record books when he scored a hat-trick of spot kicks against Millwall in November 1986. This made him one of only 11 players to net a hat-trick of penalties in first-class English football, but as his trio came in the Full Members' Cup he remains the only player to have netted such a hat-trick in that competition. No Reading player has ever scored a hat-trick of penalties, but on 4 September 1976 **John Murray** had the chance to join that select group. 'Minty' had already successfully converted two spot kicks in the game against Walsall when a third was awarded. Unfortunately, that would-be record-equalling third kick was saved by the visitors' keeper Mick Kearns, the brother of one of Murray's teammates, **Ollie Kearns**.

WORLD RECORD BREAKING ROYALS

As well as the many League and national records, Reading's two main grounds have each seen world records set, while two of the Club's pre-League grounds might also have such a claim.

CROWDED OUT

There is an old joke in football aimed at Clubs with low attendances, where it is claimed that the announcer reads out the crowd's names rather than the players, because it is quicker. It is not always a joke. On 15 November 1994 Elm Park was the venue for a fixture in the UEFA under-18 European Championship between

Latvia and Slovakia. The Slovacs won 2–0 but this mouthwatering tie attracted an attendance believed to be the lowest ever for an international fixture, with a paying gate of just nine fans.

THE LONG GAME

On 13 October 1902 Reading were losing 5–2 in a Western League game at The Dell when, with only five minutes left to play, the referee abandoned the game due to fading light. Reading acknowledged that they were unlikely to recover that three-goal deficit, but the league was insistent that the remaining five minutes be completed. Eventually it was agreed that the outstanding period would be played prior to the return fixture at Elm Park. The five minutes were played with no change to the score, but they were played on 13 March 1903, 168 days after the game kicked-off, making it, surely, the longest match in the history of the game! Additionally, as Reading went on to win the home fixture this was the only time that Reading had lost and won competitive games on the same day.

THE BLACK STUFF

There are plenty of jokes about the drinking exploits of rugby fans as well, and again Reading's ground was the venue for adding some truth to the legend. The football Club's tenants, London Irish Rugby Club, set one of the more unusual records when they staged their annual St Patrick's Day game at the Madejski Stadium on 17 March 2001. The Craik must have been special that afternoon because the Exiles fans drank an amazing 23,452 pints to set a new world record for Guinness consumption. The Madejski Stadium was the scene of another St Patrick's Day-inspired record because on 18 March 2007 London Irish's game against Wasps attracted a Guinness Premier League record attendance of 22,648, a record that was increased to 23,709 for the following year's St Patrick's Day fixture.

PITCH BATTLE

It is also possible that a third of Reading's grounds hold another world record. On 21 February 1872 Reading played their first-ever game, a goalless draw against the local grammar school, at the Reading Recreation Ground. The Club played their home games at this venue for six years, and occasionally after that, although with no facilities or enclosing features the term 'ground' is probably an exaggeration. Be that as it may, the pitch is still in use to this day and so might have a strong claim for being the oldest former ground of a national League Club still currently staging football matches. The world record for the oldest ground used continuously is certainly held by a Berkshire Club – Maidenhead United having played at their York Road ground since 1870.

FIRST PROGRAMME?

According to several sources the first football programme was produced in 1893 for the Preston North End versus Derby County game but no copies are known to exist.

Consequently, the programme issued by Reading for their FA Amateur Cup tie against one of the top sides of the day, Old Carthusians, on 17 February 1894 might just be the oldest programme in the world. The single sheet, double-sided card featured the two line ups, the season's fixtures and five adverts. In 1889 Reading had moved their ground to The Caversham Cricket Ground on the north banks of the River Thames but access was always a problem, a fact born out by one of the adverts. This read 'The most direct way to the ground is to ferry the Thames from Adam & Gyngell's Boat House – Fare 1d return.' A penny was also the cost of the programme on the day but this so-rare programme, owned by collector and Reading supporter Bryan Horsnell, would now cost several thousand pounds, if Bryan was ever willing to sell it!

LONG LEGG

A Reading player also wrote himself into the record books back in 1995. Andy Legg was a classy left-sided player who was known throughout the game for his prodigious throw-in. Andy could easily reach the centre of the pitch and his throw was a useful attacking ploy for all the teams he represented. His throw came to the attention of *The Guinness Book of Records* while he was a Notts County player, and under strict scrutiny Andy threw the ball a massive 44.54m before it hit the ground, to claim a place in the prestigious publication.

THE 106 TRIBUTE

The 2005–06 season was the most successful in Reading's long history, culminating in promotion to the Premiership for the first time, along with the setting of several League records. While the team were performing with such style, the Reading matchday programme featured a series of articles combining this book's author's eye for the unusual with a continuous stream of statistics, from Nigel 'Strap' Meek and his *Ultimate Reading FC Database*. Typically, for these two masters of the obscure, these articles featured a number of increasingly weird records that no one even knew existed! Subsequently, Alan and Nigel set themselves a task as a tribute to the players' achievements in that never-to-be-forgotten season – to find one record or obscure fact for each record-breaking point gained. Although some of the following have been subsequently bettered, all were correct as at the end of the 2005–06 season.

1 = First in the Championship, Reading's highest-ever League finish, and the most important record of all.

2 = Reading suffered only two League defeats in a 46-match season to set a new League record.

3 = There were only three League games in which they failed to score, a Club best and also a season's best.

4 = Four players, **David Kitson, Kevin Doyle, Leroy Lita** and **Steve Sidwell**, all scored at least 10 League goals, a feat that no other Club could beat in 2005–06 for a season's best.

5 = 5.2% is the portion of the entire League season Reading were behind. That represents just 238 losing minutes out of 4,140.

6 = Six consecutive away wins which was a season's best.

7 = Seven Reading players appeared in the top 11 of the Championship's Actim Index – (1) **Kevin Doyle**, (2) **Bobby Convey**, (3) **James Harper**, (4) **Ibrahima Sonko**, (6) **Marcus Hahnemann**, (8) **Ivar Ingimarsson**, (11) **Nicky Shorey**.

8 = There were eight games, from the 3–0 win over Hull to the 2–0 triumph against Leicester, all of which were won by at least two goals.

9 = The number-nine shirt did not feature once for Reading that season. Surely no Club has ever failed to use the traditional centre forward number since shirt numbers were introduced in the 1930s. We can not definitely prove it but we are claiming it anyway as a League record.

10 = There were 10 straight League victories, equalling Chelsea and Liverpool, for a season's best.

11 = They attracted 11 consecutive home League crowds over 20,000. Surprisingly, Reading's previous 'best' was a miserable two consecutive attendances over this figure. They have only achieved that four times, although in 2002–03 it was extended to three if you include their Wolves play-off game.

12 = Reading gained 12 away wins, a total only matched by Manchester United for a season's best.

13 = For 13 consecutive games from November to January in which Reading scored at least two goals.

14 = There were 14 goal assists created by **Glen Little**, a total not bettered by any other League player, so a season's best.

15 = Fifteen was **Bobby Convey**'s squad number for USA's World Cup squad in Germany 2006. On 12 June Bobby played in the States' team that faced the Czech Republic, and so became the first Reading player to appear in the World Cup Finals.

16 = For those who count these things, the Preston game was Reading's 100th consecutive 10,000-plus attendance.

17 = Reading managed 17 consecutive away games without defeat, equalling Bristol Rover's run in 1973 for the best outside the top division and equalling the divisional record.

18 = Eighteen seconds was the time it took **Kevin Doyle** to score at Luton and so net Reading's quickest second-tier goal, and also the swiftest in a Reading away game to set another Club record.

19 = Reading managed 19 League victories at Madjeski Stadium, a Club record and season's best.

20 = The last five games of September 2005 saw Reading score six goals, each scorer coming from a different country or nationality – the order of the countries being Ireland, Congo, Senegal, Iceland, Wales and England.

21 = Reading's defence kept 21 away clean sheets all season, another Club best.

22 = There were 22 home League games without defeat, a season's best.

23 = Reading managed 23 consecutive games in all competitions without a defeat, setting a new Club record.

24 = The number-24 shirt was worn by **Shane Long**, who became their youngest second-tier scorer when he netted the late equaliser at Derby (taking the honour from **Leroy Lita**).

25 = There were 25 unused substitute appearances (or non-appearances!) by **Chris Makin** – a Club record for an outfield player in one season.

26 = Back to **Shane Long**, he was also Reading's youngest two-goal sub with his brace in the Championship-winning game at home to Derby.

27 = When Shane's two goals are added to fellow sub **John Oster**'s goal in that game, it was the first time Reading have had three goals from their subs in one game. This, of course, is the true reason why everyone ran onto the pitch at the final whistle!

28 = **John Oster**'s goal against Derby came within one minute of him coming on as a substitute, the quickest Championship goal by a sub that season, so a season's best.

29 = The number-29 shirt was worn by **Eric Obina Chukwynyely**, probably the only player ever to have three names in one season! Signed under his full name, he was originally shown in the squad list as Eric Chukwynyely but played as Eric Obina.

30 = This was the shirt number of **Sekou Baradji**, who was the first Frenchman to play for Reading in the League.

31 = Reading achieved 31 League wins in the season. Another Club record and season's best.

32 = Only 32 goals were conceded; a Club record, beating the 35 let in during 1978–79.

33 = The team went 33 League games without defeat in the season. Only Arsenal and Nottingham Forest have beaten that total and so Reading hold the divisional record.

34 = Thirty-four goals is the previous second tier Reading career record, set by **Bill Johnstone** in 1930 and now extended by **Dave Kitson** to 42.

35 = There were 35 substitute appearances by **Steven Hunt** in the season, a Club record for the second tier.

36 = **Glen Little** was substituted 36 times, again a Club record at this level.

37 = **Eric Obina Chukwynyely** was also the first Reading player to feature in a national television advertising campaign (PC World) before being 'substituted' by **Bobby Convey**.

38 = Reading could have fielded a team of all different nationalities from the 2005–06 squad. During the season they used players from the USA, Iceland, Senegal, Kenya, Eire, Congo, France, Nigeria and England, plus Scottish and Welsh internationals.

39 = Three of Reading's English-born players have been capped by Eire (**Graham Stack**), Wales (**John Oster**) and Scotland (**Graeme Murty**), while two other Englishmen, **James Harper** and **Dave Kitson**, turned down the chance to represent Ghana and Northern Ireland.

40 = The only Reading player to be picked for England in 2005–06 was **Leroy Lita** at under-21 level, and he was born in the Democratic Republic of Congo.

41 = The 41 goals scored away from the Madejski Stadium was a season's best.

42 = Reading spent 42.2 per cent or 1,747 minutes in the lead during the season. Pity poor Cardiff who were behind for 159 of the 180 minutes Reading played them!

43 = Leroy Lita became Reading's first £1 million player when he joined them from Bristol City in the summer.

44 = The 44 League games without defeat in a season is another League record.

45 = The attendance of 36,167 for their match at Highbury was the highest Reading have had for a League Cup tie.

46 = The 23,726 crowd was the highest to watch a Reading player make his home debut, when they turned out to watch **John Halls** make his first Madejski appearance.

47 = That same attendance was also the highest for a first appearance in a Cup tie. Depending on how you rate **Darren Caskey**'s 'designer stubble' John may also have been Reading's first bearded player at the Madejski Stadium!

48 = For the first time in Reading's history they were watched by over one million fans in a season, 1,012,841 seeing the 54 competitive games.

49 = Not surprisingly, that season's average home League attendance of 20,234 was a Club record, beating the previous season's high by over 3,000.

50 = Similarly, they set their best away average of 17,896.

51 = This, of course, means that season also saw a record overall average of 19,065.

52 = The home game against Southampton produced a gate of 23,845 – the Madejski Stadium's highest League attendance (at the time).

53 = The number of first team appearances **Ivar Ingimarsson** made in 2005–06, 53, was the highest total of any Championship player.

54 = It took 54 minutes for **Leroy Lita** to score his first goal for Reading and so become their youngest debut scorer to end up on the losing side. (This also set a League record for the most obscure fact ever to appear in a programme!)

55 = Almost four weeks after the season ended Reading were still setting records – the 22,032 that saw the England versus Belarus game staged at the Madejski Stadium was the highest B international attendance since 1957.

56 = Reading's elevation to the Premiership made them the top flight's oldest Club.

57 = It took Reading 135 years to make it to the top flight, longer than any other Club. Thus, Reading became the second oldest top-flight Club in the world with only Kilmarnock, founded in 1869, being older. In contrast, Chelsea, the reigning champions during Reading's inaugural Premiership season, took less than 17 months from their formation to make it to the top. Reading were also the first Club beginning with 'R' to make it to the League's top division but that is just too silly to mention!

58 = There were 58 home League goals scored, an average of 2.52 per game, which are both season's bests.

59 = **Glen Little** became the first Reading player to be a substituted substitute twice in one season. Having taken the place of **John Oster**, against both Swansea in the League Cup and at Burnley in the Championship, Glen was then injured and had to be replaced himself.

60 = There were 60 points won at home, another League record.

Not all of the season's records were set in the League:

61 = When he equalised at West Brom, **Kevin Doyle** became the first Reading substitute to score a penalty in a Cup tie.

62 = As West Brom's goal was also scored by their sub from the penalty spot, this must surely have set another record.

63 = Not to be outdone, **Leroy Lita**'s sensational hat-trick in the replay was the first time a Reading player had scored three times in his first FA Cup start. Surprisingly, Leroy's hat-trick gave Reading their first FA Cup victory over League opposition since they moved to the Madejski Stadium, almost eight years earlier.

64 = Leroy's trio also made him the youngest Reading scorer of a Cup hat-trick.

65 = Of the Club's 17 outfield players who started at least one League game, only **Chris Makin** failed to score.

66 = On the other hand, Chris was unbeaten throughout his Reading League career, his 12 appearances earning eight wins and four draws to produce a healthy 28 points.

67 = Reading ended up with a goal difference of 67 – the best since this method replaced goal average in 1975 and so that is another League record.

As well as those already mentioned, the players have broken some fairly obscure individual records:

68 = **Marcus Hahnemann**'s 168 appearances in the second tier are more than any other Reading player, beating **Alf Messer**'s 162.

69 = That total meant that Seattle-born Marcus has also played more times for Reading than any other overseas-born player.

70 = The **Hunt**-for-**Convey** substitution took place a Club record 25 times.

71 = A Club high of seven different players, **Kitson, Doyle, Long, Oster, Hunt, Gunnarsson** and **Lita**, scored after coming on as substitute.

72 = Along with **Glen Little, Bobby Convey, Kevin Doyle** and **Nicky Shorey**, all reached double figures for goal assists to create another season's best.

73 = There were 22 clean sheets kept by **Marcus Hahnemann** and his defence.

Several notable milestones were reached during 2005–06:

74 = **Dave Kitson**'s second goal in the 3–1 win over Swansea was the Club's 200th in the League Cup.

75 = On 17 September 2005 Reading notched up their 1,000th home win in the League, beating Crewe 1–0.

76 = A week later Reading celebrated their 3,500th League game by winning 1–0 at Norwich City's Carrow Road. By coincidence, the Club's first game also ended in a 1–0 away win against a Club with the initials 'N.C.' – Newport County.

77 = Reading's final goal of 2005, **Shane Long**'s late equaliser at Derby, was Reading's 2,000th away League goal.

The home game against Millwall on 20 August 2005 proved as eventful for the statisticians as it did for the players!

78 = Millwall became the first team to make consecutive visits to Madejski Stadium without bringing a substitute goalkeeper.

79 = This was a record that was to cost them dearly. After Andy Marshall was sent off after only 23 minutes the Lions used defenders Mark Phillips and then Adrian Serioux between the posts. Neither could keep Reading at bay and the rampant Royals scored against all three Millwall keepers during their 5–0 win.

80 = In addition to Millwall, five teams arrived at Madejski Stadium in 2005–06 without a substitute keeper on the bench and although Swansea, Sheffield United, Sheffield Wednesday Preston and Burnley were not forced to use a stand-in goalkeeper, like Millwall they all lost. Strangely, on the five occasions over the years that Reading did not name a specialist keeper on the bench they failed to win.

81 = Although he never scored against any of Millwall's keepers in the home game, **Kevin Doyle** netted against a fourth Lion's stopper, Colin Doyle, in the away fixture. That was one of 19 goals the bargain-buy Irishman scored, the highest total for a Reading player in their League debut season.

82 = Kevin's goals helped him to a unique double, claiming Championship-winners' medals in England and in Eire, with Cork City, in the same season.

83 = Those goals also earned him his debut for the Republic, making him, along with **Ivar Ingimarsson, Brynjar Gunnarson, Graeme Murty, Marcus Hahnemann** and **Bobby Convey**, a Club record sixth current international in the same season.

84 = A further honour for the young Irishman was his being named with **Marcus Hahnemann, Imbrahima Sonko, Steve Sidwell** and **Nicky Shorey** as a member of the PFA Divisional Select Team – a Club record five players, beating the Royals trios named in 1978–79 and 1993–94.

85 = Idolised by Reading fans, Steve Coppell is also statistically the Club's most popular manager, having attracted a higher average attendance to Reading games than any other manager.

86 = Steve's success was recognised by the League Manager's Association, who named him the Manager of the Season for 2005–06.

87 = Reading's manager also topped the complex Tissot ranking system with a League Record high score of 153.

Back to more team records:

88 = Reading achieved 10 home and away 'doubles' during the season, beating the previous Club best of nine in 1951–52 and 2000–01.

89 = The Club only suffered one away League defeat all season – a Club best and a season's best.

90 = Only two Clubs, Southampton and Watford twice, prevented Reading from scoring.

91 = On the other hand, Reading conceded more than one goal on only six occasions, a Club best.

92 = Reading won promotion to Division One with a draw at Griffin Park on the last day of the 2001–02 season, but only two of that Reading team, full backs **Graeme Murty** and **Nicky Shorey**, survived to the 2005–06 Championship-winning squad. Remarkably, four of the Brentford team were involved in Reading's record-breaking season, with **Steve Sidwell**, **Ivar Ingimarsson**, **Stephen Hunt** and **Michael Dobson** all playing in that fateful game, while the Bees were managed that day by Steve Coppell and coached by Wally Downes.

93 = **Chris Makin** broke his own League record because, as well as being a part of the Reading squad that won 106 points, he was also a regular in the Sunderland team that set the previous record of 105 points in 1998–99.

94 = It had been 94 years since Reading last beat a 'First Division' side (Aston Villa in 1912) in an FA Cup home replay.

95 = By clinching their Premiership place on 25 March Reading became the earliest team to secure promotion in a 46-match season, another League record.

96 = That early promotion, courtesy of **Kevin Doyle**'s equaliser at Leicester, completed a unique Reading hat-trick. Notts County's early elevation came on 26 March 1998, thanks to a goal from former Reading winger **Mark Robson**, while Plymouth lowered the record in 2004 with another former Royal, **Lee Hodges**, scoring in the promotion-clinching victory.

97 = Reading went 97 League games without a player being dismissed. For the second season in a row Reading were the only Club not to 'see red' in the League, a season's best disciplinary record.

98 = **Sekou Baraji** is probably the least-remembered of the 24 players used in 2005–06, his 23 minutes against Sheffield United being the total of his Reading League record. He made his time count, though, as his free kick led to **Brynjar Gunnarson**'s late winner.

99 = Reading scored 99 League goals, only the second time they have set the season's best for the most goals scored.

100 = The last of those goals was the 150th Reading had scored in the Championship.

101 = That all-important goal was scored by Club captain **Graeme Murty** from the penalty spot and was only his second Reading goal in eight years with the Club. This put him level with 1960s goalkeeper **Arthur Wilkie** and

groundsman **Gordon Neate,** but on the other hand he can claim to have scored more League goals in 2006 than Michael Owen!

102 = Unfortunately, that goal still did not prevent Reading's charismatic captain from breaking **Bert Eggo**'s record of the most second-tier games without a goal, his penalty ending a run of 235 games without scoring.

103 = Throughout their 2005–06 League season Reading only conceded six first half goals in their 23 away games.

104 = When Crystal Palace's Andy Johnson scored their equaliser at Madejski Stadium on 13 September he was the last visiting player to score a League goal in the North goal that season, a run of 1,771 minutes. That run was extended to 23 full games and 2,132 minutes, before Thierry Henry broke the run 13 months later.

105 = From 1 January 2000 to the end of 2005–06 Reading had won a remarkable 538 League points, 15 ahead of the second-best Club over that period, Manchester United. So Reading were not only the team of the season, they were also team of the millennium.

106 = 106 points is, if anyone needed reminding, a League record.

FOUR – THAT'S

ENTERTAINMENT?

─────────── ON THE BOX ───────────

'ALLO 'ALLO

Reading's first appearance on television came when the BBC cameras were at Elm Park to broadcast the second half of the game played on 6 October 1954. Strangely, this was not for a vital League clash or an important Cup tie but for a friendly against Racing Club de Paris that marked the switching on of the Club's new floodlights. The second half of the game was shown live on BBC and in several European countries, the BBC getting good value for the £150 fee they paid the Club since all the goals in Reading's 3–0 win were netted after the break. The match was also an early outing for a commentator who was to become a legend in televised football – Kenneth Wolstenholme.

TV FIRSTS

Six months later Elm Park was the scene of a piece of televised football history, albeit rather obscure. In the mid-1950s the two sections of the Third Division played each other and the very first North v South game was played at Reading on 16 March 1955. The game attracted such interest that the second half was shown live on BBC television. The South were managed by Reading boss Jack Smith and included home winger **Wally Hinshelwood**, but the man who set the record was Brentford's John Rainford. He scored in the second half to become the first player to score a televised goal in a representative game!

It was over 50 years before a full Reading game was shown live on terrestrial television and this time it was an FA Cup tie. Then, having waited so long for the cameras, 'two came along at once' as the fifth-round game at Old Trafford on 17 February 2007 and the subsequent replay at Madejski Stadium were both shown on BBC.

Reading had appeared on the big screen before World War Two, their semi-final against Cardiff at Molineux in 1927 being shown on cinema newsreels, as was the home tie against Arsenal on 16 February 1935. That game at Molineux was also the first FA Cup semi-final to be broadcast live on the radio, the commentator being assisted by a colleague calling out the numbers corresponding with a chart of the pitch printed in the *Radio Times*. According to legend, these early broadcasts gave birth to the phrase 'back to square one'. By the late 1930s the final was an annual event on the radio schedules, often to the cost of Clubs like Reading. In those days the final competed with a full League programme, or perhaps that should be the other way round because the broadcast of the 1939 final between Wolverhampton Wanderers and Portsmouth cut Reading's attendance for their game against Bournemouth to 2,705. Not only was that the Club's lowest League gate to date, but it also produced receipts of just £103 and a comment from the *Berkshire Chronicle* that the attendance was 'a disgrace to the football-going public of the town.'

OFF THE AIR

Thirty years later Reading created another piece of radio history when they forced the BBC off the air! The second half of their FA Cup tie against the (then) First Division giants Burnley was being broadcast live on the radio when Reading's **Peter Kerr** scored an equaliser. The volume of noise from 'The Elm Park Roar' was so loud and sustained that the commentators, including former Reading player **Maurice Edelston**, were forced to abandon their coverage for a while until the excitement died down.

Live coverage of Reading's games has not always been viewed as a good thing by the superstitious. Before they covered every Reading game, home and away, *Radio Berkshire* restricted their live broadcasts to the second half of selected games. During Reading's play-off campaign in 1994–95 the local station chose to cover the second half of five important games, but unfortunately each of those games ended up as a defeat for Reading.

SOAP STARS

Probably the highest viewing figure to watch Reading was the 18 million that tuned in to see an episode of *Coronation Street* in 1994. The episode in question showed Kevin Webster watching his beloved Wetherfield County on the television in his sitting room, the game featured clearly being Reading's visit to Stockport County earlier that year.

COMMERCIAL BREAK

At least two television adverts have featured Reading. In 1971 a petrol advert was filmed at Elm Park using youth team players and hundreds of local students to form the crowd, plus tons of fake snow. The filming lasted all day but the eventual advert only featured Elm Park for seven seconds. More recently, PC World used action shots of Reading players for a series of adverts in 2005. Copyright prevented the use of footage from League matches so Reading were asked to provide video from a recent League Cup game, which explains why the first advert featured a lesser-known fringe player, **Eric Obina**. In a subsequent version Eric was 'substituted' for USA international **Bobby Convey**.

TV TERMINATION

Elm Park was featured regularly in Channel Four's 1989 drama series *The Manageress*, starring Cherie Lunghi as football's first female manager Gabriella Benson and Warren Clarke as her Chairman. The series ended with Gabriella's team needing to win their final home game of the season to clinch promotion. The match was staged with the actors playing a team of Reading players and, in true dramatic fashion, the fictitious team were 1–0 up when they conceded a late penalty. The script required the actor-goalkeeper to save the spot kick, and Reading's regular penalty taker **Stuart Beavon** was to be his opponent. Apparently it took 10 spot kicks before the director was satisfied with the save, and this was to have a serious effect on Reading. When the Club were next awarded a penalty Beavon's kick was saved and he blamed this failure on the fact that he had been practising missing penalties for his TV role! That miss cost Reading a victory against Huddersfield and nine days later it cost manager Ian Branfoot his job – surely the only manager to be sacked due to a television drama series.

QUESTION TIME

One of the most popular and long running quiz programmes on television is BBC's *A Question of Sport* and Reading players have featured regularly in the questions. The Club's elevation to the Premier League saw winger **Glen Little** become the first current Reading player to be featured in the 'Picture Board' round. The team recognised Glen but some years earlier Bill Beaumont, Graeme Hick and Colin Jackson could not name 'a David connected with music'. Not surprising, because **David Tune** only played one League game for Reading back on 21 September 1957. Other Reading players to be featured in the 'One Minute' round were **David** 'found in the Tower of London' **Crown**, and the obvious **Robin** 'found on a calendar' **Friday**.

In May 2008 Irish international **Kevin Doyle** became the first Reading player to appear as a panellist on *A Question of Sport*, his all-round sporting knowledge helping teammates Phil Tuffnell and Welsh rugby star Shane Williams to a narrow victory.

The rather less reverential *They Think It's All Over* once, memorably, featured **Graeme Murty**, **Sammy Igoe** and **Andy Hughes** re-enacting one of Hughes's more outrageous goal celebrations in the 'Feel a Guest' round. As the zany celebration involved the players lying on their backs and waving their legs in the air, this proved a hazardous part of the show for the blindfolded Rory McGrath and Gary Lineker.

MAKING A MEAL OF IT

Probably the most unusual television appearance for a Reading player belongs to **Jamie Cureton**. As a Norwich City player, 'Curo' was seen scoring a typical poacher's goal against Southampton on BBC2, not in a sports programme but in the cookery programme that saw the return to television of City director Delia Smith.

DAVID MAKES HISTORY

Over the Christmas 2008 period, ITV will be screening a one-off drama called *Caught in a Trap*. Starring *How Do You Solve a Problem Like Maria* winner Connie Fisher as an Elvis-obsessed traffic warden, a couple of scenes were filmed at Madejski Stadium after Connie's character comes across an old programme for a Reading game.

That programme was lent to the film unit by Reading FC historian and the Club's children's safety officer David Downs. David can claim to be Reading FC's most filmed employee, having appeared on a number of programmes, including *Collector's Lot, Esther Rantzen's Sporting Chance, The Big Breakfast Show*, plus a Sky TV advert for Pizza Hut. In addition to his television appearances, David also featured in the latest screen version of *Pride and Prejudice*, the opportunity to appear with Keira Knightly just off-setting the director's insistence that David shave of his trademark beard!

THE BIG SCREEN

Reading's cinematic involvement has not been restricted to period dramas as two of the better football-based films also boast a Reading connection. Guy Ritchie's remake of the Burt Reynolds classic *Mean Machine* not only featured Vinnie Jones in the starring role but also Reading's defensive coach Wally Downes, then at Brentford, as 'football choreographer'. This enabled Wally to provide a startling answer when a magazine asked him who was the most famous person he had in his mobile phone, as he was able to reply Madonna a.k.a. Mrs Ritchie. Wally's brief movie career coincided with **Steve Sidwell**'s loan spell at Griffin Park, and apparently the future Reading star was keen to obtain a role in the film. Unfortunately, after being given a few lines to read by Wally it was clear that the young midfielder would be better off concentrating on his playing career.

Probably the best football film of all time, *Fever Pitch*, featured a scene where a young Maidenhead-based Nick Hornby watched his beloved Arsenal play an FA Cup tie at Elm Park. Although the movie was made in 1997, when Elm Park was still in use, the scene was actually filmed at Fulham's Craven Cottage. However, the Reading connection was maintained by an appearance of 1970s defender **Tommy Youlden** as an extra in the crowd.

ROYAL CORRESPONDENTS

Several Reading players have graduated to the ever-increasing number of football pundits now appearing on the various television channels. Best known of these are **John Salako** and **Les Ferdinand,** who is a regular on BBC's various football shows as well as Setanta. Someone who has carved out a long and often controversial career on Irish television is former Reading midfielder **Eamonn Dunphy**. As an outspoken critic of Jack Charlton's managership of the Republic of Ireland team, Eamonn's opinions were not always popular with the viewers, but things became even worse when he was openly doubtful of the dramatic improvement in the performances of Irish swimmer Michelle Smith in the Atlanta 1996 Olympics. Although his doubts were proved to be correct, it did not stop Eamonn being described as the most hated man in Ireland for a time. He 'enhanced' his reputation by later becoming the host of the Irish version of *The Weakest Link*.

FANS BANNED

One programme that did feature Elm Park was Lenny Henry's comedy show, although the appearance was not as long as planned. In November 1996 Henry, a resident of nearby Henley, brought a TV crew to the Reading versus QPR match to film the crowd singing sanitised versions of popular chants. The revised words for the chants including 'The Referee's a Sweetie', 'Oooh, bad luck' and 'The toilets here are lovely' were printed in the programme but, despite the comedian's encouragement from the centre circle, the fans from both Clubs preferred the original lyrics and so little of the footage shot could be used in a family programme!

─────── SING WHEN YOU'RE WINNING ───────

There have been several attempts to launch a 'Reading' song, but to date none have really caught the imagination of the fans.

LET'S ALL SHOUT HOORAY!

The first attempt to launch a Club song was in 1935 when Jack Morgan, the musical director of the local Palace Theatre, wrote a song that first appeared in the *Evening Gazette* and the Club programme, where the fans were requested 'to try to sing the following refrain':

'Let's all shout hooray, to all who play today.
Let's be bright and gay, that's the only way.
Give our lads a cheer to help them win the game.
When they win, should they lose, cheer them just the same.

They are the hope of all the Reading fans today.
Help them on their way, make them bright and gay.
Let us all give three cheers to Reading,
And shout hip, hip, and hooray.'

Although the song inspired Reading to their first win in five weeks, the song soon fell by the wayside.

BAD START

The next Reading song did not even enjoy a winning start. In early 1964 the *Reading Chronicle* held a competition to find a new Reading song, and on 14 March the song was launched. To the tune of *You Were Made For Me*, a recent hit by Freddy and the Dreamers, Reading fans were encouraged to 'Join in and sing':

'Reading you're the tops,
Everybody knows it's true.

Reading, you're the tops,
We all have faith in you.'

As with the first song, back in 1935, a local band played the tune and the fans
(well, some of them) joined in. Unfortunately, bad weather reduced the crowd to
the lowest so far that season and a disappointing 1–0 defeat by Oldham meant that
the song was rarely heard of again.

Another competition, this time organised by the *Reading Evening Post*, looked
to find a song to help Fourth Division Reading beat double winners Arsenal in
February 1972. The winning song, to the tune of *Hello Dolly,* met the same fate
as the previous attempt and the not unexpected home defeat ended Reading's FA
Cup run and any chance the song had of catching on.

FOR THE RECORD

With the advent of home studios and readily available recording equipment,
several fans have recorded their own musical tributes to Reading with titles
ranging from *Shaka, Shaka, what's the Score* to *Go Royal Go* and *Cooking Up a
Storm*, a three-track CD that featured *Kingsley's Mix* in tribute to the Club's
mascot. The best known of these songs was made by the Club's commercial
manager Kevin Girdler and was released during the early part of John Madejski's
rule as Chairman. Entitled *The Royals' Anthem*, it started off with a classic line:
'It's 2.45 and the place is alive'. In truth, at the time it was released 'the place' was
rarely 'alive', but of all the Reading Club songs *The Royals' Anthem* has enjoyed
the longest playing life.

The failure of purpose-written songs saw Reading attempt to adopt a record
as a Club song. Towards the end of Reading's 2005–06 record-breaking
Championship season the players adopted Neil Diamond's *Sweet Caroline* as their
song and undoubtedly the line 'Good times never seemed so good' certainly
applied. The song was given a full-throated airing by a capacity Madejski Stadium
crowd at Reading's last game of that season but, like other songs, soon fell out of
use. Another attempt at choosing a Club record saw the Levellers' *500 Miles* top
an internet poll but this failed to even get started.

TANNOY TROUBLES

One record that did cause some comment was one made by local spoon-bender
and erstwhile Reading supporter Uri Geller. Played before a game against
Birmingham City in 1995, the song, entitled *My Diary*, allegedly contained
subliminal messages and the City officials were upset enough to make a formal
protest. Whatever the truth, the messages did not reach the Reading players as the
visitors won the game 1–0. That was not the first time the Elm Park loudspeakers
had caused a dispute. On 30 December 1967 Bristol Rovers complained bitterly
that they had been so put off by a tannoy announcement regarding a parked car
that it caused them to concede **George Harris**'s winning goal. Some 30 years later,

on 5 November 1994 against Burnley, a similar announcement caused more amusement than complaint, since the offending car was owned by one of that afternoon's Reading players, midfielder **Mick Gooding**.

MYSTIC MYSTERIES

Geller claimed to have more effect on a Reading game a year earlier when he announced that his power of positive thinking was responsible for Reading scoring a late winner against Bristol City on 15 October 1994. Despite his comments, the goal was still credited to **Michael Gilkes**! Always keen to promote his psychic abilities and their uses in football, the spoon-bender later claimed to have moved the ball as Gary McAllister failed to convert Scotland's penalty against England in Euro '96.

STRANGE CHOICE

The nearest Reading have ever come to having a Club song came in 2000. Concerned by the lack of atmosphere at the new ground, several supporters groups combined to stage a series of increasingly zany events. From a beach party (in February!) to the formation of a band, these all helped to increase support but it seemed that the only tune that all the band members could play was the theme from the 1960s TV sitcom *Terry and June*. As a result, this most strange of choices became a regular feature at Madejski Stadium, so much so that for the final game of the season the star of the programme, June Whitfield, was invited to lead the singing. This self-confessed Wimbledon supporter gamely did, much to the bemusement of the visiting Stoke City fans.

THIS IS MY SONG

At least three Reading players have been immortalised on vinyl. In 1972 Karl Douglas had a worldwide number-one hit with what was to be his only success, *Kung Fu Fighting*. The second verse contained the lyric 'There was funky Billy Chin and little Sammy Chung.' There is just the slightest possibility (!) that this was not the same player who replaced record scorer **Ron Blackman** as Reading's centre forward in 1952 , since Reading's **Sammy Chung** could hardly be described as little and is not known to have any martial arts expertise. There is no doubt about the other honoured Reading player. Guitarist and Brentford supporter Paul Devlin, of the group The Bluetones, named the instrumental B-side of their 2002 hit *After Hours* after one of his favourite Bees players, **Ivar Ingimarsson**. In truth, Devlin named the track *Ingimarsson* because of the sound of the Icelandic international's name, stating 'No offence, but "Dobson" hasn't got the same ring to it.' Strangely, the aforementioned Michael Dobson later joined Ivar for a loan spell at Reading. The best known song about a former Reading player is *Man Don't Give A F**k*, a tribute to then Cardiff City star **Robin Friday** by Welsh rockers Super Furry Animals.

Ingimarsson and **Robin Friday** are not the only times Reading have featured in the pop world. Irwin Sparks, lead singer of The Hoosiers, is an avid Reading fan and when recording the video for the group's 2007 hit *Goodbye Mr A* Irwin is seen playing EA Sports' *FIFA 08* as Reading against Manchester United.

WISE AFTER THE EVENT
Football is littered with team records, usually recorded in celebration of an on-the-field success and often with a celebrity supporter. But while Spurs joined Chas & Dave when they reached the FA Cup Final, and England players dueted with New Order prior to the 1990 World Cup, Reading's one visit to the recording studio was rather more downbeat. Although the title, *Time To Celebrate*, sounds an appropriate football record, the players' backing vocals to Ernie Wise's 1989 song were, in fact, to commemorate 100 years of Berkshire County Council!

FAN-TASTIC
Of course, the most likely source of a Club song is from the fans themselves, and although Reading fans are not renowned for their innovative chants, a couple of memorable ditties have emanated from the Reading stands over the years. In the mid-1960s most terrace chants were not for the faint hearted, but Reading fans performed an almost unique alteration to a popular chant by actually making it cleaner than the original. In tribute to the sports editor of the *Reading Chronicle*, the Elm Park fans reworded the rude version to sing 'He's here, he's there, he's every Roger Ware…'

Thirty years later, while the Reading players were proving that they could match the Premiership superstars during their first season in the top flight, Madejski Stadium fans were also rising to the occasion. In an end-of-season vote, the Reading fans won the Best Chant of the Season award with an amusing, if politically incorrect, tribute to their South Korean winger, **Seol Ki-Hyeon**. By a remarkable coincidence they used the same tune as they had for the 'Roger Ware' chant to sing 'He'll shoot, he'll score, he'll eat your Labrador, Seol Ki-Hyeon, Seol Ki-Hyeon!'.

IN CONCERT
Both Elm Park and Madejski Stadium have been used to stage concerts, with varying degrees of success. The first attempt took place in July 1967 when Freddy and the Dreamers headlined a programme of mainly local groups. Only 800 tickets were sold and the event was a financial failure. Artistically, it also left something to be desired since a lack of consultation among the lesser acts meant that many of them played the same songs, with one number being so popular that those who did attend still know the words to *Knock on Wood* off by heart! At least that concert took place. Three years later 'The Spring Thing' looked like being a great success. With Fleetwood Mac headlining a quality show, ticket sales were impressive, but when April showers turned into a downpour the concert had to be cancelled on safety grounds. Madejski Stadium has been far more successful with top acts like Elton John and The Red Hot Chilli Peppers turning on memorable performances in front of packed crowds.

PRE-MATCH MUSIC

Occasionally, musical acts have been used as pre-match entertainment, with the Dagenham Girl Pipers being regular visitors in the 1950s. Other such acts included The Butlins' Young Ladies and, in September 1969, the Terry Lightfoot Jazz Band. Probably the strangest choice of pre-match entertainment occurred at the FA Cup tie against Burnley on 30 January 1965, when the crowd attempted to ignore the freezing temperatures by listening to a Caribbean Steel Band!

THE READING ORCHESTRA

Over the years Reading could have formed quite an orchestra to play as the following, admittedly attack-minded, line up proves:

Cliff Walmsley: a pianist who entertained his teammates more regularly than he played in goal for the first team in the early 1930s.

Matt Forster: another pianist who, apparently, 'could play anything'. He was a pretty good full back as well.

George Horler: a fine singer who performed regularly around Reading and whose claim to fame, apart from playing in the Club's first League game, was that he was the first person to sing *Bless this House* in the town.

Jimmy Quinn: he fancied himself as a vocalist and gave an impromptu version over the tannoy of Queen's hit *We Are The Champions* after the 1994 victory over Brighton that meant Reading were, in fact, the champions.

Shane Long: an accomplished young striker plus singer and guitar player.

Fred Chandler: a popular fiddle player who once gave a concert at a Supporters' Club Smoking Evening.

Wesley Maughan: a short-sighted striker and Salvation Army trombonist.

Frank Newton: a prolific scorer in the 1930s who was, like Wes, a fine trombonist. He was good enough to play professionally at Reading's County Theatre.

Jack Whitham: he never scored at Elm Park during his one season in 1975–76 so many fans claim his best performance was a memorable concert the singer-guitarist gave in the Supporters' Social Club.

Bruce Stuckey: a contemporary of Whitham's who sang semi-professionally in a country duo with Torquay United's Dick Edwards.

Freddy Smallwood: after retiring from football, he ran a small dance band in his native North East.

Manager/Conductor, Rupert O'Donnell: although he never managed a football team, no one would want to dispute the leadership of this Southern League goalkeeper, as he was bandmaster of the Royal Marines at their Portsmouth base.

GROUNDS FOR COMPLAINT
Not all of the musical ability displayed by Reading's players has been appreciated. In October 1930 the chief constable of Reading was forced to pass on complaints from residents near Elm Park in respect of singing and piano playing emanating from the ground throughout the day.

RHYMING ROYALS
Although it is not quite singing, Reading's history has often been recorded in poetry, and not just the successes. After Reading suffered their record defeat against Preston back in 1894 the Club's mood was lightened by a poem that appeared in the local paper, linking a well-known local shop and the town's main industry with events at Preston:

When Reading team to Preston went down,
They thought to get licked but said they'd risk it.
'Eighteen' is a name well known in the town,
But eighteen to nil! It takes the biscuit.

Rather more appropriate for a celebratory poem was Reading's win over First Division Champions Sheffield Wednesday in the 1929 FA Cup. In the tradition of the times a mourning card was produced, commiserating with Wednesday:

IN LOVING MEMORY OF SHEFFIELD WEDNESDAY
WHO FELL FIGHTING FOR THE CUP

We know you have the finest steel,
And we the finest biscuit,
But it takes a darn good knife to kill,
The goodness that's within it;
So shine your steel with might and main,
This fight we are about to gain,
We know you are above the lot,
But don't forget we're getting hot.

FIVE – FRIENDLY FOES

For the first seven years of their existence Reading played nothing but friendly matches, and it was not until the formation of the Southern League in 1894 that competitive games outweighed the friendlies. From their first game, against the local grammar school on 21 February 1872, Reading played a variety of opponents. Local Clubs from Marlow, Maidenhead and Windsor were all considered stronger teams than the later-formed Reading, while local derbies against the town's other teams, Reading Abbey, South Reading and the Hornets, were all big events in the local sporting calendar. Army sides were regular opponents in those formative years and the Club played the likes of the Somerset Light Infantry, 19th PWO Regiment and the 93rd Highlanders. Another big attraction were the old boy sides such as Old Etonians and Old Carthusians, two of the biggest and most successful Clubs in those Victorian days. Some equally unlikely opponents to face Reading included Reigate Priory, the Church Missionary College, Pilgrims, Vampires, Oswaldtwistle Rovers and Oxford Cygnets.

During the early years of Reading's history the Club would play internal practice games, the teams often divided between married versus singles, local players against outsiders and, at the end of 1877–78 season, the players from the west of the town met those from the east. So that everyone was included, the east-enders fielded 14 players but still lost to the 13-man westerners.

FALSE IMPRESSIONS

Such internal friendlies continued until 1961, mainly due to the fact that, somewhat bizarrely, the Football League banned pre-season friendlies against other League Clubs until the 1961–62 season. Consequently, the week before the opening of the League season would see the Probables play the Possibles, giving fans their first opportunity to judge their team's chances for the coming season, although not always. In August 1925 the Reading reserves beat their first team 6–2, 4–2 and 5–4 in the pre-season friendlies, yet despite these worrying indications the Club went on to win promotion. Once the League relented Reading took full advantage, beating Crystal Palace 7–2 and Spurs 4–3 in their first unrestricted pre-season friendlies.

FRIENDLY CROWD

More recently, on 1 August 2001, another pre-season visit from Tottenham Hotspur saw a record crowd for a friendly turn up at Madejski Stadium. Spurs won 2–0, but it was the 21,874 fans that impressed visiting Uruguayan international defender Gus Poyet, who commented 'Could you imagine this many people at a Division Two ground in Argentina or Uruguay? It's another world.'

NAME CHANGES

The first professional team to visit Reading were Burslem Port Vale, who were touring the South over Christmas 1892 and would play anyone for a £20 guarantee. Vale had already beaten Arsenal during their tour, but Reading proved a tougher matter and they beat their illustrious opponents 2–1. The victory was the icing on the cake as a record crowd had paid £24.5.6d to watch the game, enabling Reading to make a profit as well. Other League Clubs to visit the town included Everton, Wolves, Small Heath (now Birmingham City) and Newton Heath, who managed a 2–2 draw in 1896 and only attracted a 2,000 crowd before changing their name to Manchester United.

NOT SO FRIENDLY

Not all League visitors proved perfect guests. Leicester Fosse demanded a £30 guarantee to play at Elm Park but then only turned up with eight players and had to make up their team with Reading players. Blackburn also upset the Club and supporters after a 2–2 draw in April 1900 when the First Division visitors described the home side as 'nondescript'. Despite this apparent insult, Rovers still thought that four of Reading's Southern League team were good enough to sign. Along with **Walter Whittaker**, **Michael Kelly** and **Jim Hosie**, Rovers also paid £40 for **Joe O'Brien**. This fee was presumably to recompense Reading for the loss of income that the Club received in the way of fines from this misbehaving player. During his four seasons at Elm Park, Joe was fined 'a sovereign for misconduct' £5 (about two weeks' wages) for turning up drunk for training, plus five shillings after he deliberately kicked a ball through a window in the stand, which 'much annoyed' the directors.

RECORD VICTORY

The varying quality of friendly opponents could lead to some unusual scorelines, and in a three month period either side of that Burslem Port Vale victory Reading beat St Thomas' Hospital 13–0 and Spurs 6–0, but days later were held to draws by Ilford and then Marlow. However, none of these results compare with the events that took place at Elm Park on 13 January 1897. In their first season at their new ground Reading played a representative side from the Reading Wednesday League. This league was one of the strongest in the area and it was thought they would give their professional opponents a tough test – they did not. Ten-nil up at half time, Reading refused to ease up in the second half, even though goalkeeper **Mickey Cannon** played the second half in the forward line. The keeper was one of eight different Reading scorers, with **Robert Gordon** netting eight in the 24–0 win.

GROUNDS FOR COMPLAINT

Five months earlier another big win, 7–0, had seen Reading celebrate the opening of Elm Park, but the Club's joy soon vanished. Their opponents, the snappily named

A. Roston Bourke's London XI, was a scratch team that had not been registered with the FA. This was viewed as a serious offence by the governing body, who found the Club guilty of 'wilful violation of the rules of the Association' and suspended Reading for two weeks. The town was affronted by this slur on their Club and a public meeting raised the £25 necessary to appeal against the decision. That appeal against the suspension proved successful, although the FA increased their fine to £10, a penalty that never appears to have been paid.

ZULUS LOSE

In virtually their last game of the 19th century Reading played their first game against overseas opposition when The Kafirs visited Elm Park. A team of native Africans from Basuto, they ended their four month, 37-match tour at Elm Park having suffered some hefty defeats, failing to win a game and conceding over 200 goals, and it was clear to see why, Reading going three up in as many minutes. Reports of the game were rather less politically-correct than nowadays, the *Reading Standard* stating that 'we doubt they would score a single goal during their tour if the games were taken at all seriously by the Whites', and noting that Reading spent much of the game 'trying to allow the Blacks to obtain chances'. Reading's hospitality saw the game end with a 9–5 scoreline that hardly reflected the home side's superiority.

ENTENTE CORDIALE

That generosity to visitors was demonstrated again in September 1905 when Parisienne Athletique became the first European side to play in Reading. Under the headline 'Entente Cordiale at Elm Park', the local paper reported on another mismatch that saw Reading stroll to a 13–5 victory. The report noted that the French side were remarkably small compared to the Reading team and, again, having dominated their opponents the home side eased up to make a game of it. At half time they were 6–0 up, despite a brilliant display by the visitors' keeper, and Reading again released their own goalkeeper into the forward line, **Alex Newbiggin** scoring twice. This allowed the visitors to pull a couple of goals back, each one being greeted by louder applause than had been accorded the Reading goals. Reading continued to score with ease but another change of goalkeeper allowed the Frenchmen to make the scoreline slightly more respectable.

EXTRA TIME

On one occasion, the generosity in providing goals was not down to Reading. In the early 1960s an annual event was a match against The Showbiz XI to raise money for charity. The Showbiz side contained some big names of the time and some fine players with the likes of early English rock star Tommy Steel, cricketer Brian Close and comedian Jimmy Tarbuck all producing impressive displays. Traditionally these games ended in a draw, in 1965 the match finished 7–7 and the following year the score stood at 9–9 with a couple of minutes to go. Then the

Showbiz side took the lead and Reading frantically set about getting the required equaliser but it just would not come. In the end the referee had to allow an embarrassing 13 minutes of added time before Reading made it 10–10 and so allowed everyone to go home.

DUTCH DELIGHT

Reading survived until the end of World War Two before suffering their first home defeat to overseas opposition, and even then there was an element of home involvement. As part of the Anglo-Dutch Sports Association events taking place in the town, Reading played Krooger FC. The two towns had built up a number of connections during the war but the main one as far as Reading fans were concerned was that the visitors were managed by former Elm Park favourite and Club captain **George Johnson**. As other English sides were later to experience in their games against Dutch Clubs, George's team gave Reading a football lesson, winning 5–2. The visitors were then chaired off the pitch by the many Dutch soldiers in the crowd.

JUST THE TICKET

During the second half of the 1950s, Reading staged a series of floodlit friendlies to make full use of their newly installed lights. A wide variety of opponents visited Elm Park, some with modest demands. When Raith Rovers played such a friendly at Elm Park on 9 April 1957 they asked for a share of the gate and 18 third-class train tickets. No third-class ticket was offered to Stanley Matthews earlier that season. The great winger had agreed to play for an All-Stars XI against Reading, but he was forced to withdraw by the Football Association, who wanted to save him for England's fixture against Brazil.

FAN POWER

Sometimes Reading would take the opportunity to field trialists in friendlies, but in the summer of 1987 they took this to a new level. The Club had arranged a pre-season tour in southern Spain, with 100 supporters being given the opportunity to join the Club. Those fans expected sun, sangria and soccer, but five got more than they bargained for. Partly due to an increasing injury list and partly by way of a 'thank you', manager Ian Branfoot offered five of the fans the chance to play against Malaga. Not surprisingly, Reading lost 3–0 but those fans, who included players from teams such as Chazey Heath and Pantiles Reserves, had the memorable experience of playing for the team they supported in a stadium that had staged games in the 1982 World Cup.

STRANGE KIT

Some friendlies at Reading's grounds did not feature the Reading team and in the early part of the 20th century there was a craze for such charity matches to be played in fancy dress. Among those featured at Elm Park were contests between Sweeps and Bakers plus Dairymen against the Police, all players appearing in their work 'uniforms'.

THE ITALIAN JOB

In May 1913 Reading took part in their first overseas tour when they journeyed to Italy for one arranged by their former player **Willie Garbutt**, who was now manager of Genoa. After spending almost two days travelling by train and ferry Reading played their first game on Sunday 11 May against Genoa. Despite the rigours of the journey Reading won 4–2 and, according to captain **Jack Smith**, if they had not taken it easy they could have scored 10. It took Genoa over 80 years to gain their revenge when, on 7 May 1994, they won 4–1 at Elm Park against a Reading side that had been celebrating the Division Two Championship during the week and who were, indeed, presented with the trophy and medals that afternoon.

A day after the away game in Genoa Reading faced the Club that is now known as AC Milan, and the five-times winner of the European Cup were no match for their English visitors, Reading winning 5–0. Even then Milan were one of Italy's top sides, having already won the League title three times, so Reading's comprehensive victory led to them being described in the Italian press as 'without doubt the finest foreign team seen in Italy'.

On the Wednesday Reading suffered their only defeat of the tour, losing 2–1 with a weakened team on a pitch that was well below the regulation size, one report stating that it was only 34 yards wide. Undeterred, Reading maintained their punishing schedule by playing the best Club side in Italy 24 hours later. Pro Vercelli had won the Italian Championship five times in the previous six seasons and had not been beaten in 18 months. Ninety minutes later that record had gone as Reading cruised to a 6–0 victory. The Italians did not take this humiliating defeat well, and after **Jim Morris** reacted to a particularly bad foul the home fans 'assumed an ugly attitude' and the match was only completed after the Italian captain appealed for calm.

Having beaten the best that Italian Club football could offer, there was only one thing left for Reading to do – play the national side. Played on Sunday 18 May in Turin's huge Piazza d'Armi stadium, the game attracted 15,000 fans. Italy fielded their strongest side but Reading were two up by half time and were never in danger of relinquishing that lead, even though the home side used a substitute, a first for a Reading game. **Joe Bailey**, who scored in every game, and **Ted Hanney** scored in that memorable victory and the following day the team began the 1,500-mile return journey, having been wined and dined at a banquet hosted by the president of the Italian FA. As well as the playing success, Reading made a profit of £18.2.0d, but plans of further tours were cancelled following the outbreak of war a year later.

CLUB V COUNTRY

Reading have played several friendlies against national sides through the years and, impressively, have suffered just one defeat in eight games. Included in this total are victories over two European Champions and two countries that have won the World Cup a total of five times.

WORLD CUP WINNERS VANQUISHED

Reading's triumph over four times World Cup winners Italy is detailed above in 'The Italian Job', but the other World Cup victory was over England. It was not, admittedly, the full England side, but a Young England side, managed by England boss Ron Greenwood, came to Elm Park for **Steve Death**'s testimonial on 14 November 1979 and were promptly beaten by a **Jerry Williams** goal. That was not Reading's only success over England. In September 1983 Bobby Robson's England team faced a vital European Nations Cup qualifier against Denmark at Wembley, but his preparation was in disarray due to injuries. Unable to field two full teams for a full-scale practice match at the training centre at Bisham Abbey, the England manager approached Reading for the loan of three players to make up numbers. **Jerry Williams**, **Steve Richardson** and **Lawrie Sanchez**, an English born player with an Ecuadorian father and later capped for Northern Ireland, made the short trip and played for the England 'reserve' side, helping them to a 2–1 win over the first-choice XI, both goals being scored by future Reading trialist Luther Blissett. Robson should have heeded that warning and retained the Reading trio because Denmark won that vital fixture.

DOUBLE DUTCH

In the early 1930s Reading staged two tours of Holland and on each occasion they played and beat Dutch International XIs. The first of these took place in Rotterdam on 3 February 1932 when 18,000 fans saw Reading win 3–1 and receive 2,500 Dutch florins, enabling them to show a profit of £100. Two years later Reading returned to win 6–4 in what must have been the most sporting games in the history of football since not one foul was committed during the entire 90 minutes.

The first international opponents to visit Elm Park were the Canadians, who drew 1–1 with a mainly Reading reserve side in 1919. Although billed as the Canadian national team they were, in fact, made up of locally based servicemen. There was nothing local about the next international team, the Ugandan touring side losing 2–0 in a floodlit friendly on 3 October 1956, a game best remembered for the fact that several of the visiting players played in bare feet, three of the visitors played the whole game without boots, and a fourth removed his at half time. There were no bare feet when the Danish under-21 team visited Elm Park on 3 February 1981, but it did not stop Reading gaining their biggest international win, thrashing the young Danes 5–0.

SECOND BEST

Reading's only defeat against international opposition came on 29 October 1985 when, as part of their warm-up for the World Cup qualifiers, New Zealand beat Reading 2–1. At least the home side had an excuse for this rare defeat as they were forced to play a weakened side since their team included **Martin Peters** and

George Best! These two players were involved in a little bit of football history since the game was the first ever to be sponsored by a firm of solicitors following an easing in Law Society rules on advertising. Berkshire was obviously the destination of choice for World Cup warm ups, since in August 1977 Kuwait's World Cup squad played a friendly against Hungerford. The internationals were beaten, with Town's winner being scored by former Reading forward **John Ashton**.

SIX – SPACE INVADERS

DODGY DOGS

Before the advent of the modern all-seater stadium it was a regular event each season to see a match disrupted by a stray dog. In the Club's Southern League days the Reading directors found it necessary to specifically ban dogs from entering Elm Park. Remarkably, this seemingly sensible edict was rescinded in November 1921, and soon horrible hounds were interrupting play at Elm Park again. Probably the best-remembered canine intruder came on 9 October 1974 when a greyhound disrupted Reading's fourth-round League Cup tie against First Division Burnley. The cur ran amok for several minutes until finally being caught, appropriately by Reading's greyhound racing fan, goalkeeper **Steve Death**. One dog that entered the field of play with permission was a black-and-white terrier called Jeff who, on Boxing Day 1986, was one of nine mascots for Reading's game against Birmingham. Included among the two-legged mascots were James Hunt and Jonathan Palmer, although neither of these local schoolboys has yet gone on to win a Grand Prix!

BARKING MAD

Rather less welcome, although it never made it on to the pitch, was a dog owned by a Reading fan who decked the pooch out in the Club's blue-and-white colours and took it to the 1927 Cup tie against Brentford. The game attracted Reading's record attendance and in the crush the dog bit a visiting supporter, a reaction that cost the owner, a Mr Thomas Hucker, a 22/6d fine and a warning from the judge that the dog should not be taken to football matches again 'where it was likely to get excited'.

Regular guests at football grounds during the 1960s and 1970s were the RAF police dog display teams. As well as a series of exercises to demonstrate their bravery and agility, such as jumping through flaming hoops, a regular feature was to chase and catch a well-padded 'thief' who would steal the matchball from the referee at half time. On one occasion the dogs should have stayed to the end of the game because Reading's match against Walsall on 23 January 1965 ended in a pitch invasion by fans angry at the opposition's tactics. Reading had finished the game with nine men and had several others hobbling after some tough tackling from the Walsall players. One of the visiting players was a young Allan Clarke, but by the time the future England, Leeds United and Manchester United player came to write his autobiography his memory was playing tricks on him, since he recorded that it was Walsall who were reduced to nine players.

HOOLIGAN RABBITS

If taking a dog to a football match sounds like a strange idea, what about the fan who turned up at Elm Park for the opening game of the 1898–99 season with a couple of rabbits? Midway through the game the owner decided it would be a good idea to release the bunnies, with inevitably chaotic results. It is hard to imagine what would inspire such an act, although it just may have been a protest against the referee Mr Roston Bourke who, two years earlier, had almost got Reading suspended from the FA when he brought an unregistered team to Elm Park for its opening game.

FEATHERED FANS

Not all pitch invaders have been four-legged. During Reading's home game against Gillingham on 16 April 1983, the game was held up while the visitors' keeper, Ron Hillyard, rescued a fledgling starling that had fluttered into his goalmouth. That incident proved to be the most exciting in a drab goalless draw; that was until later that afternoon when the Club announced Robert Maxwell's ill-judged plans to merge Reading with Oxford United. By a strange coincidence, that was not the first time an animal had been rescued by a Gillingham keeper on the day they played Reading – in 1970 one of Hillyard's predecessors, John Simpson, had rescued a trapped hedgehog that had been stuck in a Priestfield Stadium drainpipe.

Another goalless draw and another bird to hit the headlines was a seagull that took residence in Aldershot's penalty area when they came to Elm Park on Easter Monday 1973. The bird was rarely troubled by an ineffective Reading attack, which was just as well as it was clearly exhausted. It remained on the pitch long after the game, but when the local press discovered that groundsman Gordon Neate had 'put it out of its misery' there was uproar from animal lovers.

Birds have been put to work at Reading's grounds for opposing purposes over the years. In the days long before local radio and the internet, the directors were approached to give permission for homing pigeons to be used to relay the scores. Somewhat surprisingly, the board agreed 'so long as no obstruction or annoyance was caused'. There is, however, only one recorded instance of these feathered couriers being used, and that was by Leicester fans during their FA Cup visit in 1928. Seventy years later, the descendents of those pigeons were creating a cleaning problem by roosting in the rafters of the Madejski Stadium roof, so the Club employed a hawk to chase away the now unwanted messengers.

PEACE KEEPER

Even the modern stadiums and the size of Premier League crowds have not been enough to keep pitches free from invaders. During 2007–08 a fox was seen crossing the Craven Cottage pitch prior to the start of Reading's game while, weeks earlier, a white dove decided to take residence on the Ewood Park pitch during Reading's visit to Blackburn Rovers. The symbol of peace, the dove clearly had an effect on the players as only 16 fouls were committed throughout the 90 minutes and no one was booked. That dove obviously was not present when the two teams met at Madejski Stadium for the return match on 29 March 2008. That game saw referee Mark Clattenburg contrive to book 10 players, five from each side, and send off Reading's **Marek Matejovsky**. This was particularly galling for Reading since, despite suffering five yellows and one red card, they only conceded 10 fouls all afternoon. A couple of seasons earlier, Reading's game at QPR was interrupted when a squirrel ran across the pitch, apparently celebrating Rangers' equaliser.

At least the Fulham fox survived to enjoy the match, which is more than an invading vixen did at Elm Park back in August 1992. Guilty of digging holes in the sacred turf and eating the goal nets, the offender was shot by a pest control expert.

HORSE PLAY

When Reading signed **Alonzo Poulton** from Bristol City in 1922 the Club programme stated that 'it was doubtful if any signature had given greater satisfaction'. Not everyone at Elm Park was to agree. In the 1920s ground maintenance equipment was 'powered' by Tichey, the groundsman's horse. When not in action, Tichey would quietly keep the pitch neat by munching on the grass, oblivious of the players training around him. That pleasant scene was shattered one day when the Club joker, centre forward **Alonzo 'Jerry' Poulton**, decided it would be funny to creep up behind the poor animal and frighten it with a mighty shout. It certainly did frighten the horse to the point where Tichey no longer enjoyed the company of the players on his pitch and would chase anything in a blue-and-white shirt, resulting in the horse having to be securely tethered while the players were training. Sadly Tichey was eventually put down during the summer of 1932, the Club having decided that he was no longer fit for work. Other animals on their way out of Elm Park at that time were groundsman Fred Bartholomew's chickens, which until then had been kept under the stands and 'free ranged' on the pitch when the players left.

NATIONAL HERO

Another horse to make an impression at Elm Park was Foinavon, the 100–1 winner of the 1967 Grand National. A local horse, it only won because of a massive pile up at the 23rd fence (now known as Foinavon's Fence), but many Reading fans had backed it and it received a tremendous reception a few weeks later when it appeared before the home game against Workington. By now Foinavon was used to the noise of the crowd's cheers, but the horse's permanent stable companion, a goat, was clearly more nervous and did something disgusting in the Town End goalmouth. Although the unwanted deposit was removed, the game was memorable for two very cautious performances by both goalkeepers!

BOXING CLEVER

Occasionally it is a human who makes it unlawfully onto the pitch, but apart from the occasional hooligan, now thankfully a thing of the past, or even rarer (but more popular) streakers, most are invited. Successful sportsmen, like the medal-winning 1976 Olympic Pentathlon team or the Commonwealth Games-winning relay team, featuring popular local athlete Kathy Smallwood-Cook, have been presented to the crowd but on one occasion it caused some confusion. Prior to the kick-off of centre forward **Joe Bailey**'s benefit match against Plymouth Argyle, the teams were presented to World Featherweight boxing champion Jimmy Wilde. This must have been strange for one Reading player, who was also named **Jimmy Wilde**. To make matters worse, Reading's team also included **Jimmy Carr**, the name of the town's most famous boxer of the time.

LEGLESS FAN
One hooligan who did make it over the Elm Park walls was a Southampton supporter during their League Cup tie against Reading on 8 November 1978. The yob did not get very far before being apprehended by a policeman but the bobby was in for a surprise. As he grabbed the offender by the leg he suddenly found himself holding nothing but that limb, the thug's artificial leg having become detached in the struggle.

If artificial legs are unusual for supporters, they are virtually unheard of in players. Yet, back in September 1908, the local press was full of praise for Maidenhead Norfolkian's goalkeeper George Gyngell for his display at Elm Park against Reading Reserves. Despite ending up losing 9–1, Gyngell was clearly the visitors' star, deflecting several goal-bound shots to safety with his wooden leg. Known unimaginatively as 'Peggy', Gyngell's disability did nothing to shorten his playing career because some 20 years later he saved a penalty from Reading's Irish international **Billy McConnell** in a charity match.

ROYAL GUEST
Reading did not become the Royals until 1976, but almost 50 years earlier the players were introduced to a real Royal, one of the late Queen Victoria's sons, Prince Albert of Connaught. The prince obviously knew that the home team would become the Royals one day as his visit inspired Reading to a home victory over Oldham on 25 February 1928.

UNWELCOME VISITORS
Two invaders wished they had not tried to get into Elm Park. For Reading's final game of the 1986–87 season, against champions-elect Derby County, Reading arranged for the Royal Marines free-fall parachute team to land on the pitch prior to the game. Unfortunately, one of the team got caught up in the trees surrounding the ground and had to be cut down. One animal that definitely did not want to make it to the Elm Park pitch was the gerbil that, along with the ashes of several supporters, was buried beneath the Elm Park turf!

DROPPING IN
Others to 'drop in' on Reading include Club Chairman Frank Waller, who made a spectacular entrance prior to the game against Wrexham on 8 September 1976, landing on the pitch in a helicopter having flown from the Farnborough Air Show

in just 12 minutes. Another helicopter arrival was experienced pilot **Les Ferdinand,** who flew his own 'chopper' to the Club's Hogwood training ground to greatly impress his teammates.

HEAVEN SENT

Probably the most unusual 'invasion' of Elm Park took place in July 1972 when the ground was hired by the Jehovah's Witnesses for a four day 'Divine Rulership' convention. During that period the pitch was covered with giant tableaux depicting scenes from the Bible.

SEVEN – JUST A
COINCIDENCE

POPULAR PLAYER

One of the most popular players to appear for Reading, flying winger **Michael Gilkes** was just as popular with his managers. While at Reading 'Gilkesy' had two loan spells in 1992, one with former Reading manager Ian Porterfield's Chelsea and the other at Southampton under the man who brought him to Reading, Ian Branfoot. After he left Reading in 1997, Michael also played for Wolverhampton Wanderers and Millwall, each time being signed by another of his former Reading bosses, Mark McGhee.

PROMOTION POINTERS

⚽ Middlesbrough must regard Reading as their favourite opponent, since the six seasons they shared before the Royals joined them in the Premiership all resulted in Boro winning promotion. In 1926–27 and 1928–29 they ended the season as champions of the old Second Division, a feat they repeated in 1994–95. Runners'-up spots in 1966–67 and 1997–98 saw further promotions, while 1987–88 saw them finish in a 'lowly' third place, although Boro's 'failure' in that season was compensated by a return to the top flight via the play-offs. Boro's promotion in 1994–95 was achieved despite Reading inflicting their penultimate defeat at Ayresome Park before they moved to the Riverside. Revenge came three years later, on Easter Monday 1998, when Boro became the penultimate team to win at Elm Park, prior to Reading's move to Madejski Stadium.

⚽ An even stranger coincidence revolves around Reading's seven promotions. Each season that the Club has won promotion has seen a winner of the Welsh Cup relegated or having to seek re-election. It started in 1924–25 when Merthyr finished bottom of Division Three South, and although they survived the vote that season every subsequent Welsh winner signalling a Reading success has gone down. It took Reading 50 years to gain their second League promotion, but they made sure because the previous season saw both Cardiff City and Tranmere Rovers, one of several English winners of the trophy, relegated. After that the demise of Swansea City and Wrexham in 1982–83, Cardiff two seasons later, Chester, another English winner, in 1992–93 and then Swansea and Wrexham this Millennium all signalled a Reading elevation. With Wrexham losing their Football League status at the end of 2007–08, there is every hope that the trend will continue with Reading regaining their Premier League status.

⊕ It is well known that Spurs seem to 'always' win the FA Cup when the season ends in 'one' (well five times, anyway) but the same appears to apply to Reading winning promotion in seasons ending in 'six'. The first promotion came in 1925–26 and the second was achieved in 1975–76. Ten years later the original 'Record Breaking Royals' won the Third Division title while in 2005–06 the second 'Record Breaking Royals' reached the Premier League via the Championship title. Even Reading's reserves got in on the act, winning promotion in the Football Combination in 1965–66.

⊕ A rather less welcome coincidence is that the last three seasons ending in 'eight' have seen Reading relegated. 1988 and 1998 saw the Club lose their second tier status, while 2007–08 ended with Reading relegated from the Premier League.

⊕ A visit by Gillingham to Elm Park in the League Cup has also been seen as a good luck charm for Reading. On each of the three occasions the Gills came to the Club's old ground, Reading went on to enjoy a memorable season. In 1975–76 the pain of being knocked out of the competition by Gillingham was more than offset by the fact that Reading went on to win their first promotion in 50 years. Three years later Reading did the 'double', beating Gillingham in the League Cup before going on to win the Fourth Division Championship. The Gills' final League Cup game at Elm Park saw the season end with Reading finishing as runners-up in the second tier, only failing to make it to the Premiership after defeat in the play-off final.

⊕ By way of contrast, the last three teams to lose a League game at Reading's old ground, Elm Park, during its final season were Manchester City, who lost Elm Park's final floodlit game, Stoke City, who were the 'victims' of Reading's last League win there, and Reading themselves, all ended 1997–98 being relegated together from the old Second Division.

GROUNDS FOR CELEBRATION

Double celebrations were seen at Madejski Stadium on 20 April 2002. While Reading Football Club were winning promotion to Division One at Brentford, just a few miles to the south of Griffin Park the Club's tenants, London Irish Rugby Club, were wining their first trophy in 104 years when they beat Northampton Saints at Twickenham to win the Powergen Trophy.

DRAMATIC END

The game against Queens Park Rangers on 30 April 2006 was, remarkably, the first time since they had moved to Madejski Stadium that Reading's final game of the season did not decide a promotion or relegation issue for one of the teams involved. In 1999 Oldham needed to win to avoid relegation (they did), 2000 saw Stoke City needing to match Bristol Rovers to make it to the play-offs, (they did, as well), in

2001 Reading's final game of the season was in the play-off final against Walsall at the Millennium Stadium, 2002's last game saw Reading clinch promotion at Brentford, 2003 ended with a play-off semi-final versus Wolves, and the following two seasons saw Reading go into their last game with an outside chance of making the play-offs. After 2006, normal service was resumed to some extent as Reading travelled to their final game of their first Premier League season, needing to win at Blackburn to have a chance of a UEFA Cup place, eventually drawing 3–3 and so missing out on a place in Europe by one goal. The final game of 2007–08 was even more important. Third from bottom on goal difference, Reading had to win at Derby County and hope that Fulham did not match the result at Cup finalists Portsmouth. Reading did all they could by beating the hapless Rams 4–0, but it was to no avail as Fulham also won and Reading's two-year stay in the Premier League was at an end. One small consolation for the statisticians was that the final-day victory at Pride Park maintained Reading's record of completing at least one home and away double in every one of their League seasons, a very small consolation indeed.

That 'unimportant' last match of the 2005–06 season saw Reading break the League's points total and be presented with the Championship trophy after the final whistle.

FIRST FRANK
Frank Richardson was the first Plymouth Argyle player to score a League hat-trick, on his debut at that, and later became the first at Argyle to score four in a game. Transferred from Plymouth to Reading in 1926, he soon became the first Reading player to score four in a League match. His quartet for Reading came in the last game of that season as Reading beat Brentford 7–1 and helped them win the one promotion spot in the Third Division South, pushing Plymouth into second place, the fifth consecutive season in which Plymouth had missed out on promotion by just one place.

'KEEPER'S COINCIDENCE
Goalkeeper Geoff Crudginton achieved an unusual double against Reading. On 4 May 1971 he was in goal for Aston Villa when Reading lost their Third Division status at Villa Park. Five years later he was in the Crewe Alexandra team that were Reading's opponents in the final game of their Fourth Division promotion season which saw Reading finally return to the Third Division.

When England played Eire on 14 November 1990 future Reading loan player **Chris Woods** faced his opposing keeper Pat Bonner, who later had a spell as Tommy Burns's assistant at Reading. Virtually uniquely, the two keepers were from two of Britain's greatest rivals, Rangers and Celtic.

THE FOURTH ESTATE
Reading have 'enjoyed' three spells in the Fourth Division, and although they were spread over 13 years the Club's first and last games in the basement division were

played at the same away ground. On 14 August 1971 Reading made the long journey to Hartlepool's Victoria Road on a wet and windy day that saw nearby Darlington's game postponed and, in what could only be described as a cultural shock, were brushed aside as the home side won 3–1. Reading's last Fourth Division game was a far more pleasant experience. Having clinched promotion the week before, the Club had just one target in mind when they took to the field at Hartlepool. Two goals from **Trevor Senior** in the 3–3 draw were enough to bring his season's total to 41 goals, a Club record that stands to this day.

In 1972–73 Reading began their Fourth Division campaign with a draw at home to Crewe Alexandra and ended the season with a draw, also at Crewe. In complete contrast, the following season Reading's last two games of the season were against Chester City, winning 3–0 at Elm Park on 22 April 1974 and then drawing 0–0 at Sealand Stadium five days later. It is hard to imagine that many other Clubs have deferred their League meetings until the final two games of the season.

STARTING TOGETHER
Dick Habbin scored Reading's first and last competitive goal of the 1970–71 season, as did Peter Silvester, the player Habbin replaced, at Norwich City. In addition, former Reading players **John Docherty** for Brentford and **Colin Meldrum** at Cambridge United both scored the first League goals for their Clubs that season, Meldrum's effort being United's first goal in the Football League.

ALL SQUARE
Reading's final League record for the 1980–81 season was one of almost perfect symmetry. In the last season in which only two points were awarded for a win, Reading ended with 46 points from 46 games and won with the following record:

	Won	Drew	Lost
Home	13	5	5
Away	5	5	13
Total	18	10	10

Although they scored 39 times at Elm Park, conceding 22, while the away figures were scored 23, conceded 40, the total scored was 62, and total conceded was also 62.

SIMOD SIMILARITIES
When **Neil Smillie** produced a man-of-the-match display as Reading beat Luton 4–1 in the Simod Cup Final on 27 March 1988, he did not realise that he was on his way to completing a most unwanted double. Despite that Wembley triumph, Reading ended the 1987–88 season by getting relegated, an experience Neil had suffered five years earlier with Brighton when they made it to the FA Cup Final but lost their First Division status in the same season. Reading loan goalkeeper **Chris Woods** also suffered the same fate, winning the League Cup with Norwich City on 24 March 1985 but then being relegated weeks later.

That was not the only coincidence involving Reading's Simod Cup scorers. Smillie and Stuart Beavon were the sons of former professional players: Stuart's father Cyril played for Oxford United, and Beavon Junior was born in Wolverhampton, the Club to which the other Reading scorer, **Michael Gilkes**, was sold. Both Smillie and Simod teammate **Les Taylor**, also a former Oxford player, joined Reading from Watford after a loan period and both had previously been on the losing side of an FA Cup Final, Smillie with Brighton in 1983 and Taylor the following year with Watford. On each occasion it was their Clubs' only appearance in the final to date.

When **Mick Tait**, another Simod scorer, was sold by his first League Club Carlisle United in 1977, he was replaced by a young Peter Beardsley. Twenty-two years later, as manager of Hartlepool United, Mick's last signing for the Club was a by now somewhat older and more famous Beardsley.

Many players never get the chance to play at Wembley so it is only a very elite few that get to play in finals at the national stadium in three consecutive seasons. As another member of Reading's Simod Cup-winning team, future England international **Keith Curle** achieved that rare feat. Prior to his success with Reading, Keith had been a member of the Bristol City team that beat Bolton Wanderers 3–0 in the 1986 final of the Freight Rover Trophy before losing on penalties to Mansfield Town the following year in a game that was City's 17th Cup game of a very long season.

START AND FINISH

Reading full back **Len Vallard** began his playing career with Yeovil before spending four years at Elm Park between 1958 and 1962, during which time he suffered the misfortune of breaking his arm on his League debut. Len ended his playing days with Basingstoke, where his career was ended by a neck injury sustained at Yeovil, not only on the same ground on which he had made his debut but also the incident happened exactly 16 years to the day from that start.

FINAL DEBUT

As a schoolboy, **Lawrie Sanchez** made his League debut for Reading against Wimbledon on 1 October 1977 and was marked by Dave Bassett. Eleven years later Lawrie scored Wimbledon's winner in the 1988 FA Cup Final, when Dave Bassett's team beat Liverpool. That completed a hat-trick of Wembley Final giant-killing shocks, Luton Town having beaten Arsenal in the League Cup and Reading, of course, starting it all off by beating Luton in the Simod Cup. Incidentally, Lawrie Sanchez's debut game for Reading saw an unusual incident. Reading were awarded an indirect free kick, which was taken by **Gordon Cumming**. **Steve Hetzke** attempted to head the ball on, but at best it just brushed his hair before ending up in the net. The referee allowed the goal to stand but it has always been credited to Gordon Cumming – as the taker of that indirect free kick he was, surely, the only person on the pitch who could not have scored the goal!

ALL FOUR NOTHING

On 25 September 1983 **Kerry Dixon** netted four times for Reading against Doncaster Rovers in their Third Division game at Belle Vue. On the same day, future Reading trialist Luther Blissett was also scoring four goals for Watford. Unfortunately for Dixon, his quartet was to no avail as Reading contrived to lose 7–5. Blissett, on the other hand, was able to enjoy double celebrations as his goals helped Watford beat Sunderland 8–0 in the First Division. Kerry was not the first Reading player to score four times and still end up on the losing side. On 22 March 1939 **Tommy Tait** scored all four of Reading's goals in their 6–4 Southern Section Cup defeat at Crystal Palace. That game was a replay, the match at Elm Park having ended goalless.

FAMILIAR FINALS

Elm Park has been used as the venue for two Amateur Cup Finals, in 1903 and 1914. On each occasion Oxford City reached the final, where they met teams from the North East of England, Stockton and South Bank. Both games at Elm Park ended in draws and each replay ended with City losing by the only goal of the game.

WINNING TICKET

As a Millwall player Eamonn Dunphy purchased a golden goal ticket before the away game at Blackburn Rovers. He went on to score two minutes from time from his usual inside left position. When he returned to the dressing room after the game he looked at his ticket and discovered that it showed Visitors' Number-10, 88 minutes – he had scored to make his own ticket a winner.

OFF OFF OFF SIDE

Dunphy managed to stay onside for his prize-winning goal, which is more than Blackburn's Benni McCarthy managed during his visit to Reading on 16 December 2006. Rovers' South African striker had a hat-trick of goals disallowed before finally netting one that counted, albeit from a suspiciously offside-looking position! Not surprisingly in view of his performance against Reading, McCarthy was flagged offside more times than any other Premiership player that season. Even so, he had some way to go to match his former Blackburn teammates. In 1896 Rovers had an amazing five goals disallowed for offside (and another for entering the net after the half time whistle had been blown). As with their game at Reading, Rovers overcame these disappointments to win, beating Liverpool 1–0.

PENALTY PAIN

One of the pivotal moments in Reading's history came on 29 May 1995 at Wembley when **Stuart Lovell**'s penalty was saved in the play-off final against Bolton. A successful kick would have put Reading 3–0 up and surely into the Premier League. Five years later to the day, former Reading loanee and teammate of Lovell at Wokingham Town Darren Barnard suffered the same fate with a Wembley play-off penalty for Barnsley.

ONE IN A MILLION?

When the ball burst during the 1946 FA Cup Final between Charlton Athletic and Derby County, the match referee was famously quoted as saying that it was a million-to-one occurrence. Despite this statement, the following season the ball burst again, and yet again Charlton were involved. The only recorded instance of a ball bursting during a Reading League game took place on 28 September 1929 in an away game at, where else, Charlton. In March 1978 the ball burst during Reading A's Middlesex Border League game against Hungerford in what was an eventful game, since there was also a temporary floodlight failure.

GIANT KILLERS' MISERY

Reading have lost to four non-League Clubs on their travels in the FA Cup, with dire consequences for the winners! The first two Southern League Clubs to knock Reading out of the Cup, Guildford City in 1937 and Brentwood in 1969, both subsequently went out of business, Brentwood just two years after their memorable victory. Since then, Hendon, in 1975, and Wealdstone, two years later, have knocked Reading out of the competition, and although both are still in existence they have suffered severe financial problems, with Wealdstone being homeless for over 20 years.

DOUBLE DISMISSALS

Wealdstone's victory took place at their Lower Mead ground but they have less happy memories of their two visits to Elm Park in the FA Cup. Not only did they lose both games, played in 1976 and 1985, by the only goal of the game, but on each occasion they had two players sent off. In the second of those meetings those dismissals, plus one Reading player, came after a 20-man brawl following a terrible tackle on Reading captain **Martin Hicks** by Wealdstone's newly introduced substitute. That sub was playing his first senior game of what was to be a long and controversial career – the sinning-sub was none other than soccer hard-man Vinnie Jones.

CARELESS HANDS

Another FA Cup sinner who got away with it was Tottenham Hotspur's full back Sandy Tait. In the closing minutes of the third-round tie at Elm Park, with the game poised at 1–1, Reading sent in a fierce shot. With the Spurs keeper beaten, the ball was destined for the back of the net when visiting defender Tait made a flying save as he punched the ball round the post. Everyone in the 14,417 record crowd saw the blatant penalty, except referee Mr Green, who compounded his error by awarding Spurs a goal kick. It was a significant decision because Spurs won the replay and went on to become the last non-League team to win the Cup. Twenty-five years later Sandy Tait was back at Elm Park, putting his hands to more legitimate uses as foreman in charge of the construction of Elm Park's new grandstand.

SCHOOL FRIENDS

A star defender for Reading in the 1970s, **Paul Bennett** made his League debut with Southampton at Tottenham Hotspur, where he was required to mark Martin Chivers, a player who had attended the same school as Bennett. What made the event so unusual was that in the same game the Saints centre forward Ron Davies was being marked by Mike England, both of them also being former pupils of the same school.

GOALIE'S GRIEF

Goalkeeper **Phil Whitehead** gave sterling service to Reading either side of the turn of the millennium, but must have hated the sight of Sunderland's Stadium of Light. During 1998–99 he played there twice, once for Oxford United and then for West Bromwich Albion, and conceded a total of 10 goals in those two games, equalling the total conceded by the home side's keeper Thomas Sorensen in all 23 home games that season.

GOOD SEND-OFF

As well as being named after a legendary England bowler by his cricket-mad father, **Brian Statham** also ran up a strange hat-trick of red cards. On loan with Reading towards the end of 1990–91, Brian was sent off at Brentford in what was his final game for the Club. Within a year he joined Brentford, only to suffer the same fate by being dismissed in his final game for the Bees. Brian then moved on to Gillingham but was sent off in his first away game for them, at Griffin Park!

MANAGERIAL MERRY-GO-ROUND

Another strange hat-trick came in the manager's office at Doncaster Rovers. Minutes before the start of the 1997–98 season the Rovers board sacked former Reading forward **Sammy Chung** and replaced him with another former Reading forward, **Kerry Dixon**. Kerry was himself replaced by **Dave Cowling**, yet another former Reading forward, although he only lasted 10 days, the fifth shortest managerial career in League history. Wycombe also had three former Reading players as managers, **Paul Bence** in their non-League days and then in 1999 two Wembley scorers managed the Chairboys, **Neil Smillie** who netted for Reading in the Simod Cup being replaced by Wimbledon's FA Cup hero **Lawrie Sanchez**.

TREBLE TROUBLE

Former Reading players very nearly achieved a distinctly unwanted hat-trick of managerial horrors. Not many goalkeepers become successful managers and 1920s Reading keeper **George Irwin** can be counted among them. The first Crystal Palace player to manage the Club, George was in charge when Palace were on the receiving end of Reading's 10–2 record victory, and six years later he was in charge of Darlington when they had to apply for re-election in 1952. Darlington were re-elected but Workington were less fortunate, losing their League place to

Wimbledon in 1977, at the end of a season in which they were managed by Reading's first Player of the Year, **Colin Meldrum**. Another tough-tackling defender **Stuart Morgan** escaped the ignominy of being the manager of the first Club to automatically drop out of the League. In the final game of 1986–87 his Torquay United side scored an injury-time equaliser to beat the drop, the time famously being added for treatment to a player bitten by a police dog.

SUCCESSFUL SACKINGS

Even success as a manager does not guarantee continued employment. Reading infamously sacked Maurice Evans in January 1984, even though his team were in the third promotion spot in the Fourth Division at the time. It was a decision that so incensed the normally loyal Reading Football Supporters' Club that they immediately showed their disapproval by naming the popular Evans as a life vice-president. Similarly hard done by was former Reading youth goalkeeper **Mick Walker**, who enjoyed a long and successful managerial career, but not at Colchester United. He lost his job at Layer Road during the 1986–87 season despite having been named manager of the month the day before. In 1971–72, Blyth Spartans hit the headlines with a giant-killing FA Cup run that saw them beat Stockport County and Crewe Alexandra, defeats that cost the managers of those Clubs their jobs. Spartans actually completed a hat-trick of League managerial dismissals when they came up against Reading in the third round. Caretaker boss Jimmy Wallbanks was in charge of the game at Blyth's Croft Park, where his team earned a replay before he handed over to new manager Charlie Hurley. Unlike the other two of Blyth's victims, Reading were grateful for 'Wally's' managerial stint and he immediately reverted to his normal Reading role as physiotherapist.

NATIONAL LEADERS

Towards the end of Reading's 2007–08 Premier League season they played four consecutive Madejski Stadium matches against sides managed by former national team managers. First up was Manchester City, managed by former England boss Sven-Goran Eriksson, followed by ex-Scotland manager Alex McLeish's Birmingham City. Next was Blackburn Rovers and their former Welsh national manager Mark Hughes, the run ending with Fulham's Roy Hodgson who had managed Switzerland, Finland and United Arab Emirates over the years. During that period one of Reading's away fixtures was at Newcastle United, where they came up against Eriksson's England predecessor, Kevin Keegan.

CROWN JEWEL

Reading had tried to sign **David Crown** from Brentford in November 1981 but he moved to Portsmouth instead. Towards the end of the following season he was loaned to Exeter City, where he scored a last-minute winner on the final day of the season that relegated Reading in place of Exeter. Having made his last appearance for Portsmouth against Reading, he eventually moved to Elm Park in August 1983 and played a vital role that season in helping the Club regain the Third Division status he had cost them a year earlier. Despite relegating Reading, Crown was so popular with the Reading fans that a local football team, the David Crown Steamers, was named after him.

REGLUAR RETURNS

When **Steve Francis** was transferred from Reading in August 1993 he subsequently played for two other League Clubs, Huddersfield Town and Northampton Town. With both of these Clubs his League debut came in games against Reading.

FAVOURITE GOAL

Stylish midfielder **David Madden** scored his only goal for Reading at Christmas 1987 in the Club's win at Crystal Palace. His only other League goal had come three years earlier for Charlton Athletic who, at the time, were tenants at Selhurst Park. As a result, not only had both his League goals been scored on the same ground, but they had even been scored in the same net. Released by Reading at the end of that season, it was not surprising that Dave took the opportunity to play regularly at his favourite ground by signing for Palace.

DAUNTING DEBUTS

Neither of Reading's two modern grounds could be classed as among **Andy Gurney**'s favourites. He made his League debut for Bristol Rovers at Elm Park on 2 April 1994 and ended up losing 2–0. Things got even worse after he signed for Reading and made his debut for his new Club at Madejski Stadium on 16 January 1999. That game saw Reading suffer their heaviest defeat at their new ground, losing 6–0 to Andy's old Club Bristol Rovers.

JUST LIKE BROTHERS

Bertie Oswald Corbett enjoyed two spells with Reading in their Southern League days, either side of his one game for England in 1901. His brother Reggie was also an England international and the two of them enjoyed remarkably similar lives:

⊛ Both Reggie and Bertie won a single cap each, their internationals both achieving wins over Wales.

⊛ Both played for Corinthians and were left wingers.

⊛ Both Reggie and Bertie became schoolteachers before each died at the age of 87.

WEMBLEY STARTERS

Two Reading players appeared in the initial internationals at both the original and the new Wembley Stadium. Then a Bolton player but later to be both a Reading player and manager, **Billy Butler** was the first England player to make his international debut at Wembley when he played against Scotland on 12 April 1924. Eighty-three years later and, at long last, the new Wembley was finally ready, with England celebrating their inaugural international with the visit of Brazil. Making his England debut that day was Reading left back **Nicky Shorey**, yet despite an accomplished display his first cap was not the most memorable event for him that weekend – less than 24 hours after winning his first cap Nicky had an even bigger match, his wedding to Emily. Nicky was not the first Reading player to have appeared at the rebuilt national stadium, as his teammate **Leroy Lita** had played in the first formal game at the stadium, an under-21 international against Italy two months earlier.

Former Reading winger **Sammy Igoe** also has happy memories of a double achieved at two national stadiums. On 1 April 2007 he scored for Bristol Rovers in the final of the Johnstone's Paint Trophy against Doncaster Rovers, which was the last English final staged at Cardiff's Millennium Stadium before they reverted to Wembley. Two months later he scored in the League Two play-off final at Wembley, thus matching Didier Drogba by scoring at both venues.

LIGHT WORK

Reading had two completely different sets of floodlights at their old Elm Park ground. The first, installed in 1954, were fixed to the roof of the stands and on short poles behind the goals, while their replacements were on 60ft pylons that dominated the town's skyline. When the Football League eventually relented on the use of lights, they initially only permitted them for re-arranged fixtures, so the first competitive game played under Elm Park's lights was on 27 February 1956 for the visit of Colchester United. Sadly, it was the visitors who shone under the lights, winning 3–0. Twelve years later and the replacement lights were first used for a League Cup tie which ended with the same result. This time Reading lost 2–0 and the visitors, again, were Colchester. Strangely, Reading have been far more successful under other Club's new lights, beating Swindon 1–0 in a friendly to mark the switching-on of the County Ground's lights in October 1951. This was Reading's first game under lights and they quickly adapted to the new phenomenon, **Ron Blackman** scoring the only goal of the game after just 25 seconds. Later, on 24 February 1959, Reading thrashed Doncaster Rovers 5–2 under their new lights.

ATTENDANCE HAT-TRICKS

Liverpool almost completed a hat-trick of attendance records during Reading's first Premiership season. The very first meeting between the two Clubs took place at Anfield in the third round of the League Cup on 25 October 2006 and drew in 42,741 fans – the highest attendance to watch Reading at a Club ground at that time. Ten days later Reading returned to Anfield for their Premiership game and that record was increased to 43,741. When the Reds made their first visit to Reading on 7 April 2007, they were looking to break Madejski Stadium's attendance record of 24,122 set by Aston Villa. However, Liverpool missed out on that record – by just one fan.

Newcastle United did set a trio of attendance records, although it took them almost 107 years to achieve it. On 4 January 1969 41,210 were at St James' Park for Reading's fourth-round FA Cup tie, a figure that stood as the biggest crowd to watch Reading until their appearance at Wembley in the 1988 Simod Cup Final. Newcastle upped the record to watch Reading on a Club ground to 48,182 at their first Premiership meeting on 6 December 2006, while back on 27 January 1900 Reading's FA Cup visit to St James' Park attracted their first five-figure attendance. Unfortunately, that double hat-trick of big attendances against Liverpool and Newcastle all ended in defeat for Reading.

LEAGUE INS AND OUTS

In March 1962 Accrington Stanley resigned from the Football League, their place being taken by Oxford United. Fast-forward to the last day of 2005–06 and Oxford are beaten at home by Leyton Orient to be relegated from the League and replaced by Accrington Stanley. The Reading connection is that one of their former players, **Bill Smith**, made his last appearance of a long League career in Accrington's final game, while **Matt Robinson**, also a former Reading player, ended his League career in Oxford's final League game.

The only other Club to resign during the season in recent years was Aldershot. On 20 March 1992, the Shots played their final League game before their resignation at Cardiff City and their team included former Reading defender **Mark Whitlock** plus Reading-born Leigh Cooper, brother of Reading's **Adrian Cooper**. Sixteen years later, Aldershot returned to the Football League and the team that earned the point that clinched promotion with a draw at Exeter City included former Reading midfielder **Ricky Newman** and **Louie Soares**, previously a youth team player at Madejski Stadium. The team that the Shots replaced in the League, Mansfield Town, featured another former Reading youngster, **Johnny Mullins**, although he could not be blamed for the Stags' demise, having been voted their Player of the Year in that final League season.

EIGHT – THE NAME GAME

SO GOOD, THEY NAMED THEM TWICE

Several Reading players have changed their names during their careers. Both **George Goodman** and **Les Goldberg** changed their names, to **Getgood** and **Gaunt** respectively, while with Reading. George changed his name almost as soon as he arrived at Elm Park, but Les caused no end of problems for statisticians, playing two seasons at Reading as Goldberg and then two as Gaunt. Born Lohn, **Billy Lane** played his entire professional career under his changed name, including the 1928–29 season at Reading. He was also a popular player with Spurs, where fans spotted his initials of W.H. Lane and nicknamed him 'White Hart' Lane. He later made his name with Watford, for whom he scored a hat-trick against Clapton Orient in three minutes, and as such is one of several players with a claim to the fastest League hat-trick.

By contrast, **Graham French** changed his name after his playing days were over. His League career had begun at Shrewsbury, becoming their youngest League player when he made his debut against Reading, a Club he subsequently joined on loan for three games in November 1973. A controversial lifestyle, that included prison following a shooting incident, led him to change his name to Lafite. In Reading's Southern League days they sold **Michael Good** to Brighton in 1904, where he promptly switched his surname to **Sullivan**. A year later **Arthur Leonard** played on Reading's right wing for a season, returning in 1908 after spells with Clapton Orient and Plymouth Argyle, this time using the name **Bamford**. This did not mislead Reading's fans, who immediately recognized him from his distinctive 'little mincing steps'! It was not just surnames that players have chosen to change. Born **Frederick Anthony John Gernon**, the versatile defender chose to be known by the first name of Irvin during his playing career, which spread throughout the 1980s and included a season at Elm Park.

And it is not just players who have changed their names. Reading Chairman John Madejski was born John Hurst and he named part of his printing empire after his birth name.

STRANGE NAMES

Some players must have considered changing their names, especially their middle names. Just look at these imaginary Reading line ups that would raise few eyebrows when read out over the PA:

Pre War XI
Lancelot Holliday Richardson (1929–31)
Thomas Rollason Shipman (1937–38)
Bert Mollison Eggo (1921–29)
Jimmy Sigsworth Liddle (1932–37)

Billy Bullock Wright (1933–38)
John Birrell Barclay (1926–27)
Matt Sprott Young (1923–24)
Wilson Messina Allman (1905–07)
Ralph Slack Littlewood Allen (1936)
Herbert Ernest Saxon Cordey Lyon (1902–03)
Edgar Underwood Bluff (1903–04)

Post War XI
Willie Furness Hall (1953–54)
Andy McArthur Alleyne (1971–76)
Michael Glenis Gilkes (1984–97)
John Hilley Walker (1957–66)
Alan Hayward Wicks (1952–59)
Paul Peterson Clark (1981–82)
David Bell Grant (1963–66)
Jimmy Caird Martin (1962–64)
Willie Silcock Gardiner (1958–61)
George Larmouth Forrester (1955–56)
Gilbert Swinborne Glidden (1936–50)

THE CLUE'S NOT IN THE NAME

In addition to the above fictitious teams, neither Fred Charlton Houldsworth nor Sam Bolton Ashworth played for the Clubs featured in their names. Ashworth should probably have been named Stoke as he played for Stoke City, Stoke Nomads and Stoke Alliance plus four other Staffordshire Clubs. In 1904, with Manchester City, he became only the third amateur to win an FA Cup-winners' medal since professionalism was legalised in 1885 but, on the other hand, he was one of 18 City players found guilty of receiving unauthorised payments. Back to names, George Warrington Gale was not born in that town and Robert Broome Oswald was not a sweeper! Peter Young McLean was 30 when his Reading career ended and Harry Summers Brown was born in September, while it seems unlikely that Tommy Bastin Wilson was named after Cliff Bastin, even though the Arsenal forward had won the League title, FA Cup and been capped for England by the time Tommy was born in 1933. On the other hand, Craig Dell Maskell was probably the only player to make his League debut at the ground of the same name as his middle name. Meanwhile, the exotically named David Reno Bacuzzi and Leon Autonin Boullemier were born nowhere more continental than Highgate and Stoke respectively.

IN TRIBUTE

Reading 1991 loanee **Brian Statham** was named after the England bowler by his cricket-mad father, while legendary Royals keeper **Neil Shaka Hislop** was named after a Zulu warrior king. Sadly, King Shaka suffered from mental illness later in his life which resulted in him causing the deaths of thousands of his people, meaning that one of Reading's most popular players is surely the only Football League player to be named after a mass-murderer! But the strangest reason for the naming of their child must belong to the parents of Reading's Welsh international and member of their 1925–26 Third Division South Championship team **David Gethin Evans**. A few players have been honoured by having pubs named after them, but 'Dai' Evans was named after his parent's pub, 'The Dai Gethin'.

SAME NAME – Part One

Although 'Smith' is the most frequent surname to appear on Reading's team sheets, as it is with most Clubs, other names have also featured regularly. When they played at Preston North End on 28 December 1929, Reading fielded three **Richardsons**, Frank, Lance and Jim, in their team. The Reading game at Bristol Rovers on 15 September 1984 saw four Williams on the pitch, although only Jerry was a Reading player, appearing against Rovers' Dave, Geraint and Brian. All of this must have made it very difficult for reporters at those games, but nowhere near as difficult as the Rochdale versus Reading game played on 26 September 1970. The press box must have heaved a collective sigh of relief when Tony **Wasgstaff** went off, leaving only one Wagstaff, Tony's brother Barrie, on the pitch. But that feeling must have changed to one of horror when they realised that Reading's substitute was **Dennis Butler**, the local youngster joining two other Dennis Butlers, Reading's left back and Rochdale's midfielder, already on the pitch.

SAME NAME – Part Two

Of course, with over 800 League players and several hundred Southern League players appearing through the years for Reading, there is bound to be some duplication of names. Spanning both those eras, a forward by the name of **Jim McIntyre** spent the 1904–05 season with Reading while his namesake played for the Club at the turn of the millennium. The 'original' Jim McIntyre was to feature in Reading's history some 20 years after he left Elm Park, to his regret. As manager of Fulham, McIntyre was responsible for the transfer of record goalscorer **Frank Newton** to Reading in 1934. This led to his dismissal, the Fulham board citing the 'unprecedented action of transferring, on his own initiative, F. Newton to Reading for the impossible price of £650'. Despite this, James still had the honour of being the first manager to lead two different Clubs to promotion from the Third Division, Southampton in 1921–22 and Fulham 10 years later. Strangely, after each of these successes McIntyre left the game, on the first occasion to run a hotel and then after his Fulham dismissal he went to work in a factory.

McIntyre Senior shared his Southern League season with left-footed, free-scoring forward **George Harris**, 60 years before another left-footed, free-scoring forward named **George Harris** moved to Elm Park and immediately broke the Club scoring record for a winger. During the last two seasons of World War Two football,

Reading confused fans and reporters by fielding two **Freddy Fishers** in the same team. Fred T. Fisher was a Grimsby full back playing as a guest for the Club, while Slough youngster Freddy later signed for Reading, spending six years at Elm Park mainly on the right wing.

Apart from the two **Dennis Butlers**, the only same-named players to make League appearances for Reading are **Roy Davies**, **John Walker** and **Jimmy Martin**, plus the **Micky Murphys** featured in 'How Not To Play For Reading'. As with the McIntyres and Harrises, the two Roy Davies had similar playing styles. Both were wingers and both had moments they would probably prefer to forget. The early Davies, who had three seasons at Elm Park between 1929 and 1932, joined Reading after his contract with Wolves had been cancelled following a sending off, while the second one left Reading in 1980 for Torquay United, where he was a popular player even though the United programme commented that 'discipline was not his forte'. The Johnny Walkers both came to Elm Park near the end of their playing careers and yet played longer than expected, both finishing their League careers at Reading as full backs. The original Walker carried on playing until he was over 40 to become Reading's oldest-ever League player. Strangely, both Jimmy C. Martins were forwards, although the player Reading signed in 1924 had a career and goals total 10 times that of his successor, the second J.C.M.'s playing career virtually ending after he broke his leg in a collision with Watford's young keeper Pat Jennings on 25 January 1964. In addition to the two James Martins, Reading have also fielded a **Martin James**, this reversal of names coinciding with a reversal of position since M.J. was a centre half.

To complete the set, Reading have also had two managers named Jack Smith. Admittedly, the man who took over from Ted Drake in 1952 was christened 'John' but was always known as Jack throughout his playing career. Again, the name was not the only feature they shared – both ran pubs after they quit the manager's office at Elm Park. Finally, Reading have fielded two **Harry Millars**. The original was Reading's first-ever captain back in 1872, an important role in those days since no one could play for the Club without the captain's permission. The second Harry Millar was loaned to Reading from Bury in 1898–99 to restore his confidence after he had been barracked by the League Club's fans.

HOW NOT TO PLAY FOR READING

The two shortest Reading playing careers were both recorded by players with the first name Andy. **Andy Painter** made his one and only first team appearance for Reading when he came on for the final eight minutes of Reading's FA Cup tie against Wealdstone on 20 November 1976. Almost 20 years later, on 16 April 1996, another Andy, Freeman, reduced his namesake's record to a mere five minutes when he came on at Watford. At least Andy F. had crammed a lot into his five minutes of fame, since that period saw two goals scored and a player booked. He was not the only Reading player to have a career limited to Vicarage Road. Both **Darren Campbell** and **Peter Castle** came on as substitutes during Reading's 3–0 win at Watford on 30

April 2003. The game was doubly memorable for Castle as he was just 16 years and 49 days old and had to get his headmaster's permission to play on a school night to become the Club's youngest-ever League player. Other short-term Andys were **Andy King,** who played a mere 25 minutes as a substitute for Reading at Wigan Athletic on 17 September 1988, and **Andy Moore,** a Reading veteran with 70 minutes to his credit during the home game against Doncaster Rovers on 17 February 1982.

Another name to avoid if you want to play for Reading is Murphy. In 88 years of League football, Reading have featured three Murphys and they only managed four games and three substitutions in total. **Nick Murphy** made three starts plus two sub appearances in 1970–71, while his namesakes, both **Mick Murphys,** only managed 166 minutes between them.

So the message is clear – if your name is Andy Murphy and you are brought on as a Reading substitute at Watford's Vicarage Road you would be advised to call in at the job centre the next day!

THE SMITH XI

As with most Clubs, Reading could field a team of Smiths and the following by no means exhausts Reading's players of this name:

John Smith: was signed on trial in 1907 but only made one Southern League appearance.

Jack Smith: he made more Southern League appearances for Reading than any other player and then became the Club's first player-manager when they entered the League.

Herbert Smith: Reading's most capped English international and one of the last old-style amateurs to play for Reading in the first decade of the 20th century.

Ben Smith: his only first team appearance came as a second half substitute at Manchester City in the final game of the 1996–97 season. He later made his Madejski Stadium debut as a Yeovil player in an FA Cup tie in 1999.

Eric Smith: the only Reading-born Smith, he scored one goal during his 63 first team appearances spread over eight years up to 1956. Like Ben, he also moved on to Yeovil after he left Reading.

Neil Smith: he is a well-travelled midfielder who made over 300 League appearances in his career, 51 of them with Reading between 1999 and 2001.

John Smith: with 102 League appearances for Reading, this speedy mid-1920s winger made more League appearances for the Club than any other Smith.

Mark Smith: he played three games for Reading on loan from Nottingham Forest over Christmas 1990. All three games were won and on each occasion Mark was substituted for Stuart Lovell.

Bill Smith: despite being a versatile player who could play in almost any position, he only played three times for Reading. Said to have the hardest shot at Elm Park, he scored 40 times in a 237-game League career.

William Smith: brother of the great Herbert Smith, he only played nine Southern League games for Reading spread over three seasons at the start of the last century.

Les Smith: the shortest playing career of any of Reading's Smiths, Les's one game as a wartime guest was on Boxing Day 1944, the game at Aldershot being abandoned after only 40 minutes.

Manager: with Jack Smith 'selected' as a player, the job goes to **Joe Smith**, who left Reading in 1935 for Blackpool, where he stayed for 33 years, guiding the Seasiders to victory in the 1953 'Matthews Final'.

——————— NICKNAME NONSENSE ———————

Most fans are aware that Reading have been known by two nicknames but, in fact, a third lesser-known nickname existed long ago. When the Club was founded back in 1871 the meeting to form the Club took place in the Bridge Street Rooms, not surprisingly based in Bridge Street, close to the banks of the River Kennet. Reading played their first games at the Reading Recreation Ground, then the Reading Cricket Club Ground and the Caversham Cricket Ground, all three being situated on the banks of the Thames. Despite this the Club was known as the Kennetsiders, partly because of the site of that first meeting and partly because Victorian Reading was based around the River Kennet rather than the more illustrious Thames.

That early nickname eventually fell out of use when the Club finally moved to its own ground at Elm Park in September 1896, the Club gradually becoming known all over the country for the town's major industry as the Kennetsiders became the Biscuitmen, the Biscuits or even ye Biscuiteers. This was a gift to headline writers ('Reading Take The Biscuit') and cartoonists, with one local exponent, AREFF of the *Reading Chronicle*, embodying the Club's fans in a character called 'Ginger Nut'. It is said that at the time Elm Park opened every family in Reading had at least one member working for Huntley and Palmers, and 'The Factory' dominated the town until the early 1970s. By 1976 Huntley and Palmers had all but closed and the Supporters' Club, in conjunction with the *Reading Chronicle*, held a competition to find an appropriate replacement nickname. The undisputed winner, selected by Mr B. Palmer of Shinfield among many, was the Royals, and for the last 20 plus years fans at Elm Park and Madejski Stadium have been chanting the new name. The football Club was not the first local sporting team to adopt the Royals as their nickname, although it is unlikely that there will ever be any confusion between the professional footballers and the Reading Royals Synchronized Swimming Club!

HARD NAMES

Players have always been given nicknames by fans or teammates, many reflecting the playing style of the individual. For instance, it is fair to assume that forwards **Peter 'Elbows' Harman** and **Trevor 'Nudger' Morley** were more popular with the Elm Park faithful than they were with the opposition or, for that matter, referees. Similarly, **'Demolition' Dennis Butler**, a 1970s full back who frequently combined a powerful tackle with a loud grunt, provides a good description of the popular defender's style. An even more popular left back, **Ray 'Bomber' Reeves,** earned his nickname partly due to the awesome strength he used to good effect and partly because of the power of his kicking that led to any free kick in the opponents' half being viewed as a possible scoring chance.

One of the toughest men in 1980s football, **Mick Tait** was highly respected by Elm Park fans who, likening his challenges to those of World Heavyweight Champion Mike Tyson, borrowed the boxer's nickname so that Mick became 'Iron Mike'. Another Reading tough guy was **Fred Sharpe**. In a four-match spell in January 1970 Fred sustained a cut eye requiring stitches, reopened the wound resulting in more stitches, dislocated his shoulder and broke his nose. Despite all of these setbacks Fred was not substituted in any of those games. When, a month later, a car crash on the way to a game failed to prevent Fred from playing he was dubbed 'Iron Man'. Another tough tackler in the 1960s, **John 'Chopper' Chapman,** regularly lived up to his nickname. And when a player receives a six-month suspension from the FA there is no further need to explain why Southern League full back **Tommy Clinch** was always known as 'Terrible Tommy'!

ALL IS EXPLAINED

☺ Less physical styles of play were also recognised by fans and colleagues. **Richard 'Jammer' Evans**, a speedy Southern League winger at the beginning of the last century, was so named because in those days one of the fastest things around was a (wind) jammer sailing ship. Pre-World War One keeper **Rab Bernard** lived up to the old adage that 'all goalies are crazy' by earning the name 'Daft Rab' for his suicidal bravery when diving at forwards' feet.

☺ Rather less complimentary was the name given by Madejski Stadium fans to **Paul Brayson**. Known as 'the Michael Owen of the North East' when he joined Reading from Newcastle United, striker Paul failed to live up to this billing and after a goal in his second start after his March 1998 transfer he lost his scoring touch. By the time he left Reading two years later he had failed to add to that early goal in his 48 appearances and had earned the unwanted nickname from the fans of 'Banjo', as in 'couldn't hit a barn door with a banjo'.

❖ One player who never had a problem hitting the net was **Jack Palethorpe**. After scoring 54 goals in only 57 Reading League games, Jack was sold to Stoke City for a big fee. He immediately helped them win promotion that season, and a year later he moved to Preston North End and repeated the feat, scoring the promotion-clinching goal with seven minutes of the season left. These consecutive promotions led to Jack earning the deserved nickname of 'SOS' Palethorpe.

❖ Another popular goalscorer, 1980s Reading favourite **Kevin Bremner**'s all-action style earned him the nickname of 'Mad Max'. On the other hand **George Eastham,** who played six games for Reading during the war, was known as 'Diddler' due to his tricky play. George played for England and when his son, George Jr, was capped in 1963 they became the first father and son to be so honoured.

❖ Managers do not appear to encourage the use of nicknames, although Reading-born **Martin Allen**, the son of **Denis Allen**, has always been known as 'Mad Dog', with good reason. Former Reading Southern League star **Willie Garbutt** is credited with developing the sport in Italy where he was known as 'The English Mister.'

❖ Some players acquire their nicknames because of their physical appearance. The gangling **Rod Thornhill** put his long legs to good use in Reading's half back line during the 1960s and was known throughout the Club as 'Spider'. Another player of similar build was **Ray Hiron,** who played a vital role in Reading's 1975–76 promotion, and he was known as 'Charlie', bizarrely being named by his former Portsmouth colleagues because of his perceived likeness to the Fratton Park physio's skeleton, which was also known as 'Charlie'.

❖ Goalkeeper **Phil Burns** came out of the army to play for Reading and was promptly named 'Jack' by his new teammates, who thought he resembled Jack Nicholson. On the same lines, **Dylan Kerr** was known as 'Barney Rubble' to his teammates due to his perceived facial similarities to Fred Flintstone's cartoon friend.

❖ Another Reading lookalike was **Glen Little** who throughout his playing career has been known as 'Blakey', due to his uncanny resemblance to the inspector in the sitcom *On The Buses*. A great impersonator, Glen can even sound like his

TV character and so it was a disappointment that when he signed for Reading, the Club had already sold centre forward **Martin Butler**, thus denying 'Blakey' the chance to use his famous catchphrase 'I hate you, Butler'!

☻ Individual teammates can be credited with providing a name for a colleague, and when legendary player and manager **Maurice Evans** first joined Reading one of his fellow trainees was **Gordon Neate**. Maurice clearly thought that the Reading-born defender did not live up to his surname and consequently began calling Gordon 'Fred Karno' after the crazy silent movies star. The nickname really stuck, and although he remains a popular character at the Club over 50 years after he first joined Reading, some fans still think that the groundsman's real name is Fred Neate.

☻ Another nickname that stuck was the one given to **Stuart Lovell** by youth team boss **Bobby Williams**. During one training session, Williams (who in his playing days was known as 'Shadow' because of his ability to ghost in to the penalty area and score vital goals) told the young striker 'I used to know a player called Archie Lovell and he was bloody useless as well'. From that day on Stuart became 'Archie' to everyone and the fans' chant of 'Archie, Archie' was a memorable feature of Reading games in the 1990s.

SPOILT FOR CHOICE

Sometimes teammates have a different nickname to the one used by the supporters. **Martin Williams,** for instance, was known within the Club as 'The Kid' after he was forced to sleep in a child's bed during a pre-season tour. The fans, however, were less kind, referring to the enigmatic striker as 'Skittles' due to his regular failure to keep his feet at vital moments. **Steve Moran** had no nickname that was used by the fans but he was, apparently, known rather unflatteringly as 'Piggy' by his playing colleagues. Another player with two nicknames was **Walter Bailey**, the scorer of Reading's very first goal in the League. Known throughout his career as 'Joe', his happy personality also led to him being called 'Bubbles'.

King of the nicknamed players must be Reading's Premier League keeper, **Marcus Hahnemann**. At Fulham he was called 'Boomer' because of his prodigious kicking, but at Reading his Club nickname became 'Buddy'. However, after a spontaneous chant in response to a sensational penalty save against Watford on 23 November 2002, to the Reading fans the American international is simply 'USA'.

One of Marcus's teammates was also nicknamed after a spontaneous chant from Madejski Stadium fans. Having made a remarkably swift recovery from an ankle injury, **Ibrahima Sonko** crowned another towering display at the centre of Reading's Championship-winning team with a spectacular and brave headed clearance that saved a certain goal for opponents Ipswich Town. Immediately, the crowd began chanting 'Sonko is Superman' and the name stuck, even to the extent that the Senegalese international was commemorated with T-shirts featuring him as the super hero.

Another player, more popular even than Reading's giant American keeper, was **Phil Parkinson**, who also had three nicknames during his time at Elm Park. Phil's aggressive tackling initially earned him the obvious title of 'Psycho' shortly after he joined Reading in 1992, but as he matured into an inspirational leader he became 'Parky' and, in the local press at least, 'Captain Marvel'.

SIZE MATTERS

Ernie Watts was the first player for whom Reading paid a transfer fee, costing 2/6d (12.5p) from Tilehurst in 1896. In those days both players and the general population were physically smaller than they are today so, despite only being 5ft 10in tall and weighing 12st 8lb, he was always known as 'Big Wattie'. On the other hand, Joe Hutton was only 5ft 3.5in tall and, as the shortest player to appear for Reading, he was appropriately known as 'The Mighty Atom.'

CRUEL TO BE KIND

Other nicknames demonstrate the perverse humour that exists in football. **John Keeley** spent a month at Elm Park in February 1992, on loan from Oldham Athletic. While with the Latics he experienced a horrendous time. He failed to make their first team, partly because of three different hand injuries, broken ribs and a sending off. He had also suffered two burglaries and his car had been vandalised – what else could his teammates call him but 'Lucky'? A similar level of humour was imposed on **Robert Codner**. During one of his three short spells with Reading, Robert was mistakenly charged with possession of cocaine but, partly due to character evidence from his friend and Reading teammate **Michael Gilkes**, the jury quickly found Robert not guilty. However, this trial took place at the same time as a rather more famous court case and on his return to Elm Park as an innocent man his teammates named him 'OJ'!

DEFYING LOGIC

On the odd occasion a nickname simply defies explanation. One of the most popular players at Elm Park throughout the 1960s, **Denis Allen** was part of the well-known footballing family of that name, and yet no one has been able to explain why he was always known by the unlikely nickname of 'Daisy'. Denis was not the only Reading player with a less-than-manly nickname. A player who lost his life in World War One, **H.P. Bert Slatter** had the unlikely name of 'Little Eva', but both Denis and Bert's names are preferable to that given to Southern League winger and ex-miner **Jack Bainbridge,** who was known as 'Pretty Polly'. **Billy Walker** played for Reading for one season in 1907–08 before being capped twice for Scotland, but despite that fame no one appears to be able to identify the reason for his nickname, 'Shoogly'.

IN DEFENCE

Although not really a nickname, during their promotion season of 2001–02 Reading featured three defenders who all had the same first name of Adrian.

Messrs **Viveash, Whitbread** and **Williams** clearly did not suffer from any confusion over their shared name, as they formed a strong defensive unit that was frequently referred to as 'Adrian's Wall'!

OWN NAME

It is very rare for a player to have the luxury of choosing his own nickname, but the Reading squad were allowed that chance when they represented the Club in a charity darts tournament in March 2008 to raise funds for their partners' charity, 'Royal Families'. Inspired by the presence of darts champions Phil 'The Power' Taylor and Bobby 'Dazzler' George, some of the names chosen are obvious to Reading supporters, but with others it is probably best not to know! The nicknamed players were:

Nicky *'The Dreamer'* Shorey
Marcus *'Buddy'* Hahnemann
Glen *'Iceman'* Little
Ibrahima *'Toy Boy'* Sonko
Brynjar *'Assassin'* Gunnarsson
Steven *'The Contender'* Hunt
Kevin *'Irish Rock'* Doyle
Ivar *'Eagle Eye'* Ingimarsson
Dave *'Great Guy'* Kitson
Aaron *'The Weapon'* Brown
John *'The Hammer'* Oster

GROUNDS FOR A CHANGE

For a long time during its construction, Reading's new ground was nameless and several suggestions were bandied about in the local press. As well as the obvious but hardly appropriate 'New Elm Park', the death of Princess Diana produced a move for 'the Princess of Wales Stadium'. However, it was only appropriate that the man who made the stadium possible and guaranteed the funding should be honoured, and so the stadium was named Madejski Stadium. However, not all the suggestions during the naming process were quite so serious. With the new ground being built on a former landfill site close to an old sewage works, local jokers came up with 'Flushing Meadows', 'Dungroamin', and 'W.C. Fields'!

INTER THE NET!

Manchester United can claim, with some justification, to be the most famous Club in the world, but not as far as the internet is concerned. A Google search reveals 21 million hits for Manchester United, a mere trifle when you compare a similar search for the word 'Reading', which produces an amazing 615 million!

Similarly, it has always been claimed that Queen of the South are the only football Club to get a mention in the Bible, but at least one other is also named. The word 'reading' appears eight times in the good book, and in case anyone feels that these entries do not qualify without a capital 'R', then Deuteronomy 31.9 refers to 'The Reading of the Law' – remember, you read it here first!

NINE – I'M HONOURED

ON THE LIST

⚽ Two Reading players have been honoured by the Queen as a Member of the British Empire. **Shaun Goater** made his name with Manchester City where he was one of the Premiership's top scorers and shot himself into the record books by netting that division's faster-ever goal by a substitute. He used his fame to good effect back in his native Bermuda, where he did much to promote youth football. Indeed, Shaun remains a hero in his home island, having been awarded the freedom of Bermuda where they even celebrate a Shaun Goater Day every June.

⚽ Like Shaun, **Les Ferdinand** played for Reading at the end of an illustrious career that saw him score the fifth-highest Premier League goal total, including the competition's 10,000th goal, for Spurs against Fulham on 15 December 2001. Despite being known throughout the game as 'Sir' Les, the great forward was thrilled to be awarded an MBE in 2005 for his footballing career and charity work. Les was also voted the PFA Player of the Year in 1996 when his 29 goals fired Newcastle to second place in the Premiership.

⚽ Great Reading goalkeeper **Neil Shaka Hislop** might also try to claim that he has a day named after him as he has always chosen to use his middle name, Shaka. South Africa celebrates Shaka Day every year, not after the Reading keeper but in tribute to a 19th century warrior king who was the founder of the Zulu nation.

NATIONAL HERO

Reading full back and 90-cap Ecuadorian international **Ulises de la Cruz** has also received the highest honour of his home country. Throughout his playing career Ulises has donated part of his salary to help build amenities in his home village, Piquiucho, and his generosity has built a pipeline, a school and a medical centre. Awarded the Presidential Medal, an honour bestowed on one Ecuadorian a year, Ulises was described as a 'defender of the community'. His FundeCruz is a registered charity and, in addition to his fund-raising role, Ulises is also an ambassador for UNICEF.

STREETS AHEAD

Some honours are of a more local nature. **Sam Bartram** spent six months on trial with Reading but was allowed to leave, subsequently joining Charlton Athletic where he played over 600 games. Revered in south-east London, there is a large statue of the legendary goalkeeper outside the Valley, while nearby a road is named

Sam Bartram Close. However, Reading cannot be blamed for missing out on a player described as the best uncapped goalkeeper in the country because his time at Reading was spent playing as a wing half, and he only became a goalkeeper after returning to his native North East. Another player slightly more famous for his service with another Club rather than his one appearance for Reading in a friendly was **George Best**! He can also outdo Sam Bartram's road since the legendary Manchester United forward has been immortalised by having Belfast's airport named after him.

STRANGE HONOURS

In 1907 Reading's **Ellis Gee** was honoured by having a poem in tribute to his wing play printed on the front page of the country's main sports paper *The Athletic News*, having previously become Chesterfield's first three-figure transfer when he joined them from Everton in 1898.

An even stranger honour was bestowed on free-scoring forward **Trevor Morley**. In 1999 television playwright and West Ham supporter Tony Grounds,wrote a series for BBC2 entitled *Gone to the Dogs* in which the main character was named Jim Morley, as a tribute to Trevor. However, even the more unusual honours can be withdrawn. Shortly after he had left Reading for Newcastle United in 1995, **Shaka Hislop** was asked to play for Trinidad & Tobago, the country in which he grew up. The giant keeper declined, hoping that his Premiership appearances would earn him a call-up for England, but this angered the Trinidadian authorities who promptly withdrew Shaka's picture from a set of phonecards depicting local sporting heroes!

I AM A FREEMAN

Neil Webb won numerous honours during his playing career, particularly with Manchester United, Nottingham Forest and England. However, one of his highest honours came before his professional career was underway. In 1978 he was awarded the freedom of the town of Reading – unfortunately for Neil it was not the town of his birth but Reading, Pennsylvania. The award was made to all members of the local Maiwand Lions youth team that toured America in that year.

MANAGING SUCCESS

More conventional awards have been heaped on Reading over the last three seasons which saw the Club win the Championship in style and then reach eighth place in the Premier League. The success was masterminded by manager **Steve Coppell**, and he was rewarded by winning the League Managers' Association Manager of the Year Award in both 2005–06 and 2006–07, the first manager to win the award in successive years. Other Reading managers to win the divisional award of Manager of the Year were **Maurice Evans** in 1978–79, after guiding Reading to the Fourth Division title, **Ian Branfoot** in 1985–86, and **Mark McGhee** in 1993–94, for winning the third tier. McGhee was also honoured as a player, being voted Scottish PFA Player of the Year in 1982 while with Aberdeen.

SPORTING AWARDS

⊕ Reading's recent success also saw Club captain **Graeme Murty** named BBC South's Sports Personality of the Year, while **Kevin Doyle** was the Young Irish Player of the Year for 2006 and the Championship Fans' Player of the Year. The following year, Kevin was nominated for the PFA's Young Player of the Season, eventually losing out to **Christiano Ronaldo**, but having the consolation that his thunderous left-foot shot against Croatia in the European Championship qualifier was named Ireland's goal of 2007.

⊕ Another Reading player to be honoured in the Republic of Ireland was the Club's former classy right back **Dave Bacuzzi** who, on leaving Elm Park, became player-manager of Cork Hibernians and guided them to a League and Cup double that led to him being named Eire's Sports Personality of the Year for 1974. Across the border in Northern Ireland, **Jimmy Quinn** was similarly honoured when he won the Bingham Trophy as Northern Ireland's Football Personality of the Year in 1993, the same year in which his long-range goal against Eire was Ulster's Goal of 1993.

⊕ Another Reading player who was highly thought of beyond Berkshire was **Richie Bowman**. The complete player, Richie was named the best player in the Third Division after he topped the 1979–80 match averages in the *Sunday People*, only Spurs' **Ossie Ardilles** getting higher marks than the Reading star. The award earned Richie a £500 cheque and a silver salver, presented by **Bobby Charlton**.

CUP CHEER

Another unusual, but creditable, honour was bestowed on Reading's Australian goalkeeper **Adam Federici**. As deputy to the reliable **Marcus Hahnemann**, Adam's chances were restricted to the knock-out competitions, but he took those few opportunities well, and never more so than on 17 February 2007. Playing in Reading's 'second string' FA Cup side at Old Trafford, Adam pulled off a number of impressive saves from Manchester United's all-star attack to earn his side a surprise 1–1 draw in the fifth round in front of BBC's live cameras. It was a performance that earned him the Player of the Round award and so guaranteed him a seat at the first FA Cup Final at the new Wembley Stadium. The only other player with a Reading connection to be so honoured was **Paul Brayson**. The former Royals striker was never likely to receive any awards while with Reading, but he scored hat-tricks for Northwich Victoria in 2005–06 FA Cup triumphs over Frickley Colliery and then Morecambe to become the first to be named Player of the Round on two occasions.

FAMILY FORTUNES

Reading midfielder **Steve Sidwell** was named as the best player outside the Premiership in a 2004 poll by readers of *Four Two Four* magazine, but that was not the only honour won by the Sidwell household. In 2007 ITV ran a reality series entitled *WAGs' Boutique* in which two teams of players' wives and girlfriends competed with each other to run a fashion shop. Not only was Steve's wife Krystell a member of the winning team, but she was also voted the most popular WAG in the series.

HE'S A STAR

One of the most unusual awards was given to **Jamie Cureton** after he had scored the last-gasp goal that won promotion for Reading at Brentford on 20 April 2002. With the Supporters' Club having switched to trust status, the new Supporters' Trust At Reading honoured the scorer of that vital goal by utilising their acronym and naming a star after Jamie Cureton.

WALKING IN TRIBUTE

In 1994–95 Reading enjoyed their best-ever season at that time, finishing second in the newly renamed Division One for their, then, highest League finish. Many tributes were paid to the team that had exceeded everybody's expectations by reaching the play-off final, but surely the greatest tribute was that of the Club's Chairman, **John Madejski**. One of the richest men in the country, he was generous to the team, paying for a break in the sun for his squad, but he felt another tribute would be even more appropriate. So, the man with a collection of performance luxury cars that would make any Formula One driver envious decided that he would walk the 40 miles from Reading to Wembley for surely the ultimate gesture from a Club Chairman.

PERFECT PITCH

The final home game of Reading's debut season in the top flight saw a presentation to **Gordon Neate**, who had recently celebrated 50 years with the Club as a player and then groundsman. After a nationwide search Gordon was named Barclay's Local Hero, an honour that also saw him featured on BBC's *Match of the Day 2*. Gordon had already received the Canon Loyalty Award, presented by the then Football League sponsors, as far back as 1985. This is not, however, Gordon's only honour. In November 1972 a competition was held to find the Football League player with the hardest shot. A testing machine was sent to each League ground, but at Elm Park the wayward shooting of Reading's Fourth Division players meant that few registered a reasonable speed. However, with the machine momentarily vacant, groundsman Gordon had a go and beat the rest of the playing staff with a 60mph-plus effort.

One honour Gordon Neate failed to secure was that for the best playing surface in the League. Elm Park achieved that accolade back in March 1938, long before Gordon was in charge of the pitch and almost 40 years before the popular groundsman's most embarrassing moment. During the pre-season preparations for Reading's first season back in the Second Division for 55 years, Gordon mistakenly sprayed the pitch with undiluted (Neate?) weed killer, with disastrous effects. The pre-season friendlies had to be cancelled and for most of the season the predominant colour of the Elm Park pitch was brown rather than green.

WAR HEROES

All the honours accorded on footballers throughout their playing careers pale into insignificance when compared to those earned during wartime. **Joe 'Bubbles' Bailey** was a goalscoring hero at Elm Park either side of World War One, but during those hostilities he proved to be a true hero. Entering the Footballers' Battalion as a private, Joe was discharged as a captain, his rise through the ranks being earned by several acts of bravery. During his four years fighting in Europe, Joe was awarded the Distinguished Service Order and the Military Cross with two bars. Apart from two amateur international caps for England, Joe never won any football awards, but he is surely the most honoured player in the Club's history. Another Reading player to be honoured for his bravery during World War One was **Joe North** who was, like 'Bubbles' Bailey, awarded the Military Cross.

PLAYERS PLEASED

✪ In 1974 the Professional Footballers' Association launched its seasonal awards, voted for by its members. As well as voting for their Player of the Year and their top team of players, awards were made to produce a select team for all four divisions. That first season saw Reading's goalkeeper **Steve Death** and centre half **John Hulme** voted into the Fourth Division side that also included future Reading manager **Ian Branfoot** for his displays at full back with Lincoln City. Death was to be selected again in Reading's Fourth Division Championship season of 1978–79, along with **Gary Peters** and **Richie Bowman**.

✪ In total 24 Reading players have been honoured with a divisional team selection but only **Trevor Senior** and **Steve Sidwell** have matched Death's double nomination as Reading players. However, **Kerry Dixon,** with Reading in 1982–83 and Chelsea the following season, **Shaka Hislop,** in 1994–95 with Reading and nine years later with Portsmouth, **Jimmy Quinn,** also with Peterborough United, **Martin Butler,** first with Cambridge United and then with Reading in 2000–01, and **Nicky Forster,** with Brentford and Reading, have all been selected twice with different Clubs. However, the most successful Reading player in these awards is **Scott Murray,** who was selected three consecutive seasons as a Bristol City player before signing for Reading in 2003.

✪ 2005–06 was a bumper season for Reading with **Marcus Hahnemann, Ibrahima Sonko, Steve Sidwell, Nicky Shorey** and **Kevin Doyle** all being selected for the Championship select side. In addition, two future Reading signings, **Sam Sodje** and **Greg Halford,** were selected for the Division One side as players with Brentford and Colchester United respectively.

FANS' FAVOURITES

Since 1966 Reading's fans have had the opportunity to vote on their own Player of the Year and it has to be said that their choice has not always been the obvious one! For instance, in those 42 votes Reading's top scorer has only won the award nine times. Later to play for England, **Kerry Dixon's** 32 goals in an injury-hit relegation season were enough to make him the top scorer in his division but not good enough to edge full back **Steve Richardson** out of top spot. Another future England international, **Neil Webb** is arguably the greatest Reading-born player in the town's history, but even an impressive 15 League goals from midfield in 1982 could not take the trophy from **Jerry Williams**. Even **Trevor Senior's** Club record 41 goals in 1984 were not sufficient to take the trophy from that man Richardson again. Senior top scored in all but one of his eight seasons but still had to wait six years for his only Player of the Year award. Like Senior, 40 goals in a season were not enough for **Jimmy Quinn** to overtake another full back, **Dylan Kerr**, in the fans' vote of 1994.

BRIEF SUCCESS

Seemingly the most unusual winner was the first recipient of the fans' approval. The previous year had seen the trophy awarded for the first time by the *Reading Chronicle* to **Colin Meldrum**, who had topped the paper's players merit points table in 1964–65. The choice was opened to the fans the following year and although to an outsider the choice of **Jimmy Wheeler** was a strange one, he was in fact the clear and well-deserved winner. Strange, because Jimmy had only made two first team appearances that season, but deserved because, as an inspirational captain and manager, the Reading legend had guided the Club's young reserves to a dramatic promotion in the Football Combination. With crowds for the reserve games exceeding those for League matches it was an obvious choice; well, it was to Reading's fans anyway.

UPS AND DOWNS

Another seemingly strange choice came in 1971 when **Terry Bell** was the deserving winner despite the fact that his first act as newly elected Player of the Year was to head an own-goal in the final game of the season at Aston Villa that relegated his Club to the Fourth Division.

MULTI-WINNERS

As far as Player of the Year votes are concerned, **Steve Death** leads the way with four triumphs, the first, back in 1969–70, coming while he was still a West Ham player, such was the success of his loan spell at Elm Park. The next best total belongs to **Mick Gooding**, who won three times, his final success coming in 1995–96 despite the pressure of being joint player-manager. **Robin Friday, Richie Bowman, Phil Parkinson, Steve Richardson, Steve Wood** and **Graeme Murty** have won twice, with only the Club's Premiership captain not winning his awards in consecutive seasons.

FANS' SELECT XI

Despite the occasional quirkiness of the fans' choices, a quality team could still be formed from their selections over the years:

Goalkeeper:	**Steve Death** (1970, 1973, 1974 & 1977)
Right full back:	**Graeme Murty** (2002 and 2004)
Left full back:	**Steve Richardson** (1983 and 1984)
Centre back:	**Martin Hicks** (1990)
Centre back:	**Steve Woods** (1985 and 1986)
Right wing:	**Gordon Cumming** (1972)
Left wing:	**Mick Gooding** (1992, 1993 and 1996)
Centre midfield:	**Richie Bowman** (1978 and 1979)
Centre midfield:	**Phil Parkinson** (1998 and 1999)
Centre forward:	**Robin Friday** (1975 and 1976)
Centre forward:	**Trevor Senior** (1989)

Those Player of the Year presentations are usually made before the kick-off of the final home game of the season, but in 1998 there were two. As well as the Reading award going to **Phil Parkinson**, the visiting fans from Norwich City also presented their trophy to **Robert Fleck**, even though he had been a Reading player for the last seven games of the season.

MAN OF THE MATCH

In addition to a Player of the Season, the town's other newspaper, the *Reading Evening Post*, launched a Player of the Month in September 1996, when the first winner was full back **Martin Booty**. They also name a Man of the Match in each report and occasionally the match reporter's choice is as unusual as those of the fans. When Reading clinched promotion at Brentford on 20 April 2002, **Jamie Cureton** was named Man of the Match even though he had only been on the pitch for 23 minutes. He had, however, scored the vital promotion-clinching equaliser during that short spell. Cureton's period on the pitch, however, was excessive compared with **Nicky Forster**'s substitute appearance a year earlier. Out for most of the season with a cruciate knee injury, Forster came on in the play-off semi-final against Wigan with just nine minutes to go. A goal down at the time, Forster turned on one of the all-time great substitute appearances, setting up Reading's equaliser, winning a penalty and then slotting home Reading's winner from the spot kick's rebound. As well as Man of the Match awards, both Jamie and Nicky were both given 10 out of 10 in the match report ratings.

The most controversial award took place after Reading's League Cup defeat at Cambridge United on 10 September 2002. In that season Reading exceeded all expectations by reaching the Division One play-offs, but their display against a team two divisions below them was their worst of that season. The poor reporter struggled to find any positive features from the team and so named young Reading midfielder **Joe Gamble** as his Man of the Match – for his performance as match summariser for a local radio station!

AMERICAN STARS

Some Man of the Match awards were more obvious. During the summer of 1976 local youngster **Steve Hetzke** spent several months on loan with Vancouver Whitecaps, playing in the North American Soccer League. A series of impressive displays against some famous names culminated in Steve being named Man of the Match against Toronto Metros when he marked Portuguese legend Eusebio out of the game. Hetzke was not the only Reading player to be honoured in the States. In 1975 stylish local-born forward **Peter Silvester** spent a season playing in the N.A.S.L. with Baltimore Comets, Washington Diplomats and San Diego, being voted the North American Player of the Year. Three years later former Reading defender **Bobby Lenarduzzi** won the same award for his displays with his home-town Club Vancouver Whitecaps.

TOP 100

As part of the celebrations of 100 years of League football in 1988, the Football League named '100 League Legends'. Although no Reading players were included, several who had played for the Club were. World War Two guests **Joe Mercer**, **Frank Swift** and **George Hardwick** were there, as were, not surprisingly, **Martin Peters** and **George Best**, both of whom played for Reading in a friendly against New Zealand on 29 October 1984. An even shorter Reading career for one of those 'Legends' can be claimed by Spurs and Wales great Cliff Jones, who played in the first half of the testimonial game for his old National Service friend Dick Spiers, against West Ham United in May 1970. The final Reading-related nomination belongs to **Ted Drake**, who managed the Club after a spectacular goalscoring career with Arsenal and England.

BEST OF BRITISH

Another occasion, the return of the four home countries to FIFA after World War Two, was celebrated by a friendly between a Great Britain select team and the Rest of Europe. Played at Hampden Park, the match attracted a massive 135,000 sports-starved fans, who saw the home countries beat the European side 6–1. Included in the Great Britain side were four of Reading's wartime guests: **Frank Swift, George Hardwick, Ron Burgess** and **Archie Macaulay**.

THANK GOD IT'S FRIDAY

How could a pigeon-toed asthmatic who had recently escaped death by inches when he was impaled on a metal spike become if not Reading's greatest player then certainly the most talked about? **Robin Friday** had been turned down by most London Clubs by the time he came to Elm Park on trial in November 1973, yet within weeks a legend had been born.

HONOUR AFTER HONOUR

In only his second League game, at Barnsley, rumour has it that the home Club sent on a late substitute with specific instructions to ask the still-amateur Friday to sign for the Yorkshire Club. A week later, a sensational home debut led to the *Reading Evening Post* commenting 'Friday showed such ability and guts, such enthusiasm and willingness to take on opponents that the main thing worrying fans was how long can we keep him?' That early form was no flash in the pan and he was subsequently voted Reading's Player of the Millennium, a member of the Club's All-Time Greatest XI, made the BBC's Cult Hero team (in midfield!) having been voted both Reading and Cardiff City fans' cult hero and the Professional Footballers' Association's greatest Reading player. That latest award was slightly surprising as he was never named in the PFA Divisional teams, due to the fact that he was never a member of the players' union. Sadly, all of those awards came posthumously, Robin dying a drug-related death aged only 38.

A hugely talented, wild extrovert on the pitch, Robin lived his life off the pitch in the same way and it is appropriate that his rock-and-roll lifestyle has inspired two tributes from pop stars that sum up both sides of Robin. Former Oasis bassist Paul McGuiggan wrote a best-selling book on Robin entitled *The Greatest Footballer You Never Saw*, while the Super Furry Animals' hit single about Robin was equally appropriately titled *Man Don't Give a F**k*.

The following are just a few of the 'Best of the Worst of **Robin Friday**'

- A notoriously bad trainer, Robin once shocked Reading manager **Charlie Hurley** by being one of the first home after a cross country run. What the manager had not realised was that Robin had hitched a ride most of the way on a lorry.
- Robin's dress sense, or lack of it, was legendary, and while other players would arrive at games in slacks and blazers, Robin always wore jeans and a T-shirt, plus a kaftan coat. After one night on the town Robin arrived at a Reading nightclub wearing his usual kaftan coat, but when he took it off he had nothing on underneath except for a pair of hobnail boots!
- Despite being booked 23 times while with Reading and sent off once (after each of Bournemouth's back four had been booked for fouling him), Robin was more sinned against than a sinner. He also had less violent ways of winding up opponents – he would knock goalkeepers' hats off, pull defenders' shorts down and even plant kisses on his markers at corners.
- A more famous kiss came when he scored a last-minute winner against Rochdale on 9 April 1975. It was just a simple tap in, something of a rarity for Robin, but he was so delighted that he ran behind the Tilehurst End goal and planted a smacker on unsuspecting PC Brian Miller.

- Appropriately, in view of his surname, Robin played for Reading on every different day of the week, and on 16 October 1976 he made every newspaper sub-editor's dreams come true when they were able to use the headline 'Friday Plays Wednesday on Saturday' for Reading's home game against Sheffield Wednesday.
- Robin is widely recognised as having scored Reading's greatest-ever goal – a 20-yard shoulder-high volley against Tranmere Rovers on 31 March 1976. Refereeing that game was World Cup official Clive Thomas, who said of the goal, 'Even up against Pelé and Cruyff, it still rates as the best goal I have ever seen.'
- When his off-the-pitch behaviour became too much, Robin was sold to Cardiff City. On his first day at his new Club he was arrested at Cardiff Station, having travelled from Paddington on just a platform ticket. He learnt from this mistake and subsequently he would knock on train toilet doors claiming to be a ticket inspector, and when an unsuspecting passenger slid their ticket under the door for inspection Robin was off with a valid ticket.
- Robin's debut for Cardiff was every bit as spectacular as his Elm Park start. He scored twice against Fulham, leaving his marker, Bobby Moore, shell-shocked, not least because Robin 'introduced' himself to the England legend by grabbing him by the testicles.
- At one team meeting Robin turned up with a swan under his arm, having 'borrowed' it from the Club hotel's lake.
- Robin walked out on Cardiff and football after being sent off at Brighton for kicking Mark Lawrenson in the face. Allegedly, his last act was to leave a 'bodily deposit' in the BBC pundit's kitbag.

FRIDAY ON MY MIND

The Teammate:
'He certainly could have been a Premiership player if he had been spotted earlier. Robin was one of those wonderful footballers with great strength and a great eye for goal.' – **Eamonn Dunphy**.

The Manager:
'Are there any more like him? Actually, if there were you'd have to have 20 of them because you could never get them all to turn up!' – **Charlie Hurley**.

The Coach:
'Basically, he was a smashing lad who was easily led by stupid people.' – **Maurice Evans**.

The Man Himself:
'On the pitch I hate all opponents. I don't give a damn about anyone. People think I'm mad, a lunatic. I'm a winner.'

TOP OF THE WORLD

✸ On 12 June 2006 Berkshire was the unofficial 51st State of America when Reading fans cheered on **Bobby Convey** as he became the first Reading player to appear in the World Cup Finals when he played against the Czech Republic. Although the United States failed to survive 'the group of death', Bobby did himself, and Reading, proud. His free kick led to the States' equaliser against Italy, the only goal they conceded on their way to the final, and he was named Man of the Match in the Italian daily *Gazetta dello Sport*.

✸ What those fans did not know was that two more players appearing in Germany would soon be moving to Reading. During that summer the Club signed South Korean star **Seol Ki-Hyeon**, who had become a national hero four years earlier when his goal helped beat Italy in one of the shock results of the 2002 tournament. Also moving to Reading was Ecuadorian defender **Ulises de la Cruz**, whose last game of the tournament was in England's 1–0 win in the second round. Even so, Bobby and goalkeeper **Marcus Hahnemann**, who was an unused member of the USA squad, were by no means the first (occasionally tenuous!) connections with this stage of tournament.

✸ If Reading's two players needed any advice about playing in the World Cup Finals they only had to ask their manager **Steve Coppell**, who made four appearances for England during the 1982 competition in Spain. Who knows, he may have even mentioned his part in the build-up to Brian Robson's opening goal against France that was scored just 27 seconds after the kick-off, the fastest scored in the finals.

✸ The Reading connection dates back much further than that though. In fact, it goes back to the home countries' first entry into the World Cup in 1950. The old Home International Championship was used as the qualifying round, and Reading's 1960s manager Roy Bentley scored the goal that clinched England's top spot. FIFA had agreed that the country finishing second would also qualify for the World Cup Finals but with Scotland stating that they would only go to Brazil if they topped the group, England were Britain's only representatives. Roy played in England's first two World Cup Finals matches, including their notorious 1–0 defeat by USA.

✸ Bobby and Marcus nearly missed out on their 'first' because, in 1958, Reading keeper **Dave Jones** was named in the initial 40-man Welsh squad but their manager Jimmy Murphy, the father of early 1970s Reading fringe player **Nick Murphy**, did not include Dave in his final 22. One player who did make the finals was Spurs winger Cliff Jones, who as well as playing in all four games for Wales also played for Reading in Dick Spiers' testimonial match some 12 years later. Other near misses include **Allenby Chilton**, a

World War Two Reading guest (and scorer of an own-goal for Reading in their 1955 FA Cup tie against Manchester United), who was in England's 1954 squad but never got to play. Like Jones, **Kevin Dillon** was on standby for England's 1982 squad, while **Tony Rougier** was even more unlucky – he was named in the initial 24-man Trinidad & Tobago 2006 squad but when it had to be reduced to the maximum allowed of 23 the former Reading forward was the player who missed out.

⊛ Throughout the 1980s and 1990s Reading were well represented by former and future players, with **Jim Leighton**, one of the Club's very best loan signings, falling into both categories by playing in four World Cups. Jim also holds Scotland's appearance record for World Cup Finals with nine games. Other Royal Scots include **Steve Archibald**, a scorer against New Zealand in 1982, and **Robert Fleck** in 1990. That year also saw **Ray Houghton** and **Pat Bonner**, Tommy Burns's assistant manager, play for Eire while **Neil Webb** became the first Reading-born player to appear in the World Cup Finals. Four years later Houghton scored one of the goals of the tournament, at USA '94, when he netted a spectacular long-range winner against Italy.

⊛ Making an even bigger impression in the US was **Bobby Mihailov**, who was rated the best keeper in the competition as Bulgaria made it to the semi-finals, just months before he signed for Reading. In total, Bobby made a Reading record 11 appearances in that tournament as Bulgaria reached the semi-finals before being beaten by Italy. In the third-place play-off match Bobby earned an unwanted record when, having conceded four goals by half time, he became the first keeper in the World Cup Finals to be the 'victim' of a tactical substitution.

⊛ The 1986 tournament in Mexico was a bumper year for Reading fans as they had an interest in four countries, even if it required the benefit of hindsight. As well as **Jim Leighton**, **Kerry Dixon** played for England, albeit for just six minutes at the end of England's game against Poland, but that was longer than **Jimmy Quinn** managed as a non-playing member of Northern Ireland's squad. Playing in all three of his country's first appearances in the finals was Canada's **Bob Lenarduzzi**, although the former Reading favourite failed to finish on the winning side.

⊛ Even more tenuous Reading connections exist for the previous World Cup in Mexico, held in 1970. Both **Peter Bonetti** and the late **Peter Osgood** made appearances for England in the finals, having both been at Reading in the late 1950s, after trials in Harry Johnston's days as manager. Bonetti eventually returned to Elm Park when his playing days were over, becoming the Club's goalkeeping coach during the 1994–95 season.

⊕ Also playing for England in 1970 was **Martin Peters** who, of course, scored one of their goals in the 1966 World Cup Final at Wembley. And what was going through Martin's mind as he put England in front against West Germany? Was it 'This could win us the World Cup?' or 'I bet that impressed former Reading player Maurice Edelston, who is commentating on the final for BBC Radio'? No, the thought that flashed through Martin's mind was surely 'This must clinch my place in the Reading side to play New Zealand in a 1985 friendly!'

⊕ Peters was not the first 'Reading player' to score in the World Cup Finals; that honour belongs to **Jimmy Murray**. The Hearts forward played seven games on loan with Reading in 1954 while he was stationed locally during his national service. By 1958 he was a Scottish international, and on 8 June 1958 he scored Scotland's equaliser in their opening game in Sweden against Yugoslavia.

⊕ Of course, **Bobby Convey** and **Marcus Hahnemann** did not have the monopoly of Reading support in the 2006 World Cup. England came up against 1990s Reading favourite, goalkeeper **Shaka Hislop**, while **Kelvin Jack**, a triallist in 2004, was in goal for Trinidad & Tobago in their final game.

AFRICAN ADVENTURE

Reading were represented for the first time at the 2008 African Cup of Nations, staged in Ghana. Although **Ibrahima Sonko** was an unused substitute for Senegal, **Emerse Faé** played three times as the Ivory Coast reached the semi-final but contracted malaria during the tournament, which caused him to miss several Reading games. **Andre Bikey** had a very mixed tournament, playing in every game for Cameroon up to the semi-final when, with the 'Indomitable Lions' leading 1–0 in the last minute, Andre was involved in a bizarre incident with a stretcher bearer and was sent off, which meant he missed the final.

——————— GOING FOR GOLD ———————

With talk of a Great Britain team competing in the 2012 Olympic games, the organisers will, presumably, be looking to Reading to provide assistance in view of the Club's past success in the tournament.

FIRST WINNER

Football was first played in the second of the modern Olympics, staged in Paris in 1900, when it was featured as a demonstration sport with Britain represented by Upton Park. The first competition was held, appropriately, in England with games staged at the White City, and although the home team was named 'United Kingdom', it was, in reality, an England side. Reading's legendary left back **Herbert Smith** played in all three games (only six teams entered) as England won gold quite comfortably, scoring 18 goals and conceding just one. Controversially as far as Reading fans are concerned, Smith's participation was recorded by the FA as being as an Oxford City player, the officials presumably preferring to show the amateur Club for which he occasionally played rather than the professional side he captained. Playing alongside Herbert in the 1908 Olympics was **Harry Stapely**, a centre forward who had previously played for Reading. Interestingly, despite being the most popular sport in the world, by not being included until 1908 football was beaten to being an Olympic sport by such events as live pigeon shooting, rope climbing, and even rugby.

TED'S BIG ADVENTURE

There was no such 'ownership' dispute four years later when Wokingham-born Reading centre half **Ted Hanney** was a member of the squad, which this time was recorded as England. Ted played in the semi-final, England having been given a bye in the first round, and helped his country to a 4–0 victory over Finland. Unfortunately, he sustained an ankle injury and missed the final victory over Denmark. Ted's one Olympic appearance saw an incident that demonstrates the different culture that existed in those days. Leading 2–0, England were awarded a penalty, but 'the leaders seemed to consider that this was altogether too severe a punishment and the ball was ostentatiously put over the cross-bar.'

DIFFICULT CHOICE

International football is riddled with Club versus country dilemmas, and so it was for Reading's **C.W. 'Ginger' Harbridge**. Selected for the Olympic squad to play in Antwerp, the left half had to choose between his country and playing for Reading in their first League game following the Southern League's transition into the Third Division of the Football League. 'Ginger' elected to go for gold, but with Norway knocking out his team in the first round for the shock result of the games he should probably have stayed at home.

YOUNG OLYMPIAN

A disagreement between the FA and FIFA over 'broken time', the payment for lost time playing amateur football, left a gap of 16 years before Britain re-entered an Olympic football tournament, staged in Berlin. By then, the amateur game had moved on and Great Britain were no longer the dominant force. Even so, a 16-year-old **Maurice Edelston** was a member of the squad and played in the victory over China in the first round, but Britain were knocked out in the next. The 2008 Beijing Olympics also saw Reading represented in the soccer tournament, with goalkeeper **Adam Federici** being a member of the Australian squad and defender **Andre Bikey** playing for Cameroon.

NO BRONZE FOR COPPER

After World War Two the first games were staged in London in 1948 and the GB squad was managed by former Reading wartime guest Matt Busby, who, fondly remembering his times at Reading, used Elm Park as the training base for his squad. It was these training sessions that transformed England from no-hopers to possible finalists in a matter of weeks. Wins over Holland and France saw the home nation reach the semi-finals, where they were beaten by Yugoslavia. Qualifying for the third-place match against Denmark, the Great Britain side included Reading's flying policeman **Bill Amor**, and he became the first Reading player to score in the Olympics, pulling the score back to 2–2 with a coolly taken penalty. Unfortunately, the Danes scored three more times to take third place.

FINAL FLING

Gradually Britain ceased to be any sort of force in the Olympic tournament and with the difference between amateurs and professionals being removed in the 1970s, the last time Great Britain entered the tournament was for the 1972 competition. Forced to qualify to go to Munich, Great Britain faced Bulgaria in a two-leg play-off. As preparation the squad played a series of trial matches against League Clubs, and on 11 January 1970 they won 2–0 at Elm Park against a weakened Reading side. These trial games appeared to have done the trick as Britain won the home leg against Bulgaria 1–0 at Wembley (in front of a crowd of only 3,000). Unfortunately, the return game saw Bulgaria storm to a 5–0 win. Featuring in that away game was Reading winger **Micky Mellows**, who as well as playing in the last British Olympic team to date was, as the second of England's two substitutes, also the very last player to appear in the British Olympic team.

DOUBLE GOLD

Reading can claim a further two Olympic gold medals, but not in football. Decathlete **Daley Thompson** won gold in 1980 and 1984, 10 years before he played two friendly games for Reading, against the rather contrasting opposition of Leatherhead and Real Sociedad, having joined Reading for their pre-season training in the summer of 1994.

———————— INTERNATIONAL STARS ————————

Like most Premier League Clubs, Reading could currently field a team of full internationals with players coming from all over the world, and yet this is only a recent phenomenon. When **Bobby Lenarduzzi** played for Canada on 3 August 1973 he was Reading's first full international for 50 years, and the first of only three players to be capped for nations outside the four home countries during Reading's time at Elm Park.

Since the move to Madejski Stadium 10 years ago the foreign invasion has escalated to such an extent that 36 players have now been capped while playing for Reading. To emphasize the variety of the nationalities involved it is possible to make up two very varied teams of Reading internationals:

EUROPEAN XI

Borislav Mihailov
(Bulgaria)

| **Graeme Murty** | **Adie Williams** | **Ivar Ingimarsson** | **Nicky Shorey** |
| *(Scotland)* | *(Wales)* | *(Iceland)* | *(England)* |

| **Jos Davies** | **Marek Matejovsky** | **Bryjar Gunnarsson** | **Stephen Hunt** |
| *(Wales)* | *(Czech Republic)* | *(Iceland)* | *(Eire)* |

Jimmy Quinn   **Kevin Doyle**
(Northern Ireland)   *(Eire)*

REST OF THE WORLD XI

Marcus Hahnemann
(USA)

| **Andy Bernal** | **Ibrahima Sonko** | **Andre Bikey** | **Ulises de la Cruz** |
| *(Australia)* | *(Senegal)* | *(Cameroon)* | *(Ecuador)* |

| **Tony Rougier** | **Emerse Faé** | **Bobby Lenarduzzi** | **Mass Sarr** |
| *(Trinidad & Tobago)* | *(Ivory Coast)* | *(Canada)* | *(Liberia)* |

Shaun Goater   **Seol Ki-Hyeon**
(Bermuda)   *(South Korea)*

But the above team is fictional, unlike the 16-man squad that faced Everton on 18 August 2007, which contained 14 internationals. The 14 were:

Andre Bikey (Cameroon)
Ulises de la Cruz (Ecuador)
Nicky Shorey (England)
Emerse Faé (Ivory Coast)
Graeme Murty (Scotland)
Bryjar Gunnarsson and **Ivar Ingimarsson** (Iceland)
Seol Ki-Hyeon (South Korea)

Bobby Convey and **Marcus Hahnemann** (USA)
John Oster (Wales)
and **Kevin Doyle, Stephen Hunt** and **Shane Long** (Eire)

The two non-capped players were **Adam Federici**, who had already been an unused substitute for Australia, and **James Harper**, who could have played for Ghana but declined the invitation.

⊛ The two fictitious sides could be managed by any of several Reading managers and players who have gone on to manage at international level. Just after World War Two ended former Reading player and manager **Billy Butler** coached Rhodesia (now Zimbabwe), and **Charlie Hurley** had a short spell as player-manager of Eire before taking charge at Elm Park. Following a very successful period as a wartime guest with Reading, **Matt Busby** had been offered the job of Joe Edelston's assistant at the Club but, 'surprisingly', he chose to take up the role of manager at Manchester United. As well as his success at Old Trafford, Matt also managed Scotland and the 1948 Great Britain Olympic team. Former left-sided Reading midfielders **Bobby Lenarduzzi** and **Lawrie Sanchez** both went on to manage national sides, Lenarduzzi his native Canadian side while Sanchez managed Northern Ireland.

⊛ The uncrowned king of international management is, however, **Ian Porterfield**. A loan spell at Elm Park preceded a year as the Club's manager between 1989 and 1991, but after that he began to roam the world. As well as Club management, Ian was in charge of the national sides of Zambia, Saudi Arabia, Oman, and Trinidad & Tobago and was coaching the Armenian national side up to his premature death in 2007, aged 61.

⊛ Three other overseas players enjoyed short Reading careers in addition to those featured in the fictional teams. Recommended to the Club by Matt Busby, Norwegian **Od Rojan** played two wartime games in 1943–44, which is one more than **Billy Straus**, a South African international who was guesting from Aberdeen. A lightning-fast winger, **Attolia Nicoli** was on a school exchange visit from his native Switzerland when he joined Reading on trial in March 1939, making one appearance in the Division Three South Cup against Crystal Palace before returning home.

⊛ As well as the four England internationals capped while with Reading, **Edgar Haygarth, Johnny Holt, Herbert Smith** and **Nicky Shorey**, other players have gone on to be capped by England after leaving Reading. Two of them can claim to be hard done by as far as their international careers were concerned. **Johnny Brooks**, the first Reading-born player to be capped by his country, won just three caps despite scoring two goals and ending on the winning side each time.

Even more unlucky was **Phil Bach,** Reading's first professional captain, who won his only England cap a couple of years later as a Sunderland player. Phil's one game saw England beat Ireland 13–2, making him, surely, the only player to be dropped after such a comprehensive victory. Bach was able to make sure that such an injustice was not repeated, since upon his retirement he became a long-serving member of the England selection committee. In fact Reading players have proved something of a good luck charm for England. All four of Smith's appearances ended in England victories, Holt's one cap as a Reading player was his last of 10, none of which saw an England defeat, so Nicky Shorey is the only Reading player to have tasted defeat with England.

IN A STATE

One player who can have no complaints about his short international career is **Doug Farquar.** Born in Scotland, Doug played for Reading in the early 1950s before emigrating to the US. He continued his professional playing career in America, making a number of representative appearances before being selected for the USA side that played England on 28 May 1959 and lost 8–1. Not surprisingly, Doug never played for the States again.

ASIAN ALLEN

Another 'overseas' player with an unusual international career is **Denis Allen.** Dagenham-born Denis Allen was a member of the famous London Allen footballing family, and as a youngster he captained his local youth team which included Bobby Moore. Denis also beat his illustrious teammate to international honours, gaining his caps during his national service. Posted to Malaya, Denis's skills caught the attention of the local football selectors and he was picked twice to play for Malaya. The only European in the games against Peru and Mexico, Denis scored twice during his brief international career.

TEN – WORDS OF WISDOM

IN OTHER WORDS

The potted history of Reading Football Club by those who were there when it happened.

Football's First Mention – 1628

'John Barker junior and Willyam Booth seeing the playeing of souldyers at football in the Forberye did endeavour to fetch the ball from them whiche caused much trouble to the constables and officers and danger of hurt to many.'

The Diary of the Reading Corporation reveals the first record of football (and football hooliganism!) in the town 243 years before Reading Football Club was formed.

Club Rules – 1871

'The colours of the Club shall be dark blue and white cap and blue knickerbockers.'
Handling of the ball was not allowed *'under any pretence whatever.'*

Also banned was *'Hacking'* – *'Kicking an adversary intentionally'* – whereas *'Tripping'* – *'Throwing an adversary by the use of the legs'* – was perfectly acceptable.

First Match – 21 February 1872

'A large concourse of persons were present. Play...resulted in a 'draw' neither party gaining a goal. The [Reading Grammar] school were rather superior to their opponents in skill, but were inferior in weight and strength.'

The *Reading Mercury*'s reports on a 0–0 draw, even though both sides lined up with six forwards.

First Criticism – 20 October 1872

'At the commencement of the game Reading were somewhat at fault, not having studied the association rules.'

Possibly sour grapes from Henley Town after they had a 'winning goal' disallowed for hands.

First Competitive Goal – 7 November 1877

'Field got hold of the ball from the centre of the ground, made a brilliant run down and by a clever kick scored the first goal for Reading amid much applause from the spectators.'

A local report records an historic goal as Reading open their FA Cup account.

Record Defeat – 27 January 1894

'Innocented [sic] of the tactics which guide the great football Clubs, Reading were sunk without trace in a sea of mud.' Harsh, but obviously true words, from *The*

Athletic News report of Preston 18 Reading 0. A Sunday paper was even less kind, commenting *'The amateurs were totally devoid of the finessing, the judgement and subtleness which is indispensable in first class Association Football.'*

Opening of Elm Park – 5 September 1896
'A ground second to none in the United Kingdom.'
Reading's Member of Parliament Mr C.T. Murdoch says the right thing during his opening of the Club's new ground.

First Southern League Goal at Elm Park – 19 September 1896
'Reid assisted the sphere on its course and Cunningham put on one finishing touch to the effort by completely beating Clare with a splendid shot amid deafening cheers.'
The local press describes the goal that beat Northfleet.

First League Victory – 28 August 1920
Joe Bailey's header was *'guided delicately out of Cooper's reach'*.
Reading Standard recalls the Club's historic first League goal, a header that was enough to win the game at Newport.

Third Division South Championship – 1 May 1926
The supporters *'made the welkin [sky] ring'* as *'an altogether historic scene was created'* and *'the greatest possible pleasure was evinced'*.
The Berkshire Chronicle describes the scene as Reading beat Brentford 7–1 to clinch promotion to the Second Division.

FA Cup v Manchester United – 8 January 1927
'Sheer ineptitude, lack of control and failure to check rough and dangerous play.'
The Club minutes reveal that the Reading directors blamed the referee, Mr Collins, for the violent play during the third-round FA Cup tie against Manchester United in 1927 and this resulted in the Club making an official complaint to the FA.
And:
'Reading played with the utmost coolness and such subtlety that Manchester were left guessing.'
Those same minutes confirm that it was not the Reading players who were at fault during this heated match.

Record Crowd – 19 February 1927
'It was pleasant to mix with such nice supporters.' And
'The packed terraces were good to see, though one wondered whether all the folks felt as nice as they looked. Personally, I should choose a density per acre that permitted the occasional lighting of a cigarette.'
Two Brentford fans' views of the 33,042 fans who saw (or maybe did not) Reading beat their Club in the fifth round of the FA Cup.

League Champions Beaten – 26 January 1929

'Somehow Reading kept them [Sheffield Wednesday] out: men went down like felled oaks and they did not score. Then – and the crammed crowd gasped with disbelief before it cheered – Johnstone scored, and Reading were in the lead. Why Wednesday did not score, only heaven and Joe Duckworth could tell you – and I suspect that Duckworth would not be too certain.'

Reading supporter John Arlott's article *Reading: A Supporter's Piece* described Reading's dramatic victory over Sheffield Wednesday and goalkeeper Joe Duckworth's part in that success.

Record League Defeat – 13 September 1930

'A disgraceful exhibition, we deserved the nasty thrashing administered.'
The Club cannot find any excuses for Reading's 8–1 defeat at Burnley.

Record FA Cup Win – 30 November 1936

'It was time well spent because we got to use that move nine times!'
Corinthians centre half Bernard Joy, later a famous journalist, refers to a special kick-off routine, devised using salt and pepper pots in the train buffet on the way to their game at Elm Park. As Reading won 8–3 Corinthians kicked-off nine times!

The Club's First Advert – 1936

'Roll up in your thousands to cheer the lads on to yet another two points. The more people watching, the better the team will play.'

First Non-League Defeat – 27 November 1937

'In quite the poorest, scrappiest and most dismal game I have seen this season, Reading took their knockout blow in the FA Cup at Guildford.'
Never ones to mince their words, the local press were unimpressed with Reading's 1–0 FA Cup defeat at Guildford.

Cup Triumph – 26 October 1938

'A wash out.'
Hardly the comment you would expect to be made at the presentation of Reading's first Cup final victory since joining the League. However, having beaten Bristol City in the Southern Section Cup, the two-leg final attracted a total of just 1,897 fans so the remark seems justified.

Record League Victory – 4 September 1946

'The home attack pleased as a whole with the possible exception of Chitty.'
Faint praise from the local press for Reading's 10–2 victory over Crystal Palace, while Wilf Chitty pays for failing to get on the score sheet.

Record Home Defeat – 31 January 1967
'Oh, Oh, Seven'
The Reading Chronicle combines the latest James Bond craze with Manchester City's 7–0 FA Cup replay win at Elm Park.

Thames Valley Royals Merger – 30 April 1983
'We don't want this blend of Maxwell House.'
A fan's banner during the peaceful protest march sums up the town's feeling towards Robert Maxwell's ill thought-out planned merger with Oxford United.

Simod Cup Semi-final – 2 March 1988
'As I walked towards the goal it appeared to get smaller and smaller.'
Reading fans would have been less confident if they had known Michael Gilkes's thoughts as he prepared to take the vital shoot-out kick against Coventry City.

Mark McGhee's Shock Departure – December 1994
'We have lost the conductor but we still have the orchestra.'
John Madejski sounds more philosophical than he probably felt after Mark McGhee walked out on the Club.

Madejski Stadium Opening – 22 August 1998
'The only corner of heaven on earth can now be formally identified. It is an old rubbish tip beside the drumming infinity of the M4 in the Royal County of Berkshire. Rival claims will not be entertained for the time being.'
Legendary reporter Bryon Butler will not find any Reading fans disagreeing with his comments in the *Daily Telegraph* following the new ground's opening.

Unbeaten Run – February 2006
'This lot would kick the board over at Monopoly.'
Captain Graeme Murty explains the winning mentality of his teammates during their record-breaking run to the Championship title.

Championship Champions – 1 April 2006
'There are more people on the pitch than live in the whole of Iceland.'
Ivar Ingimarrson is suitably impressed with the fans' post-match celebrations after the title is clinched against Derby County.

Chelsea Death Threats – December 2006
'Anyone brave enough to meet him down a dark alley should be armed with a chunk of Kryptonite.'
Reading coach Wally Downes does not appear to be too worried by the death threats made by Chelsea fans against Reading defender Ibrahima 'Superman' Sonko.

England Call-Up – May 2007
'She's delighted but our wedding preparations are in chaos.'
Nicky Shorey's England debut the day before his wedding proves a mixed blessing for his fiancée Emily Bailey.

THE BRIGHAM CARDS

Nowadays, a Club that wins promotion will issue a whole swathe of souvenirs, ranging from T-shirts to DVDs and even books. Back in 1911, Reading's very first promotion, from the Southern League Second Division back to the First, was commemorated by the issue of a set of cigarette cards!

However, these were no ordinary cards. Produced by local tobacconist and cigarette manufacturers Brigham & Company to advertise their Gold Flake cigarettes, the set is now one of the most collectable in the world of cartophily. Featuring 14 players, trainer Billy Beats and the Second Division trophy, each individual card can fetch over £100, that valuation being partly due to the phraseology used on the back of the cards, the best of which read:

H. Lee – *'a dashing player. He plays a clean game.'*

Len Andrews – *'is a local product and a credit to his town. Reading hopes great things of him.'*

J. Hewitt – *'He is a most successful and accurate shot.'*

R. Greer – *'Was born 22 years ago in the Land of Cakes [Scotland]. A great favourite with the spectators.'*

F. Bartholomew – *'The hotter the fight the better he plays. He weighs 12st 3lbs, but he can move.'*

W.H. Mayo – *'Good utility forward. Although not one of the biggest Billie is one of the best. He hails from Caversham, or if you prefer it, North Reading.*

H.P. Slatter – *'"Little Eva" is still with us.'*

E. Hanney – *'Has promised to play regularly this season as an amateur. We hear Teddy can use his hands.'*

The Trophy – *'It is needless to say that all Reading Sportsmen wish the Club the best of good luck now they are again playing in the first division and the issuers of the series hope they may be able to publish a picture of the Southern League Championship Shield as a Reading trophy next year.'*

THE FRANKLYN DIARY

Some 40 years before the issue of those Brigham cigarette cards another legacy of Reading's history was produced. During the demolition of Elm Park in 1998 a dusty old book was found behind a filing cabinet, which turned out to be a diary of Reading's 1880–81 season.

It transpired that the document was produced by **W.L. Franklyn**, who had played in Reading's very first FA Cup tie in 1877 and had taken over as Club captain two years later after the tragic death of the previous captain, **Henry**

Rogers. It appears that part of the captain's duties was to keep a record of Club matches, a tradition that is carried on to this day as most programmes feature a column by the Club captain.

Franklyn's diary went much further in that it also listed Club members and reports of other local Clubs, not just Reading. These reveal that as well as the Reading Club, the town also boasted at least another five teams bearing the town name – Rovers, Eagles, Wanderers, Ramblers and Abbey. The members' listing revealed that, not surprisingly, most of the players lived in the town centre, including **Stanley Hayward**, who was one of the Club's first players and whose address of 14 Bridge Street might well have been the venue of the Club's formation meeting. A few players had addresses from out of the area, such as Cambridge, Southall and Eltham, while two, ominously, were simply shown as 'Inland Revenue'. Another outsider was **Frank Sparks**, shown as a Clapham Rovers player, who the previous season had captained England and had averaged a goal a game during his three-match international career.

Hayward himself was described by the *London Football Star* as 'a charming half back', but he was far harsher on himself in the first report in his diary. Commenting on the team's display against Old Philberdians on 9 October 1880, he stated frankly 'The only one not in the game was the captain, but in justice to myself it is the first time I have played forward in a match and am not in condition for forging ahead play.'

Two weeks later Hayward resorted to using a press report in his diary for the game in Slough against Swifts, a report that included the remarkable comment 'the [Reading] centres did not avail themselves of the chance and were much too slow in passing and playing the ball, otherwise several goals must have been got at the beginning of the game, THE SWIFTS NOT HAVING A GOALKEEPER UNTIL LATER ON.'

Another press report, this time covering Reading's game against the area's other top team, Marlow, also reveals how different football was in the 19th century. Reporting on Marlow's attempts to equalise Holbrook's goal it stated 'a capital scrimmage took place in front of goal, the ball nearly going under the tape, but was splendidly prevented by Hayward.' At this point a gentlemanly dispute took place, the Marlow players claiming that the ball had gone under the 'tape' (no nets in those days, of course, as they were not 'invented' for another 10 years) but the Reading umpire deciding it was not a goal, and the Marlow umpire 'held the reverse.' The report went on: 'There being no referee, the matters remain a vexatio question.' Hayward's hand written entry reflected the dispute, recording the result as 'Reading 1 goal to 1 goal disputed.' The FA had actually introduced the use of crossbars back in 1875 but they were clearly not always used for non-competitive games. Consequently, six weeks later, the diary records that Reading's Berks & Bucks Cup tie against Reading Abbey featured crossbars.

There is no comment on the reaction to this dispute from the Marlow fans but another cutting on the same page reporting on Marlow's game at Maidenhead, remarked that 'There was a very large number of spectators from Marlow, several of whom behaved very rudely and riotously throughout the game towards the umpires and players on either side.'

Although the diary included reports on matches in the Berks & Bucks Cup and the FA Cup, the majority of the games that season were friendlies, some against top local sides of the day but others against the likes of Church Missionary College and Bradfield College, a local school that had the temerity to beat Reading 2–1. The college fully deserved their moment of fame since, far from fielding a weakened side, Reading, led by Franklin, played what was essentially their first team and included England international Edgar Field who, just six months earlier, had helped Clapham Rovers win the FA Cup.

Not surprisingly, reporting styles were somewhat different 128 years ago and as well as 'scrimmages', goals were 'rushed through the posts', while Holbrook's goal against Hendon was recorded that he 'sent the leather under the tape'.

———————— GOING OVERBOARD ————————

In times gone by the directors of Reading Football Club were not slow to pass an often outspoken opinion on their own players, the opposition and referees:

ON THE SAME SIDE?

Having written to captain **Ted Hanney** regarding his 'unnecessary talking which was not always in good taste', the board almost immediately announced in 1923, 85 years before the 2008 'Respect' campaign, that 'the captain's voice should be sufficient while play is in progress'.

The directors did not mince their words when a player displeased them, as **Charlie Leively** found out when they described his display on Good Friday 1922 as 'palpable inefficiency aggravated by studied and persistent lack of effort amounting to misconduct.'

September 1928 was a bad month, with a 1–0 home defeat to Southampton being described as 'a most discouraging exhibition by two very poor teams. Reading were devoid of any redeeming factor', while the trip to Oldham Athletic was 'another sorry exhibition'.

The board could offer praise when due, describing the team's display in their victory over League Champions Sheffield Wednesday on 26 January 1929 as 'every player was a man to be proud of.' It did not last long and six weeks later a 5–0 defeat at Stoke was 'a wretched display all round, the forwards played so badly as to beggar description.' A month later another defeat, at home to Nottingham Forest, was described as 'the most humiliating and sadly disappointing display for many years – a lack of zest and effort.'

Occasionally, the board even suggested what was the cause of the poor performances, revealing in December 1929 that 'some players had kept late hours, taken more to drink than men in training should and run unnecessary risks in motor cars'.

Of course, the directors could always take action if displays were not satisfactory, and they did. After a 5–1 defeat at Cardiff City on 5 September 1931, in which 'the team as a whole played brainless football', an immediate response resulted in the Club writing to the Great Western Railway Hotel in Cardiff about the cost of their meals!

OH, REF!

'Reading suffered again at the hands of referee Wiltshire who is so inefficient as to be incompetent of properly controlling any Football League or Cup tie. His personal vacillations and errors re foul play and offside caused bad spirit among the players, and gave dissatisfaction to the management of both sides.'

THE OTHER SIDE

There was no Christmas spirit on either side for Reading's trip to Millwall on 21 December 1929, with the Reading board claiming 'the ground, the crowd and opponents were all objectionable.

Played on a filthy ground in pitilessly wet weather, from which there was absolutely no shelter for onlookers, was the most miserable, all-out failure imaginable.' Using your powers of deduction, try to decide from this quote as to whether Reading won this FA Cup tie at Aberdare in 1923 or not!

———— I WISH I HADN'T SAID THAT! ————

❂ At the start of 1930–31 the Reading board were confident of a successful season, revealing to the Club's Annual General Meeting that 'a good start, a willing band of players and plenty of big gates is what we wish for, with a run in the Cup and a real bid for promotion'. Reading lost 7–1 at Spurs on the opening day of the season and ended up being relegated.

❂ Reading Chairman **Bill Lee** proved why directors should leave player selection to the experts when he described 1930s Reading player **Frank Newton** as giving 'a disgracefully weak exhibition', and that he was 'the worst centre forward ever seen in the Third Division.' Newton went on to score 31 goals in just 34 games for Reading, part of a League career that saw him net 193 goals.

❂ The first ever floodlit football match staged in Reading was not at Elm Park but at the old Oxford Road Greyhound Stadium. Played on 25 September 1934, the game was between the stadium staff and the Ancient Order of Foresters, a side that included former Reading favourites **Bert Eggo** and **Billy McConnell**. Although the game attracted a crowd of about 3,000, the *Berkshire Chronicle* were unsure of the future of floodlit football, stating 'as an interesting spectacle the match was a success but it is hardly likely that floodlit football will become a vogue'.

❧ *Reading Standard* reporter J.A.L. was probably wise to remain anonymous as he was not very popular at Elm Park after likening Reading's efforts against Clapton Orient on 9 January 1937 to 'a blackberry jelly trying to pierce its way through a wooden door'!

❧ More press criticism was heaped on the Reading team as they struggled at the start of the 1955–56 season, a local reporter stating 'it is hoped that youngsters did not try to model their play on this harem-scarem, ball-bashing Reading team.'

❧ In the days when reporters dictated their copy over the phone there was the occasional mistake when words were misheard over crackling lines. Few were as embarrassing as *Reading Evening Post*'s Sports Editor Pat Forrest's comment on a game between Reading and Wrexham, which appeared in print as 'The ball was swung into the rectum area'!

❧ 'We can win this.' – Trainer **Jimmy Wallbanks**'s half time rallying call to his players at Brighton on 27 April 1957. It was intended to inspire Reading to overcome a 2–1 deficit – they lost 8–3.

❧ Reading's programme for their game against Queen's Park Rangers, played on 5 April 1963, featured pen pictures of the visiting players who included '**Roy Bentley** – Former England centre or inside forward, he played centre half before switching to full back.' Nothing wrong with that description, except for the fact that Roy had been Reading's manager for almost three months at the time.

❧ **Charlie Hurley** had a great turn of phrase, and having been recommended to watch a young Hayes striker by his coach, **Maurice Evans**, the Reading boss, unimpressed with what he had seen, came out with one of football's great quotes – 'He couldn't trap a bag of cement on a rainy day.' Or it would have been a great quote if **Cyrille Regis** had not gone on to enjoy a prolific goalscoring career and play five times for England!

❧ When it was first suggested that Reading move from Elm Park to the Smallmead area of the town that now houses the Madejski Stadium, the following home fixture in October 1982 saw fans waving a banner stating 'We Won't Go To Smallmead.'

❧ **Robert Maxwell**'s ill-conceived plan to merge Reading and Oxford United into the Thames Valley Royals met with total disapproval from both sets of fans. His arrogant attitude did not help, his overconfidence leading him to state 'The Thames would flow backwards before the merger failed'.

❧ Interviewing footballers live is a risky business, as *Radio Berkshire* found out when they joined the team on their open-top bus tour to celebrate promotion in 1985–86:

Radio Berkshire reporter: 'Michael Gilkes, live on *Radio Berkshire*, please tell the listeners how it feels to have won promotion.'
Michael Gilkes: 'F**k**g brilliant!'
RBR: We're live, Michael.'
MG: 'Oh, yes. Great, then.'

Newer Reading fans can replace Sammy Igoe's 2001–02 promotion 'speech' that included a similar 'adjective' for the same effect.

⊕ When Reading crashed to a 3–0 home defeat against Barnsley on 11 March 1995 it looked as if their hopes of a Division One play-off place were gone. *Radio Berkshire* reporter Steve Beddow certainly thought so, stating 'If Reading make it to the play-offs now, I'll walk to Wembley.' They did and, to his credit, Steve kept his word and walked the 40 miles to Wembley.

⊕ 'The referee's blown his watch.' An excited **John Southall** tells *Radio Berkshire* listeners that Reading have secured another vital win at Luton at Easter 1995.

⊕ 'He scored three goals, other than that I kept him pretty quiet.' **Michael Duberry** may have slightly missed the point of marking Liverpool's £20 million striker **Fernando Torres** during the 4–2 League Cup defeat on 25 September 2007. But he was not the first. Cardiff boss **Alan Durbin** made a similar comment about **Trevor Senior** after the Reading striker's trio secured an away win at Ninian Park but not the match ball, which the home boss refused to give to Reading's hat-trick hero unless he paid for it.

⊕ 'We are not going to win the FA Cup and I don't give two sh*ts about it to be honest.' The consistently outspoken **David Kitson** added more fuel to the January 2008 controversy over the use of 'weakened' FA Cup teams.

⊕ But, of all the quotes that turned out to be far from the truth, the winner is…

Mark Lawrenson for his grim determination to make his wayward prediction come true. Prior to the start of Reading's first-ever Premiership season the BBC pundit gave the Club no chance – 'It's going to be tough and I'm afraid I think Reading will be relegated. I'm not sure Reading's strikers will make the transition to the higher standard. I look at them now and they just haven't got enough.'

Throughout the season, Reading proved all their critics wrong but 'Lawro' grimly stuck to his view via his weekly prediction column. Ignoring Reading's permanent place in the top 10, Mark continued to predict defeat after defeat for the Club, and if his weekly predictions had come true they would have won a total of just 29 points, compared with the 55 points they actually won, leaving Reading second from bottom in Lawro's mind.

The following season, Lawrenson had learnt from his mistake and predicted that Reading would not be relegated in 2007–08. Sadly, that prediction was just as wrong as his first one.

PRAISE INDEED?

⊛ Indian-born Reading keeper **Rupert O'Donnell** was selected to play for England Amateurs in 1909 but declined the invitation, replying by telegram 'Many Thanks but begorra am for Ireland.'

⊛ The excellent *Century of English International Football 1872–1972* provided a perfect description of Reading's most-capped England international **Herbert Smith** –'Burly left back whose dextrous left foot was almost legendary. A brilliant defender and, in spite of his physique, scrupulously fair.'

⊛ Another Reading England international **Johnny Holt** was a rather different player as a contemporary pen-picture revealed – 'A peculiar built little man with a rather long neck perched on bottle shoulders. Heading due to timing, judgement and getting an extra lift via his opponents' shoulders.' The lightest England centre half, weighing in at just 10st 4lb and standing 5ft 4in, this did not reduce his effectiveness since the cap he won as a Reading player saw him become the first England international to make 10 appearances without finishing on the losing side. As well as all that he is said to have invented the sliding tackle.

⊛ **William H. Barnett** was one of Reading's early amateur players, although he was once described by *The London Football Star* as having 'little or no style but a good forward'. Mr Barnett's talents obviously lay elsewhere as he was also Club treasurer and secretary until 1890.

⊛ Language in those Southern League days can be quite unusual. For instance, defender **Frank Stokes** was described in a pen picture that he 'tackles prettily', although it added that he 'kicks with accuracy and judgement.' After two seasons at Elm Park, Frank was sold to Birmingham in 1903, where he 'tackled prettily' in over 200 games. Despite this, he had the bitter experience of not being selected for his own testimonial game!

⊛ Another Southern League star **Arthur Hadley** was described as 'one of the pluckiest of football players and this is rather surprising when his slight build [he was only 9st 10lb] is taken into account. He is one of the fastest wingmen in the country and once he gets past the opposing half back, the ball is certain to find its way into the vicinity of the goal, if not actually through it.' An interesting quote, tactically, as it indicates that at the end of the 19th century it was the half back's job, not the full back, to mark the winger.

⊛ In April 1898 Reading suspended **James Cockshutt** and **R. Barr** for life, announcing 'These men from the North would be made to know that they could not do what they liked.' Those suspensions were never rescinded despite the fact that the Club let it be known that Barr had written 'quite piteously' asking to be reinstated.

⊛ Equally uncomplimentary was the finding of an FA disciplinary board who fined future Reading player **Teddy Gettins** £10, about a month's wages, while he was with Middlesbrough. The damning statement accused Teddy of being 'loyal to his directors and disloyal to his conscience'.

⊛ Watford's fan website *Blind, Stupid and Desperate* provided a quite-possibly accurate description of the dietary requirements of Watford hard man **Roger Joslyn**, whose playing career ended through injury at Reading in January 1982. 'Between matches Roger had to be kept in a reinforced steel cage and the Club had to employ a full time keeper. He was fed on raw meat, seasoned with a sprinkling of broken glass and rusty nails. As an occasional treat, a Christian was thrown to him, secretly supplied by the Club chaplain.'

⊛ When asked by a local reporter what his role in the team was, Reading winger **Gene Carney** replied 'to protect the linesman from the crowd on my side of the pitch!' He obviously took these duties too seriously as he failed to scored in 22 Reading games and was released in January 1924 after just eight months with the Club.

⊛ On the same lines, **Brian Kirkup** began his League career with Reading in 1955, retiring from League football at Aldershot, stating he knew it was time to quit 'when the linesmen started to overtake him'.

⊛ Possibly, the prize for the strangest sporting headline should go to the *Berkshire Chronicle*'s leader in April 1950 which read 'He can sit down for the first time since 10 Dec.' The strange comment has a serious background, referring to a career-threatening injury suffered by Reading goalkeeper **George Marks**, that resulted in him being encased in plaster from his neck to ankle following a very bad thigh injury sustained in a friendly against Rotherham United. Fortunately, Marks, once the world's most expensive keeper at £5,000, made a full recovery.

⊛ **Frank Eaton** cost Reading a record fee of £1,750 in June 1930, but this did not stop Reading fans making him 'the butt of jokes and ribald remarks one would expect to hear from a third-rate comedian, not so-called sportsmen'. It was not just the fans either, as Frank forced an apology from a local paper after it had unfairly criticised his play.

⊛ There were mixed views on **Attillo Fresia**, Reading's 1913 Italian international signing – **Vittorio Pozzo**, manager of Italy's 1934 and 1938 World Cup-winning teams thought he was 'one of the most skilful players in Italian football'. On the other hand, a local Reading newspaper reporter described the forward as being 'just useful on hard ground and almost useless on soft going'.

⊛ One of the all-time Reading greats and a hero in Reading's Third Division South Championship side, right back **Bert Eggo** was clearly a bargain as a contemporary cigarette card thought Sheffield Wednesday 'were very hasty when they transferred him to Reading for the price of an old song'.

⊛ A colleague of Eggo's and just as highly regarded, wing half **David Evans** was described in the Reading programme as 'a clean and clever player admired by friend and foe alike'.

⊛ Also from a pen picture in the Reading programme, written by a member of the Supporters' Club for his benefit game in 1934, came a comment that described Reading left half **Charlie Barley** as 'one of the cleverest ball manipulators who has ever donned a blue-and-white jersey'.

⊛ Another 1930s cigarette card made a non-politically correct comment about 5ft 4in Reading winger **Billy Cook**, describing him as 'another of football's great midgets. A dazzling winger up to every trick with twinkling feet.' The same card then gave a clue why Billy only won three Scottish caps, commenting 'sometimes inclined to over-elaborate'.

⊛ Only **Trevor Senior** scored more Reading goals than **Jimmy Wheeler,** and with the goals flowing again at the start of 1960–61 the *Reading Standard* commented 'With five Jimmy Wheelers in the forward line Reading would rocket into the Second Division.' As 'Jimmy Wee' ended up scoring 31 League goals that season, that assumption was probably correct!

⊛ Chelsea's young star **David Lee** spent a sensational month on loan to Reading in February 1992. During that time he scored five goals in as many games, a fact that was even more remarkable because he was playing as a central-defender. Not surprising, then, that local reporter and editor of the Reading Club programme Maurice O'Brien described the player as 'the nearest thing to Superman'.

⊛ Never one to mince his words, either in his playing days or as a BBC pundit, **Ian Wright** was nevertheless unstinting in his praise for another player who ended his League career at Elm Park: Welsh international **Jeff Hopkins**. In his autobiography he described Jeff as 'one of the most dedicated and underrated players I have ever met. I've never met another player who could match Jeff for honesty, courage and commitment.'

⊕ 'English, half goose, professional footballer with Reading' – **Steve Sidwell**'s *Wikipedia* entry demonstrates that anyone can update the internet encyclopaedia with impunity. The culprit was never discovered but the now Aston Villa midfielder's chief suspect remains Club joker **Glen Little**.

⊕ In his brilliant article *Reading: A Supporter's Piece*, Reading fan and cricket commentator **John Arlott** gave a vivid description of **Alf Bacon**, the player who once scored a Club-record six goals for Reading versus Stoke City – 'With a shaving-brush tuft of hair growing out from a shallow forehead above a mighty jaw. His chest was like a drum, his thighs hugely tapering, and he has two shooting feet which he threw at footballs as if with intent to burst them.'

⊕ Finally, that same article by John Arlott contains a quote that sums up a feeling that many Reading fans have experienced over the years – 'There are many times, when, as a guest in the board room of some mighty First League Club, I find that the Third Division results are not read out – they stop at the Second Division. Then it is that I face superior smiles or the loud laughs and ask, with my heart in my mouth, anxious as ever, "How did Reading get on?"'

I'M IN CHARGE

Harry Matthews – 1902 to 1920
'Mr Matthews was one of the greatest assets of the Club and as long as he remains at the head of it they could never exclude the possibility of having a successful season. The remuneration he received was absolutely inadequate and incommensurate with the services he rendered.'
Praise indeed from the Club's Chairman at the 1909 Annual General Meeting.

Harry Marshall – 1920
'Mr Marshall's methods might seem a trifle heavy-handed but that is the way of Northerners.'
Comment from a Club director at the October 1920 Annual General Meeting, presumably one of the board members who voted for Marshall's dismissal, two days before Christmas.

Jack Smith – 1920 to 1922
'Jack Smith be appointed player-manager of the Club definitely until May 1922, the terms to be £1 more than his present wage.'
Proposed by director Mr Royle and carried unanimously, managers were clearly worth less than they are today.

Arthur Chadwick – 1923 to 1925
'The manager is to undertake to see that more tidy and wholesome conditions prevail in the guests' tea room.'
The man who signed most of Reading's great team of the mid-1920s and, for a short time, was the first to be allowed to pick his own team and was clearly lacking in some of his more important responsibilities, according to the Club's minutes.

Harold Bray – 1925 to 1926
'A deputation of senior players approached the board with a strange request. They felt the Club would be better served if no new manager be appointed until the end of the season.'
The official Club history reveals that player power is not always a bad thing. Former schoolteacher Harold Bray was paid an extra £1 to add managerial duties to those of Club secretary, and proved good value for this extra payment as he guided Reading to the Third Division South title that season.

Angus Wylie – 1926 to 1931
'The board accepted his resignation with regret. Mr Wylie displayed zealous, conscientious and always honourable hard work who would never fail to be a friend to Reading Football Club.'
Having survived two votes of no-confidence, Andrew Wylie's resignation was still a disappointment to the Club's directors.

Joe Smith – 1931 to 1935
'42 years old, married, free of all Clubs and willing to move home to Reading if given the job.'
Reading's prospective manager lists the details of his CV that persuaded Reading's directors to appoint him as manager.

Billy Butler – 1935 to 1939
'We have striven to make their [the players'] stay in Reading very happy and hope that by doing so to get repaid by a wholehearted team spirit on the pitch.'
Reading's innovative young manager was forced to defend the building of a gymnasium at Elm Park at the 1936 Annual General Meeting.

Joe Cochrane – April 1939
'The town was alive with rumours as the shock news spread, with the popular, but unsubstantiated, opinion alluding to the fact that the 'flu that caused his absence from the home game against Crystal Palace was just a euphemism.'
No official reason was ever given as to why Joe Cochrane's managerial career at Reading lasted just 13 days but the official Club history hints at the fans' thoughts.

Joe Edelston – 1939 to 1947

'A very fair and democratic arrangement. Clubs that do well should help those who are not so fortunate.'

Reading's boss's fair-minded comment on the distribution on the Football League wartime pool that saw Reading receive less than they had contributed.

Ted Drake – 1947 to 1952

'The happiest years of my life.'

Ted Drake may have won League titles as a player with Arsenal, managed Chelsea to their first Championship and coached Barcelona, but his heart was always in Berkshire.

Jack Smith – 1952 to 1955

'I want to see some fight, some grit and some determination.' And
'Mr Smith had been instructed to take one month's leave of absence as he is obviously feeling the strain of the past few weeks.'

The new manager's first comments and the directors' final remarks reveal the toll that managing cash-strapped Reading had on the manager's health.

Harry Johnston – 1955 to 1962

'Harry Johnston has a wealth of talent on his books.'

No Reading manager gave young local players their chance in the League more than Harry Johnston, and it was recognized by the fans and the *Reading Standard*.

Roy Bentley – 1963 to 1969

'A team manager, who would be solely responsible for the training and coaching of players, to select teams, and to secure the transfer of players.'

The Club's directors give the job description for the revised manager's role at Reading so there were no administrative duties for Roy Bentley.

Jack Mansell – 1969 to 1971

'The directors are conscious of their responsibilities to the loyal supporters of the Club and decided that immediate action was essential.'

Part of the Club announcement informing the press of Jack Mansell's dismissal.

Charlie Hurley – 1972 to 1977

'The greatest human being who ever lived. Constructed entirely of pre-cast concrete, he often played when fatally injured with his head missing.'

The *Sunderland Gazette* provides the reason why their local fans voted the former Reading manager as the Black Cats Player of the Millennium.

Maurice Evans – 1976 to 1984

'Player, Manager, Gentleman, 1936 to 2000.'

The Supporters' Club plaque outside Madejski Stadium ticket office perfectly sums up the man who coached, scouted and managed Reading as well as playing 459 times for them without ever being booked.

Ian Branfoot – 1984 to 1989
'He got us into this mess, he can get us out of it.'
Hardly a vote of confidence from Chairman Roger Smee, but at least Ian kept his job after Reading's relegation in 1987–88.

Ian Porterfield – 1989 to 1991
'Ian was a real gentleman, such a nice man who did what every schoolboy dreams of by scoring the winning goal in a Cup final.'
Sunderland Cup final teammate Richie Pitt remembers his late colleague.

Mark McGhee – 1991 to 1999
'A track-suited manager who would rarely be seen wearing his best clothes and shaking hands with people who don't matter to the game.'
Reading's chief executive Mike Lewis sets out the criteria that Mark McGhee was to provide.

Jimmy Quinn/Mick Gooding – 1994 to 1997
'I've had eight Clubs and nine managers – if I can't take a training session by now, I never will.'
Quinn allays fears of the managerial duo's lack of experience.

Terry Bullivant – 1997 to 1998
'If it doesn't work out, I can always go back to driving taxis.'
Not quite the inspiring call to arms that Reading fans were expecting from their new manager.

Tommy Burns – 1998 to 1999
'Where's the noose?'
Tommy Burns's opening remark to the press conference following Reading's 6–0 home defeat to Bristol Rovers.

Alan Pardew – 1999 to 2003
'We have to come through it stronger, and we'll do better next season. Perhaps it wasn't our destiny this time, but next year we'll make damned sure it is.'
The manager was positive after Reading's 2002 play-off final defeat and kept his promise by clinching promotion 12 months later.

Steve Coppell 2003 to Date
Humourless according to some of the national press, but Reading fans nevertheless appreciate their manager's dry sense of humour:

'I learned very quickly that you don't pick fights with Scotsmen who are bigger than you.'
On another hostile reception for former Reading boss Mark McGhee on his return
to the Club.

*'He's [Glen Little] damaged his elbow and couldn't straighten his arm. I think it's
so he can't reach his pocket to buy a drink.'*

'I'm a man of few words but most of the ones I said to the players began with F.'
After a 4–1 defeat at Wolverhampton on 4 December 2004.

'I'm not going to make it a target but it's something to aim for.'

*'When you hear some of the sh*t they come out with, you might as well let them
talk about promotion.'*
Denying that he banned talk of promotion during 2005–06.

HOME SWEET HOME
What was said about Elm Park over the years.

'The atmospheric conditions were in every way favourable.'
Reading Standard reports on the first competitive game at the Club's new ground
on 19 September 1896.

'A capitally equipped ground.'
From the Reading history included in the *1905 Book of Football.*

*'First impressions of Elm Park is certainly disconcerting. The numerous stands
and shelters takes one's mind back to some of the suburbs of Ypres.'*
The tone of the Chelsea programme for their FA Cup replay against Reading in
January 1921 is possibly due to the fact they had a last-minute penalty saved!

'Barracking of match officials cannot be tolerated in any circumstances.'
A Club warning issued in 1927 following 'rare' criticism of a referee by Reading fans!

'A stadium somewhere in the Home Counties.'
Fans trying to find Elm Park in June 1944 to watch World Heavyweight
Champion Joe Louis box a demonstration bout would have to have relied on
their sat navs rather than these wartime restricted directions!

*'Over 13,000 saw the match but what a funny crowd they were. I've heard more
noise on a golf course when I squared up to a foot putt.'*
Former Arsenal player Alex James is not impressed with the 'Elm Park Roar'
during the game against Exeter on 19 March 1949.

'It would be hard to find a more fair-minded and sporting bunch of fans than that at Elm Park.'
A Wisbech fan confirms Reading supporters' suspicions following their FA Cup defeat on 7 December 1957.

'Ooh, what a lovely lawn.'
Freddie Garrity, of Freddie and the Dreamers, comes up with the only memorable moment during Elm Park's first pop concert in July 1967.

'The least interesting ground in the League. One of the most depressed grounds in the country without an ounce of spirit or verve.'
Author Simon Inglis made this scathing criticism in his 1980s *Football Grounds of Great Britain*. At least he modified his view in the reprint.

'The hotdogs border on the erotic.'
A more favourable review in the 1990s *Supporters' Guide to Football League Grounds*.

'During the Gulf War, a scud missile went off course and hit Elm Park, doing £2 million worth of improvements!'
Manager Mark McGhee jokes at a press conference at the start of the 1994–95 season.

'The inside of this unaesthetic study of blue corrugated iron and wood is like most grounds used to be.'
The Daily Mail assess Elm Park's potential as a Premier League ground during Reading's run to the play-offs in 1994–95.

'Elm Park – crap ground, crap fans. Reading – dump of a town, joke of a ground.'
After four consecutive, costly and humiliating defeats, a Midlands fanzine reveals that Wolves fans do not appear to enjoy their trips to Berkshire anymore.

Finally, Reading actually played at a ground in the 'Elm Park' area of the town two years before their ground was built. That game, played on 24 November 1894 against Grenadier Guards, was described as being at the home of Reading Temperance, and a contemporary report shows how the language of football has changed, stating that *'the sphere had a disagreeable tendency to pass outside the uprights'*, and commenting on *'the ubiquitous movements of the visiting minder who was barely keeping the perpendicular'*.

ELEVEN – SIX OF THE BEST

No book on football would be complete without a list of Club bests so, in the tradition of Miss World, in reverse order, here are the Reading 'bests'.

FIGHTBACKS

⚽ 6 – Reading v Luton Town 27 March 1988

OK, so coming back from 1–0 down to win is hardly anything special, but this was the Simod Cup Final at Wembley against First Division opposition in front of 61,740, the biggest crowd ever to watch Reading at the time. Few people outside Berkshire gave Reading any chance, and when Mick Harford gave the red-hot favourites Luton the lead after only 13 minutes it seemed that Reading's dreams were over. But with **Michael Gilkes** in top form, the flying forward soon equalised and then won the penalty that enabled **Stuart Beavon** to give Reading the lead. Second half goals from **Mick Tait** and **Neil Smillie** completed what turned out to be a rout as Reading humbled the team that, three weeks later, were to return to Wembley to beat Arsenal in the League Cup Final.

⚽ 5 – Reading v Watford 8 December 1982

Destined to be relegated that season, Reading faced a full strength Watford side that eventually finished second in the First Division in the quarter-finals of the Football League Trophy. Again Reading were given little chance to progress and, again, early indications pointed to the inevitable home defeat as Luther Blissett scored after only three minutes. Although **Gary Donnellan** equalised for Reading, John Barnes scored twice to put the game apparently out of Reading's reach. Still 3–1 down with four minutes to go, Reading staged a remarkable recovery, when first **Peter O'Sullivan** and then Donnellan again scored to earn an unlikely 30 minutes of extra time. Six minutes into the extra period Donnellan, a former Watford player, completed his hat-trick and then **Kerry Dixon** put the result beyond doubt to make it 5–3 to Reading.

⚽ 4 – Reading v Middlesbrough 19 August 2006

After 135 years of waiting, Reading at last made their debut in the Football League's top flight when Middlesbrough visited Madejski Stadium for the Club's first-ever Premiership game. Twenty-one minutes later Reading were wondering what they had let themselves in for as first Stewart Downing and then Josef Yakubu scored to give Boro a 2–0 lead. Sparked by **Nicky Shorey**'s runs from defence Reading clawed their way back, and in a mad but memorable five minutes before half time **Dave Kitson** and then **Steve Sidwell** scored to make it 2–2 at the break. The comeback was completed on 56 minutes when **Leroy Lita** grabbed what proved to be the winner. There may have been more dramatic comebacks in Reading's history, but none more memorable.

⊕ 3 – Chesterfield v Reading 13 May 1989

Relegated from the Second Division at the end of the previous season, a run of six successive defeats had seen Reading facing a second consecutive drop when they travelled to Chesterfield for the final game of the season. By half time Reading were 2–0 down and occupying one of the four relegation places. On 51 minutes **Trevor Senior,** without a goal in seven games, chose the perfect time to end his goal drought, then **Lee Payne** equalised on the hour. Within six minutes the result was settled as **Stuart Beavon** converted two penalties to ensure Reading's Third Division safety and send Chesterfield down in their place.

⊕ 2 – Reading v Plymouth Argyle 21 December 1985

Reading had once come back from three goals down to win back in 1953, but that does not compare with the events that took place at Elm Park on 21 December 1985. Top of the Third Division after their record-breaking start, Reading faced their toughest test in the visit of in-form Plymouth. The visitors certainly maintained their form, storming into a 3–0 lead after 48 minutes. Manager Ian Branfoot's response was one of the all-time great substitutions. Bringing on **Glenn Burville,** he moved **Kevin Bremner** into the forward line with dramatic effect. Within four minutes Bremner was fouled and **Dean Horrix** converted the resulting penalty. Despite still being 3–1 down the players and fans believed that Reading could still get something from the game, a feeling that was doubled when **Trevor Senior** pulled back a second goal. A minute later he made it 3–3 and there was only going to be one winner now. A Plymouth defender later described the second half as 'like being at the Alamo', and with the fans reaching near hysteria the winner came four minutes later. Appropriately it was scored by Bremner, whose man-of-the-match display gave ample proof as to why he was known as 'Mad Max'.

That other three-goal comeback had seen visitors Coventry City go 3–0 up after only 20 minutes play before a **Wally Hinshelwood** hat-trick plus a goal from **Dennis Simpson** earned Reading a dramatic home win. Even more remarkable is the fact that on the same day Reading's A team imitated the first team, also coming back from a three-goal deficit to beat East Cowes Victoria 7–4 in the Hampshire League.

⊕ 1 – Southampton v Reading 6 January 1940

Wartime games were often high-scoring affairs, and the six War League South games prior to Reading's visit to The Dell had seen 31 goals scored. An icy pitch was always going to favour forwards and early on it was the home side who had the advantage, going two up in the first quarter of an hour, and after only 40 minutes the Saints led 5–1, **Wilf Chitty** having scored what seemed to be Reading's consolation goal. Then Reading scored through **Bill Layton** and **Jack Deverall** to make it a remarkable 5–3 at half time. Even by wartime standards that rate of goals could not be maintained and it was not until the 70th minute that the next goals came, **Johnny Sherwood** scoring twice in quick succession to put Reading on level terms at 5–5. The game stayed all-square until the final minute when Wilf Chitty sent over a great cross for Layton to head in Reading's winner and make the score Southampton 5 Reading 6. The game was a personal triumph for Wilf Chitty as he had scored one and made the other five. Those 11 goals were watched by under 2,000 fans, who paid just £82 in total to watch this most remarkable game.

THE ONES THAT GOT AWAY

✪ 6 – Stan Collymore

As a young striker stuck in the Crystal Palace reserves, Stan Collymore caught the eye of Reading manager Mark McGhee as a replacement for **Trevor Senior**. Palace's manager wanted £100,000 for the untried player and that proved too much for Reading. Shortly after, Southend United took a chance on Collymore and his career was in the ascendancy. During an often turbulent career, he played three times for England and generated transfer fees in the region of £16 million.

✪ 5 – Albert Gudmunsson

A legend in Iceland, Albert was the first player from his country to make a career as a professional footballer. While with Racing Club de Paris, Reading manager Ted Drake travelled to France to look at the player and was impressed but was put off signing the free-scoring forward when he was told of the problems involved in dealing with French Clubs. Strangely, in view of their recent transfer policy, that warning came from Arsenal! Gudmunsson went on to play for AC Milan and several other French Clubs before returning to Iceland to embark on a political career. He rose to become Minister of Finance until 1987 when he formed his own party and then subsequently became Iceland's ambassador to France.

✪ 4 – Miah Dennehy

Early in his managerial career Charlie Hurley received a number of tips of promising players from his Irish homeland. One such tip related to a young Cork Hibernian player whom the 'scout' believed would adapt well to English League football. As desperate as Reading were for new talent as they wallowed in the Fourth Division, Hurley decided not to follow up on the lead, mainly because his informant was serving time in an Irish prison. Dennehy soon made his own headlines, scoring the first hat-trick in the history of the FIAI Cup Final, and almost immediately he was on his way to Nottingham Forest. He played throughout the 1970s, also winning 11 caps for the Republic of Ireland.

Miah was not the first player whom Reading had been recommended via prison. An officer at a young offenders institute suggested that Jack Mansell should take a look at one of his 'clients' but the Club failed to follow up on the 16-year-old **Robin Friday**. Fortunately, Charlie Hurley did not repeat the mistake when Friday came to Reading's attention the second time.

✪ 3 – Sam Bartram and Vic Woodley

Two of the greatest goalkeepers of the 1930s and 1940s, both Sam and Vic could have been Reading players. Woodley played for Windsor & Eton, coming to Reading's attention when he played for the Berks & Bucks select team. Offered a trial at Elm Park, Vic gave a series of impressive displays in the reserves but was not signed, and within three months of leaving Reading he signed for Chelsea. He soon established himself in their first team, winning 19 caps for England up to the start of World War Two. Still playing when formal football recommenced, Vic won his only major trophy in 1946 when he helped Derby win the FA Cup.

The story of Sam Bartram is very similar, but with one major exception. Also on trial in 1931, Sam played a few reserve games for Reading before being allowed to leave and return to his native North East. A year later he was back in the South with Charlton Athletic, who quickly signed him. Although he was kept out of the England team by Woodley, Sam became a legend at the Valley, making over 600 appearances for Charlton. Like Woodley, he also saved his best moment until after the war when he won the 1947 FA Cup with Charlton. Unlike Vic Woodley, Reading boss Joe Smith has an excuse for not spotting Sam's goalkeeping skills while he was at Elm Park. Sam played all his games as a left half, only going in goal after he left Reading.

✪ 2 – Peter Bonetti and Peter Osgood

What is it about Reading and top goalkeepers? The two Chelsea legends both attended Harry Johnston's highly rated youth training sessions in the late 1950s and the Club were sufficiently impressed with the young keeper to want Bonetti to attend on a regular basis. Unfortunately, the promising keeper lived in Worthing and the train journey from the Sussex coast was just too arduous so the future England goalkeeper decided to train with, and subsequently sign for, Chelsea.

Osgood was another matter. A local boy from Windsor, he had been seen playing a youth match at Elm Park and was invited to attend those same training sessions. There, however, he failed to impress, and even after he had scored four goals in the Berkshire Boys Club win over Birmingham at Elm Park in May 1964 Peter was allowed to join Chelsea, where he became one of their greatest and certainly most popular players. Ossie never forgot that rejection by Reading and when his life story was serialised in a Sunday paper the first instalment carried the headline 'Even Reading Didn't Want Me!'.

✪ 1 – Jimmy Hill

In the 1970s and 1980s there was not a more powerful person in English football than Jimmy Hill, and he too almost became a Reading player. As a youngster Hill played in Reading's youth team, alongside players such as Johnny Brooks, Ray Reeves and Maurice Evans. Reading's manager, Ted Drake, was a shrewd judge of a player and as a former centre forward himself he felt that the young Londoner did not have enough to make it as a professional. Hill joined Brentford before making his name, playing alongside Johnny Haynes at Fulham, as well as leading the Professional Footballers Association to the verge of strike action over the abolition of the maximum wage. His playing career over, he became an innovative manager at Coventry City, transforming the Club. He then commenced an outspoken career in television and was responsible for introducing the panel of pundits that is now a fixture at all televised games.

TWO TIMERS

☺ 6 – Billy Henderson

The Club's Southern League days were full of players coming, going and then coming back again, but tough defender **Billy Henderson** liked the town and Club so much that he had three spells with Reading. This was despite the fact that he was warned by the directors about rough play on several occasions. After four seasons at Elm Park he moved to Southampton, where he was mainly deputy to the legendary all-round sportsman C.B. Fry. He returned to Reading for the 1904–05 season to help the team finish second in the Southern League, but his final spell with the Club was not so happy as it ended in relegation in 1909–10. A teammate of Billy at Elm Park was Welsh international **Jos Davies**, who had two spells with top Welsh Club Chirk followed by three with Manchester City, although the first two were under their previous name of Ardwick.

☺ 5 – Roger Smee

Born in Reading, Roger also had three spells with his home-town Club, but only two were as a player. It was his third spell with the Club that had the most dramatic effect on Reading. By 1983 Roger was a successful businessman and he acted as the figurehead to drive the town's objections to Robert Maxwell's planned merger with Oxford United. With the Thames Valley Royals banished to history, Roger guided the Club to its then most successful spell, winning the Third Division title in 1986 and the Simod Cup two years later. Returning to Reading appears to run in Roger's family, as his brother-in-law, **Peter Silvester**, returned on loan to Elm Park in 1975, six years after he had left Reading for the first time.

☺ 4 – Alan Judge and Gary Westwood

Reading have a history of signing goalkeepers after a loan spell, with **Steve Death** being the most obvious example. Death's replacement, **Alan Judge**, had two loan spells at Elm Park in August 1982 and again later in that season before returning for a third, permanent spell. Alan's replacement in the Reading green jersey was **Gary Westwood**, who also had a successful loan spell with Reading before coming back to the Club on a permanent basis. Both keepers were vital parts of a Reading promotion season, Judge in 1983–84 and Westwood two years later.

☺ 3 – Mike Kearney

Few Reading favourites have had a more varied career than **Mike Kearney**, and he owes it all to Maurice Evans. All five of Mike's transfers in the Football League involved Reading's great talent spotter. Signed by Evans, as manager of Shrewsbury Town, from the Scottish junior Club that had produced Robert Fleck and Kenny Dalglish, he was then sold to Chester City, from where Evans, now manager of Reading, signed him for the Club for the first time. In 1980 Mike felt unsettled in the South, so the Reading boss reluctantly sold him back to Chester. Almost immediately, the striker realised he had made a mistake and three months later Maurice Evans rescued him, signing him for a third time. Converted to a classy defender, Mike's League career was ended by a foot injury in 1982. Eight years later he returned to Elm Park for a third time to run the Club's social Club. When Reading relocated to Madejski Stadium, Mike became promotions manager and he is now the facilities manager at Reading's Hogwood Park training centre.

☉ 2 – Adie Williams

One of Reading's most popular players, many of the Club's fans will be surprised when they realise that Adie has signed for the Club four times. He initially joined the Royals in 1986 as an apprentice, graduating to become an integral part of the great Reading side of the 1990s and becoming the third Reading-born player to be capped as a full international when he played for his father's homeland, Wales. After four injury-hit years with Wolves, Adie returned to Reading on loan in February 2000. Initially the Clubs could not agree on an extension to that loan period so Adie returned to Molineux. A week later the loan deal was back on so Adie signed for a third time, before making it four in the summer when he returned permanently to Reading.

☉ 1 – Michael Thorp

Rather less well-known than Williams, Michael only made five starts plus another four appearances as substitute, and yet he has one of the strangest careers in football. The great-grandson of pre-World War Two favourite **Len Darnell**, the central-defender began his Elm Park career as a 10-year-old before being released by Mark McGhee. On their appointment as joint managers, Jimmy Quinn and Mick Gooding made Michael their first signing. He soon made his League debut, against McGhee's Leicester City but was released in May 1997 as the Quinn–Gooding partnership's last managerial decision. Remarkably, two months later he became new Reading manager Terry Bullivant's first signing, but at the end of that season he left the Club for good.

THE TWO-TIMERS XI

These six are by no means the only players to have two spells, or more, with Reading so here is a team made up of players who had two stabs at a career with Reading:

Jimmy Caldwell: was a well-educated Scottish goalkeeper who made 75 Southern League appearances for Reading in three different spells with the Club between 1909 and 1915.

Gary Peters: began and ended a very successful League career with Reading, winning promotion during both stays.

Steve Morrow: had two separate loan spells with Reading from Arsenal, making his full international debut for Northern Ireland while at Elm Park.

Robert Codner: actually had three spells with Reading in 1995, 1997 and 2000 yet only made five first team appearances during that time and failed to complete 90 minutes in any of them.

Martin Hicks: Reading's record appearance holder, but all 603 of them came in his second spell with the Club which lasted from 1978 to 1991. His first time at Reading saw him released by Charlie Hurley a year before Maurice Evans resigned the great centre half.

Ted Hanney: the first real 'two timer', Ted was sold to Manchester City for a record fee in 1913 before returning to captain his local League Club in 1921–22.

Dave Cowling: having won both his games on loan with Reading over Christmas 1987, it was not surprising that Reading signed Dave permanently when Huddersfield released him four months later. Despite playing in a side on their way to relegation, Dave had an impressive record of only two defeats in his nine Reading starts, but he was still released at the end of that season.

Colin Duncan: a star of Reading's youth team, Colin was somehow allowed to join Oxford United. He made 345 League appearances but only 59 of those were for Reading after, in 1983, he returned to the Club that should have signed him in the first place.

Robin Friday: the same could be said of Robin, who played for Reading's youth team during Jack Mansell's days. After trials with virtually every home counties Club, Robin returned to Reading and the rest is history.

Trevor Senior: talking of history, Trevor Senior is one of the most popular players ever at Reading, topping the Club's scorers in seven of his eight seasons, spread over 1983 to 1987 and 1988 to 1992. For such a prolific scorer with Reading, it is strange that he barely netted with either Watford or Middlesbrough in his 'wasted' 18 months away from Elm Park.

Hugh McMahon: left winger Hugh made his League debut with Reading during a trial in 1932 but moved on to Southend United before returning to Elm Park two years later. His second chance was not a great success but he still managed to play on until he was nearly 40 having made 157 League appearances in total with six League Clubs.

Manager – Billy Butler: no manager has really had two spells, but having resigned in March 1939 Billy Butler returned two weeks later after the shock departure of newly appointed Reading boss Joe Cochrane and took charge of one more game before a replacement, Joe Edelston, was in place. As an alternative, John Docherty became a successful manager in the 1980s with his two spells on the coaching staff at Brentford, bringing his total different spells at Griffin Park to five and, as such, John had more different spells with one League Club than anyone else. Another candidate would be Reading's most successful manager Steve Coppell, who, prior to guiding the Royals to the Premier League, had four spells in charge at Crystal Palace.

RUMOURS

This book is full of facts, but the following do not fall into that category!

✲ 1 – Jimmy Dickinson

Without a doubt, **Jimmy Dickinson** is regarded as Portsmouth's greatest player, having made all his 764 League appearances for them as well as winning 48 caps for England. Twice he helped the Fratton Park Club to the League Championship and was awarded the MBE in 1964, but he could have been a Reading player, or could he? There was a persistent, but never confirmed, rumour that Jimmy had a spell at Elm Park during the war before joining Pompey in 1944. We will probably never know the truth as Jimmy died in 1982, while Reading's records were lost when a bomb destroyed the Club's town-centre office in 1943.

✲ 5 – Johnny Cochrane

Appointed as Reading's manager on 31 March 1939, Johnny Cochrane was considered a great capture for the Club, having guided Sunderland to the League title three years earlier and then the FA Cup the following year. At a wage of £1,000 per annum and a three year contract, he was expected to be the man to return Reading to the Second Division, yet just 13 days later he had left Elm Park. After four games, one of which he missed due to 'flu, his contract was terminated by Reading without explanation, and even the Club's minutes give no indication as to the reason. Of course, the town was alive with rumours but, as with all good rumours, nothing was ever confirmed.

✲ 4 – Robin Friday

Anyone who supported Reading in the mid-1970s, or just lived in the town, could not avoid the tales of **Robin Friday**'s wild lifestyle. Almost every week a new, more outrageous story would become public, and most of these tales were true. But one persistent rumour had an innocent explanation. Barely a game would pass where supporters would announce that Robin had been drinking in the Spread Eagle, Elm Park's nearest pub, until minutes before the kick-off. The truth was that Robin had a twin brother, Tony, who rarely missed any of his brother's games for Reading and it was he who was sighted, pint in hand, not his illustrious brother.

⊛ 3 – Uwe Hartenberger

The giant German forward was one of Reading's first overseas signings of modern times when he joined the Club from Bayer Uedingen in September 1993. Manager Mark McGhee had played for S.V. Hamburg and was confident that, with his smattering of German and Uwe's limited English, language would not be a problem. Rumour has it that, initially at least, that was not the case. The day after signing, Uwe was named as a substitute for Reading's game at Swansea. A goal down, McGhee decided to throw his new recruit into the fray with instructions to, so the story goes, 'run at the full back'. Although Uwe understood the words he took them literally, charging his 13st frame at the unfortunate defender time after time. Remarkably, this misunderstanding still produced the desired effect as the shell-shocked defender miscued a back pass to allow Uwe to score Reading's equaliser.

⊛ 2 – Borislav Mihailov

Another overseas signing, another misunderstanding – allegedly. After a series of stunning displays in the 1994 World Cup that took Bulgaria to the semi-finals, it was clear that **'Bobby'** Mihailov would move to a bigger Club than his Bulgarian team, Botev Plodiv. Consequently, there was some surprise when the brilliant keeper chose to join Reading. The rumour is that when Bobby was shown a video of Reading, the game sent to him was the Club's play-off final match against Bolton and he assumed that Wembley Stadium was the Club's home ground! If this is true, one can only imagine his shock when he arrived to meet his new teammates at Elm Park.

⊛ 1 – Club Colours

This qualifies more as an urban myth than a rumour, but it has often been stated that, as the Royal County of Berkshire's only League Club, Reading do not have to change their shirts when there is a colour clash (a similar myth exists in respect of Preston North End, the reasoning being that they were the League's first champions). Of course, this is untrue and the Club regularly change their strip, even if on occasions it has caused problems. Games against Wigan Athletic have been a problem in this respect. When Reading travelled to Springfield Park in 1986 they had brought their away kit, but the match official decided that he would not be able to differentiate between Wigan's all blue and Reading's yellow-and-blue hoops. The problem was resolved by the Royals borrowing one of Wigan's Heinz variety shirts. By a strange coincidence, when Wigan had visited Elm Park on 2 November 1985 they did not bring a change of shirts, and when the referee decided that their strip clashed with Reading's the Latics had to borrow Reading's all-yellow Courage-sponsored shirts.

Reading must have believed the myth because when they visited the Hawthorns on 25 October 1930 they did not think that their blue-and-white striped shirts would not clash with West Brom's identical shirts, and so were forced to go out and buy a set of white shirts from a local shop. They were subsequently to be more frugal in such circumstances, for example when, on 16 December 1961, they travelled to Coventry City without a changed strip again they borrowed the home Club's away strip, but in those days, before Club badges and sponsors names on shirts, the players simply tucked in the white colours and cuffs so no one noticed. Reading were more prepared on New Year's Day 1952 when they travelled to Villa Park for a second FA Cup replay against Southport. Back in the 1950s, a colour clash in a Cup tie required both teams to change from their 'home' colours, but as Reading and Southport's change strips clashed as well, Reading borrowed a set of shirts from Portsmouth to overcome the problem.

Most of these enforced changes were little more than an inconvenience, but on one occasion a colour clash caused Reading problems. When they played Notts County at Meadow Lane on 17 January 1948 the referee decided that Reading's blue-and-white hoops clashed with the home side's black-and-white stripes. Reading were forced to wear dark blue shirts and this set up another colour clash, as Reading were reported to have tried to pass to the referee on several occasions. Not surprisingly, this did little to help their play and the visitors ended up losing 5–1.

However, perhaps that urban myth regarding Reading shirts is true, if another rumour is to be believed. The story goes that before a game at Brighton's Goldstone Ground the referee informed Reading that his linesman could not tell the difference between the two strips, so Reading would have to wear Brighton's away strip. Rumour has it that Reading Chairman, and owner of shirt sponsor Autotrader, John Madejski, suggested that if the linesman could not differentiate between Reading's blue-and-yellow hoops and Brighton's blue-and-white stripes, then it was the official that should be changed not Reading's shirts!

OWN-GOALS
Perhaps this next half dozen should be featured under 'Simply the Worst'!

✪ 6 – Costly Catastrophes
Deservedly in last place are the goals that cost Reading either promotion or relegation. On 25 April 1931 Reading faced a win-at-all-costs game at home to Bury, in which anything other than a win would see the Club relegated. As it was, Reading lost 4–3 with Bury's second goal being scored by Reading left back **John Richardson**, who headed past his namesake, Lance. Richardson, either of them, could hardly shoulder all the blame; Reading had a goal disallowed for offside against a player other than the 'scorer', missed a penalty and conceded the winner even though Bury had been reduced to 10 men when they lost their captain with a broken leg.

Even less to blame for a vital own-goal was Trinidadian international **Tony Rougier**, in the 2001 Division Two play-off final against Walsall at the Millennium Stadium. With the game three minutes into the second half of extra time and Reading leading 2–1, disaster struck. An increasingly desperate Walsall attack was broken up by Reading central-defender **Barry Hunter**. His thumping clearance was intended to reach the opposition's half, but as he hit the ball Rougier, back helping his defence, collided with a Walsall player and fell into the path of Hunter's clearance. The ball cannoned off Rougier's head and, from the edge of the penalty area, the ball looped up and over **Phil Whitehead** in Reading's goal for a fluke Walsall equaliser. Reading could not recover from the shock of that catastrophe and Walsall went on to score a winner, delaying Reading's return to Division One for another 12 months.

These two were not the only times that Reading suffered from important own-goals – see Number One.

❀ 5 – Double Trouble

One of Reading's greatest centre-halves, **Martin Hicks** was a threat at both ends of the pitch as his record of 26 goals for Reading goes to prove. However, he could be dangerous at the wrong end as well. When Reading faced Darlington on 23 November 1985 they had won 17 of their 19 League games, and consequently the result appeared to be a foregone conclusion. So, when the news announced a 2–0 scoreline with a goal from top scorer **Trevor Senior** and the other from Martin Hicks, the impression was that it was another win for the Royals. However, these two Reading stalwarts had both scored past **Gary Westwood** in the Reading goal for a rare home defeat. The goal was particularly annoying for Senior since Darlington were one of the very few Clubs that he failed to score against in his Reading career.

During the 1981–82 season Hicks had the misfortune of scoring own-goals for Huddersfield in both of their games against Reading. Although his 'oggie' was responsible for the Terriers winning 2–1 at Elm Park early in the season, his error hardly mattered in the return fixture since Reading lost the away game 6–1. Martin was not alone that season as Huddersfield received five own-goals during the campaign.

❀ 4 – Two Timers

Of course Reading have been the recipient of plenty of own-goals through the years, and on two occasions they have been helped out twice in one game. On 28 December 1963 they received belated Christmas presents from visitors Colchester United. First John Fowler and then Keith Rutter netted their own-goals that were enough to give Reading a 5–3 home win. During Reading's 2003–04 FA Cup tie at Preston North End, Claude Davies netted in the wrong net, and then followed a second own-goal from Michael Jackson, who no doubt felt *'Bad'* as his goal gave Reading a replay after a 3–3 *'Thriller'*!

Three players have scored twice for Reading in different games, with Notts County's Ian Richardson being the most recent, netting the Madejski Stadium's first own-goal 35 years to the day after Colchester's double, and then netting two years later at Meadow Lane. Strangely, after Reading moved to Madejski Stadium three of the first four own-goals they received were scored by Notts

County players. Other two own-goal scorers for Reading's benefit were Bury's Chris Lucketti in the mid-1990s and Bristol Rovers' Matt Mahoney, who scored in consecutive seasons before the start of World War Two.

Two other own-goals in Reading's favour deserve a mention. Being 2–1 down to reigning champions Chelsea on Boxing Day 2006, defender Ashley Cole's clearance ricocheted off Michael Essien into the home side's goal for an unlikely, but deserved, Reading equaliser. What made this goal even more special was that the combined cost of Essien and Cole was approximately £43.5 million, making it by far the most expensive Reading goal ever scored. Rather less important, but equally dramatic, was the own-goal that Grimsby Town's Alan Pouton scored in the final minute of Reading's 3–0 win at Blundell Park on 5 October 2002. This was a truly spectacular effort as he blasted beyond his own keeper from the halfway line.

⚽ 3 – Both Sides Now
There have been several instances of players scoring for both sides in the same game. Barrie Wagstaff netted Blyth Spartans' consolation goal as well as one of Reading's six in the 1972 FA Cup replay that earned Reading a fourth-round home tie with double winners Arsenal. **Kerry Dixon** repeated this feat 10 years later against Bristol City, completing an unusual hat-trick as he scored twice for Reading and once for the visitors. However, the prize must go to **David Lee**, since not only did the on-loan Chelsea defender score for both Reading and Peterborough at London Road on 1 February 1992, but this double came on his Reading debut.

⚽ 2 – Three Goal Losers
Which Club scored all three goals in an FA Cup tie but were still defeated? The answer is Reading in their fourth-round FA Cup tie against Arsenal on 5 February 1972. The Gunners were reigning League Champions and FA Cup holders, but in a game immortalised in Nick Hornby's *Fever Pitch,* they very nearly came unstuck against Fourth Division Reading. After 55 goalless minutes a George Armstrong cross appeared to pose no threat to the Reading defence, but centre half **Stuart Morgan** misjudged his headed clearance, placing it firmly beyond a stunned **Steve Death**. At least most observers thought Morgan had misjudged his header – after the game the defender claimed that the ball 'went exactly where I'd aimed it'! Reading soon grabbed a deserved equaliser through **Barrie Wagstaff**, but with Arsenal holding on in the final minutes a hopeful 30-yard shot from Pat Rice hit Reading defender **John Harley** on the shoulder, deflecting the ball into the net for a heartbreaking Arsenal winner.

⚽ 1 – 1970–71
To most people Christmas is the season of goodwill, but to Third Division teams playing Reading it also refers to the 1970–71 season. Top scorers in the League the previous season, manager Jack Mansell simply had to make his porous defence and

his free-scoring attack operate at the same standard to move out of the Third Division. Mansell achieved both of these targets but not as Reading fans would have wished. With goals at a premium at the start of the season, Reading travelled to Doncaster Rovers hoping that any of their players would score, and **Barrie Wagstaff** quickly obliged, unfortunately into his own net. Equally unfortunately, this was the start of a sorry trend. Within a month the own-goal total was up to four, and shell-shocked keeper **John Pratt** had been replaced by **Steve Death**. In Death's first game he conceded a spectacular diving header from **Fred Sharpe**, the second own-goal from the veteran defender in four weeks and double the total of goals he scored for Reading in two years.

Reading entered 1972 with a New Year's resolution not to add to their, by now, five own-goals. That resolve lasted six minutes before **Steve Death** decided to join in the fun by allowing a shot to slip through his hands in a Cup tie at Watford. A trip to Reading's bogey Club Bury was always going to be a testing time and, for the second time that season, Reading scored two own-goals in a game as the home side completed a 5–1 home and away double. This inspired Club Chairman Frank Waller to put the entire playing squad up for sale. This had the desired effect as March and April went by without another own-goal, although that was the only thing Reading had to be happy about as those two months saw Reading concede 30 goals and score just six. Obviously, such a run had left the Club in relegation trouble, and when Reading travelled to Aston Villa for their final game of the season they needed a draw to avoid relegation.

With 25 minutes of the season remaining, Reading had the point they needed, drawing 1–1 when **John Pratt** was bundled over his goalline. Surprising even the most ardent Villa fan, referee Leo Callaghan decided to celebrate his last League game by awarding the home side a corner. Equally surprising was Reading's reaction; they actually brought a forward back to help defend the set-piece. As the ball came over that defender, **Terry Bell** jumped highest, but as he was about to head clear he received a mighty push in the back from Villa's Geoff Vowden and the ball ended up in the net. It was the most blatant of fouls, so much so that it was mentioned in *The Guinness Book of Football Blunders*, but the goal was allowed to stand and Reading were down.

In total Reading had conceded nine own-goals during the season, and had they not been scored the Club would have finished a comfortable 15th in the League. Their two games against Villa had seen Reading score seven of the 11 goals, yet lose both games. So, Reading had been relegated by an own-goal, scored by their Player of the Year, in their centenary season!

BETS

❀ 6 – Phil Parkinson
Out injured, **Phil Parkinson** still travelled with the Reading team for their game at division leaders Middlesbrough on 4 February 1995. Although his replacement, the elegant **Paul Holsgrove**, could not have been a more different player from the

all-action Parkinson, the injured player still fancied a bet on the match and put £3 on Holsgrove to score the first goal of the game at attractive odds of 33/1. Parkinson's judgement was every bit as good as Holsgrove's, since the midfielder did indeed score the first goal of the game, a calm finish that won Reading the three points as well as Parky's bet.

✪ 5 – Steve Coppell
During the 2007–08 season, 12 football managers and TV presenters competed in the NSPCC Tipping Challenge. Despite claiming to know little about horse racing, the Reading boss topped the competition with an impressive £18,000 profit, well ahead of the rest of the 'field'. Surprisingly, well-known racing aficionado Portsmouth boss Harry Redknapp only managed approximately half of Steve's total, while racehorse owner Alex Ferguson trailed in with only £3,600 to his credit. In total, the competition raised an impressive £97,000 for the children's charity.

✪ 4 – Phil Bach
A fine player, Phil became Reading's first professional captain when he joined the Club shortly after they gave up their amateur status in 1895. After an illustrious playing career, Phil became one of the game's great administrators, and in 1936 he played a major role in resolving football's uneasy relationship with the football pools companies. Until then the pools companies had used the fixture lists for their coupons without paying a fee. It was Phil's suggestion that the Football League copyrighted their fixture list so they could receive a fee. At first the pools companies refused, so the League abandoned the fixture list, only announcing the revised fixtures the day before they were due to be played. This was unsatisfactory for all concerned, but the pools firms soon agreed to pay for the use of the League's fixtures and normality, and a new revenue source for the Clubs, was introduced.

✪ 3 – Harry Johnston
When Reading were drawn to play against Norwich City in the first round of the 1959–60 FA Cup, few gave Reading a chance of making it to the next round. Not only were Norwich leading the Third Division South, they also had an impressive Cup pedigree that had seen them reach the semi-finals the previous season. One local reporter was so sure that Reading's Cup season was over that he made an unusual bet with manager Harry Johnston. After a draw at Carrow Road, Reading won a memorable replay on 18 November 1959. Honouring his bet, the reporter arrived at Elm Park the following day with Harry's winnings – an appropriate yellow canary in a cage.

✪ 2 – Joe Edelston
On similar lines, Reading boss Joe Edelston and Arsenal's George Allison had known each other for years, so when their two Clubs met at Elm Park on 30 January 1943 they decided to add a bit of spice to the meeting. A bet was struck

with the loser 'paying' the winner with a new hat and, a great wartime rarity, three newly laid eggs. In a stunning opening first half display, the Gunners stormed to a 5–0 half time lead, three of the goals being scored by future Reading player **Les Henley**. Possibly inspired by the bet, Joe's half time talk nearly had the desired effect as his side fought back to almost grab an unlikely draw, eventually just failing by losing 5–4. Joe honoured his bet thanks to an anonymous donor, who supplied Joe with the three eggs.

✪ 1 - Kevin Doyle

Chris Kirkland's father made the headlines when he collected a 100/1 bet made when Chris was 11 that his son would play for England. **Kevin Doyle's** father made a similar bet, but although he received the same odds he did not have to wait nearly as long to collect. Shortly after Kevin moved to Cork City, his confident father obtained odds of 100/1 that the young striker would play a competitive game for the Republic of Ireland. Mr Doyle Snr probably did not think he would be claiming his winnings quite so quickly, as Kevin made his international debut within eight months of joining Reading, playing in the Euro 2008 qualifier in Germany on 2 September 2006, thus earning his proud father €10,000.

PENALTIES

✪ 6 – Graeme Murty

One of the best and most popular players in Reading's history, the right back's popularity was not due to his goalscoring ability. With just one goal to his credit in the eight years up to the end of 2005–06 season, everyone at the Club wanted their captain to score a second goal to cap the Championship season. Towards the end of that season, every time he crossed the halfway line the crowd roared for him to shoot, and it became known that the next penalty was going to be taken by captain Murty. Unfortunately for Graeme, the next penalty came in the one game for which he was rested, so the opportunity went to another Reading player. Then, with just six minutes remaining of the final game of the season, a Queen's Park Rangers player handled in the penalty area and Murty's big moment had arrived. After the usual delaying tactics, Murty appeared to be the calmest person in Madejski Stadium as he blasted home the perfect penalty to put Reading 2–1 ahead and so break the League's points record. It was the most popular goal of a great season, except with Club mascot Kingsley Royal, who had been the chief tormenter of the captain's lack of goals and paid the penalty (!) by being mobbed by Murty and the rest of the Reading team.

✪ 5 – Marcus Hahnemann

Usually a penalty is just that, a penalty against the offending side, but on the odd occasion it turns out to be a let-off. Take the incident that took place at Madejski Stadium on 23 November 2002. A Watford cross struck Reading's **James Harper** on the arm and was deflected into the Reading goal. Fortunately for Reading, the referee had blown immediately for the handball and so the visitors' 'goal' was replaced with a penalty. To rub salt into Watford's wounds, **Marcus Hahnemann** pulled off a wonderful save to prevent Watford from taking the lead, and Reading later won the game with a wickedly deflected shot from **Kevin Watson**.

At least this cancelled out the similar injustice that befell Reading 53 years earlier at Elm Park. The Club's highest-ever League crowd of 29,092 was present to see England centre forward Tommy Lawton and his table-topping Notts County side. With the visitors having scored the only goal, Reading appeared to have equalised when Gordon Brice headed the ball into the County net, only for County defender Rigby to claw it out of the back of the goal. Despite Reading's protests, the referee only awarded a penalty, which the usually reliable **Ron Moyse** put wide of the post.

✪ 4 – Paul Bodin

Penalty misses can be very costly, as **Paul Bodin** found to his cost on 17 November 1993. With Wales needing to beat Romania in their final World Cup qualifying match to make it to the US for the finals, they were awarded a crucial penalty. Paul was brave enough to take the kick but his fiercely struck shot hit the bar and cannoned to safety, and Wales missed out to their opponents. Paul subsequently joined Reading in 1996 but, not surprisingly, never offered to take a spot kick for the Royals.

Reading had their own penalty horror on 25 April 1931. They needed to beat Bury at Elm Park to have a chance of avoiding relegation from the Second Division. Early in the second half, with Reading disastrously trailing 2–1, **Frank Eaton** was fouled and a spot kick was awarded. Eaton took the kick himself but the Bury keeper pulled off a brilliant save, and Reading eventually lost 4–3 and were relegated. Not that all of the blame should fall on Eaton, as **Jock Richardson** scored an own-goal and 'the players, lacking in proper Club spirit, gave a typically disheartening display.'

✪ 3 – Trevor Morley

It is a mark of a great penalty taker that he still scores when he misses! **Trevor Morley** had scored six penalties out of six, and when Reading were awarded a spot kick early in their game against Huddersfield Town on 28 January 1997 he was looking to add to his total. He had reckoned without the skills of former Reading goalkeeper **Steve Francis**, who pulled off a brilliant block. As the ball bounced up, Morley reacted the swiftest, heading the ball beyond Francis to open the scoring and become only the sixth player to head in a League penalty.

✪ 2 – Syd Crawford

Syd developed a unique style for saving penalties by standing at one side of the goal to encourage the taker to shoot for the wider gap so the keeper always knew which way to dive. It clearly worked as Syd is said to have saved over 50 penalties during his long career, but none was more dramatic than the save he made on 8 January 1921. At home to First Division Chelsea in the FA Cup, struggling Reading pulled out a determined display to keep the game goalless for 89 minutes, but all their efforts seemed to be to no avail when the visitors were awarded a last-minute penalty. Meehan took the kick but Syd's system worked and he pulled off a sensational save. The tension was so great that several fans fainted as Syd made his save, including Cannon Gilmore, Club director and vicar of the town centre church St Giles, and Syd's wife. The director recovered in time to join the rest of his board, each of whom are said to have kissed the hero keeper in thanks for winning a money-spinning replay. The board had already shown their appreciation to the turnstile operators on duty that day, rewarding them all with a drink and a pork pie!

✪ 1 – Simod Shoot-out

There is no doubt about the best penalty in Reading's history and it was not, strictly speaking, a penalty since no offence was committed. After 120 tense minutes of football on the evening of 2 March 1988, Reading and Coventry City were still all-square at 1–1 in the semi-final of the Simod Cup, with a place in the final at Wembley still at stake. That place would belong to the team winning Elm Park's first penalty shoot-out. Rumour has it that several of Ian Branfoot's original five-man shoot-out line up did not fancy it when it came to the crunch and, certainly, some of the five who eventually stepped up would not have been many fans' choice. One unlikely choice was **Keith Curle**, who rarely ventured out of his own half, and those fears were realised when his kick was saved. Reading were 2–0 down but regular spot kickers **Stuart Beavon** and **Dean Horrix**, with his last goal for the Club, plus a save from **Steve Francis**, made it 2–2. **Jerry Williams** made it 3–3 with his only penalty as a professional. Then Francis made another great save to leave **Michael Gilkes** with the chance to win the tie. A huge roar as Gilkes walked to the spot died to a complete hush as he prepared to take the kick. With a choice of placement, power or sending the keeper the wrong way, Michael went for all three, blasting the ball to Ogrizovic's right, sending the keeper the wrong way and Reading to Wembley.

REFEREEING DECISIONS

✪ 6 – Not me, guv!

As far as UEFA are concerned, mistaken identity should be the only reason for reviewing a referee's decision, but on at least two occasions Reading preferred to let the original error stand. You can hardly blame the ref for getting it wrong when Reading faced Wealdstone in the FA Cup on 16 November 1985. A reckless tackle by Wealdstone's substitute, a certain Vinnie Jones, on Reading captain **Martin Hicks** sparked a mass brawl that resulted in two of the visiting players being dismissed, along with Reading's **Glen Burvill**. The Reading midfielder had not been the guilty party, but as he was only a fringe player the Club preferred Glen to take the suspension rather than the first team offender. Similarly, when centre back **Gareth Davies** gently tousled the hair of a Wolves forward, he was shocked to see the player go down as if he had been caught by a heavyweight champion.

The visiting player's reaction was hardly in the Christmas 1997 spirit, but not only did it fool the referee, the official somehow managed to mistake blond **Paul Bodin** with the ginger Davies and sent the full back off in error. A shortage of central-defenders meant that Bodin had to take the blame, a decision that disappointed the player because he had never been dismissed before in his career.

⊛ **5 – Time, gentleman, please**
Referees have a tough job and about the only easy task they have is to make sure each half lasts 45 minutes – or is it? When Reading Schools played Andover at Elm Park on 4 November 1974, the referee played eight minutes extra in the first half after his watch broke. The same thing happened when Reading visited Nottingham Forest on 22 October 1949 as the second half went on and on, until a linesman ran on to tell the official that he had played 50 minutes. There were no complaints from the BBC, who were broadcasting the second half live on the radio and so received good value for their fee.

On the other hand Mr Coultas, the referee of Reading's game against Colchester United on 28 November 1953, tried to blow for half time after only 38 minutes of play. The howls of protest from the fans and another intervention from a linesman persuaded the official to restart the game to complete the outstanding seven minutes. Reading were less fortunate on 18 September 1946 at Selhurst Park. Having beaten Crystal Palace 10–2 two weeks earlier, Reading found themselves 2–1 down, but their attempts to force a late equaliser were cut short when the referee blew for time after 85 minutes' play. The Club's protest to the official were to no avail and a subsequent request to the Football League for the match to be replayed was similarly declined.

The most significant timekeeping dispute took place at the City of Manchester Stadium on 24 November 2007 when Manchester City's Steven Ireland scored a dramatic last kick winner, four minutes into two minutes of added time. Disappointing as it was at the time, that was nothing compared with the fact that the season ended with Reading being relegated by the one point that Ireland's late, late goal had denied Reading.

⊛ **4 – Three Heads Better Than One**
Reading's visit to Ninian Park for their game against Cardiff City on 16 March 2004 proved an eventful evening for the match officials. The original referee, Mark Warren, hobbled off on 37 minutes and then his replacement, Steve Habgood, went off in the second half, leaving a third referee to see out the game with a local Club official running the line. This led to 10 minutes of added-on time, during which Reading's **Dean Morgan** scored the final goal in a 3–2 Reading victory. Incidentally, all three Reading goals had been headers, netted by players scoring their first goal for the Club.

When Reading's A team faced Burnham in a Middlesex Border League fixture at Elm Park on 4 October 1975, one of the match officials failed to arrive. With no obvious replacement available in the sparse crowd, the two officials present decided to jointly referee the match. The system worked without any problems and although it has regularly been suggested that two refs are better than one, the experiment has never been put into practice.

☉ 3 – Worst Decision?

Back at Cardiff, almost 70 years earlier on 16 March 1935, Reading were a goal down with three minutes left to play. A long clearance from the Reading defence found forward **Tommy Tait** 'at least 20 yards offside', according to the reporter from the *South Wales Football Echo*. Tait appeared to agree since he brought the ball under control with his hand before playfully knocking it into the Cardiff net. To everyone's surprise the referee allowed the goal to stand for an unlikely Reading equaliser, a decision that caused the same local reporter to state 'Never in the whole of my experience have I seen a worse decision.'

☉ 2 – All Change

Another late decision that had a dramatic effect was the one made by referee George Cain during Reading's League Cup quarter-final match against Middlesbrough on 6 January 1998. With the game still goalless as it entered its final minute, Reading winger **James Lambert** began a mazy run. He was tripped by a Boro defender but continued until an even more obvious foul stopped him, the referee immediately blowing for an offence. Reading lined up to take the free kick and the visitors packed their penalty area, when suddenly the referee pointed in the opposite direction and allowed Boro to take a free kick. With most of Reading's defence in the opposite penalty area for the expected free kick, the ball made its way to an unmarked Craig Hignett who finished Reading's hopes with a last-gasp goal. After the game Mr Cain claimed he had given the free kick for dissent by **Trevor Morley**, but there was no doubt in the minds of Reading's players and fans that they had been robbed by an indecisive referee.

☉ 1 – The Goals That Never Were

On Boxing Day 1922 Reading were drawing 1–1 with Southend United when they were awarded a last minute penalty. **Jerry Poulton** took the kick, and although the visitors' goalkeeper blocked his spot kick Jerry reacted the quickest to fire home the rebound, apparently sealing a Reading victory. Consequently, most Reading fans had a shock when they read the following day's newspapers and saw that Reading had only drawn the game. What no one had realised was that the referee, Mr T. Harding, had blown for full time in the spilt second between the keeper blocking the original kick and the rebound hitting the net. Reading promptly wrote to the FA, complaining about the ref's 'egragarious blunders and sheer incompetence', and the Association clearly agreed, removing the hapless official from the League list.

A team trains for several weeks for the opening of a new season, then travels from Lancashire to Reading for the opening game of the season full of hope. At

3.10pm that hope is shattered. That is what happened to Rochdale on 16 August 1975. After an uneventful start to the first game of the season, Reading were awarded a free kick 30 yards from the visitors' goal. Defender **Tommy Youlden** took the kick, striking it hard and low but just wide of the Rochdale goal. Fans applauded politely, someone from the Reading bench shouted 'Nice try, Tommy', and the two teams lined up for the resulting goal kick, but it never came. Referee Mr Harvey, in charge of his first League game, thought that the ball had gone into the net and, remarkably, the only other person to agree with him was his linesman, so the goal was awarded. That was about the last decision the misguided linesman made, as shortly after he fell awkwardly and injured his ankle. He was replaced by local official Alan Porton, and although Alan was an ardent Reading fan he could hardly have been more biased towards Reading than the previous official. That goal proved to be the first of a season that ended with Reading winning promotion, thanks to what is widely known in Reading (and, presumably, Rochdale) 'the goal that never was.'

ABANDONED GAMES

✪ 6 – Torquay United 1 November 1972 and Bristol Rovers Boxing Day 1962

Sometimes the abandonment of a game does not affect the eventual outcome. Take Reading's game against Torquay United on a misty Wednesday on 1 November 1972. With Reading leading 3–0, the mist turned into fog, forcing the referee to call the game off with 25 minutes remaining. When the game was replayed at the end of February it made it to the full 90 minutes this time, but the score remained the same. The scorers were different since neither **Percy Freeman**, with two goals, or **Barrie Wagstaff** played in the original match. The abandonment proved particularly galling for the hardly prolific **Tommy Youlden**, who had scored a rare goal in the original game.

Boxing Day 1962 saw the start of what became known as 'The Big Freeze' that crippled the country for weeks. The snow was falling at Elm Park throughout the game against Bristol Rovers, and it turned into a blizzard at the start of the second half, leaving World Cup referee Ken Aston with no choice but to abandon the game on the hour. Reading were leading 1–0 at the time, but that was the last time the team played for two months as football ground to a halt. It was also the last time Harry Johnston was in charge for Reading, so by the time the game was finally re-arranged Roy Bentley had taken over. This led to the season being extended but Reading entered May facing seven vital games in 18 days, vital because the Club entered that last month bottom of the Third Division. A series of gritty displays, including a repeat of the 1–0 win over Rovers, eventually saw Reading escape the drop, but only on goal difference, at the expense of Bradford Park Avenue.

✪ 5 – Elm Park's Opening 5 September 1896

In August 1997 Derby County's first League game at their brand new £28 million Pride Park was abandoned when the floodlights failed, but they were not the first

Club to suffer such an opening-day embarrassment. A hundred and one years earlier, the slightly less expensive Elm Park (£1,300 plus £100 a year rent) was opened with a prestigious friendly against an all-star team. In the opening ceremony the ground was described as 'undoubtedly admirably adapted for the purpose', but unfortunately that did not prove to be the case. As the game progressed, a thunderstorm developed, and despite the fact that the new ground had been built on what was a gravel pit, the drainage could not cope with the deluge and was abandoned on the hour with Reading leading 7–0.

✪ 4 – Bury 24 October 1995

Bury have inflicted considerable heartache on Reading over the years and are still regarded as the Club's bogey team, but things were levelled out when the two Clubs were drawn together in the third round of the 1995–96 League Cup. As with that opening game at Elm Park, this tie was played in torrential rain but, despite being two divisions lower than Reading, it was the visitors who adapted the better to the worsening conditions. As puddles began to appear all over the pitch the Third Division side splashed into a 2–0 lead before the referee decided to call the players off. Groundsman Gordon Neate and his colleagues attempted to disperse the standing water without success, leaving the referee with no alternative but to call the game off after just 28 minutes, making it Elm Park's shortest game. When the game was replayed some of the Bury players began their pre-match warm up with forks, indicating that Reading might not have done all they could to continue a game they were losing! That was the last reason the visitors had to smile as they were knocked out of the competition by an own-goal and a last-minute winner by substitute **Jimmy Quinn**.

✪ 3 – Travel Trouble

It was not always the weather that caused Reading matches to be abandoned, as during the war years erratic transport often resulted in delayed kick-offs and premature ends. Even though matches were arranged on a regional basis, cancelled trains still meant that arrival on time could not be guaranteed. Reading's late arrivals in 1943–44 to games at Charlton and Brentford, virtually a local derby, led to only 27 and 22 minutes being played. A year later, the short trip from Aldershot proved too much and the visitors' late arrival, and the darkening skies, allowed just 40 minutes' play. Even so, the fans still had four goals to cheer as the game ended with Reading leading 3–1. But it was not just the war that caused transport problems. Way back in Reading's first full season they travelled to Maidenhead on 5 March 1873 but the game, 'owing to the GWR timetable, only lasted a little over 70 minutes'.

✪ 2 – Millwall 14 January 1933

Having taken four games to get past Coventry City in the second round, Reading were drawn away to Millwall in the third round of the 1932–33 FA Cup. The visitors were two goals down when a thick fog descended over the Den, forcing the referee to abandon the game with just 17 minutes left to play. As the Reading players discussed their good fortune in the dressing room, it was noticed that keeper **Dick Mellors** was missing. A search was launched and the keeper was eventually found, still guarding his goal, peering into the fog for the next Millwall attack, blithely unaware that the game had been called off several minutes earlier. This story is also told about 'Reading reject' Sam Bartram with Charlton. The restaged Millwall–Reading game ended in a 1–1 draw, but 'justice' was done when the Lions won the replay at Elm Park.

Another FA Cup tie that failed to finish due to fog was Reading's visit to Layer Road to play the then Southern League Club Colchester United. Played at the end of November 1949, the tie attracted a huge 19,072 fans, an attendance that will remain a ground record as United have moved to their new ground for the 2008–09 season. Unfortunately, those fans saw just 35 minutes play before the lack of visibility resulted in the referee being forced to call a halt. The score was 1–1 at the time, but Reading swept through in the rearranged game, winning 4–2.

The shortest game in Reading's history was also restricted due to fog, despite the efforts of the referee. When Reading faced Sheppey United on 2 January 1897, the Southern League game should never really have started due to the terrible visibility, but the match official decided to try. The conditions worsened almost immediately and by 15 minutes of play the ref was forced to call a halt, especially as the Club officials of both sides rejected his suggestion that the game might be continued if both goalkeepers held lighted candles!

☉ 1 – Dry Finish – Good Friday 1904

Over the years Elm Park was used to stage local Cup finals, and at the turn of the previous century a whole day was set aside for such games. To break up the competitive finals, charity matches were also included but few games can have come to such an end as the match that took place at the Club's old ground on Easter Monday 1904. As a charity game featuring two teams in fancy dress progressed, a player went down injured and, in the days before sports scientists, the trainer revived the victim with a bottle of beer. This proved to be a mistake! As soon as the other players realised the treatment that was on offer, both teams started going down at increasingly frequent intervals. Soon the trainer's supply of beer ran out and the teams refused to carry on without their 'medicine', causing the game to be abandoned – surely the only match ever to be called off due to a lack of alcohol.

LOAN STARS

☉ 6 – Temporary Managers

Three Reading loan players have gone on to manage the Club, or, to be precise, one of those actually managed the Club and later became a loan player for Reading. **Adie Williams** was part of the five-man committee that managed Reading against Wolverhampton Wanderers on 18 December 1994, later returning to

Reading on loan from, of all Clubs, Wolverhampton, some five years later. With a win in his one game in charge and regarded as one of Reading's great players, Adi's playing and managerial careers were more impressive than either those of **Ian Porterfield** or **Terry Bullivant**. Ian's five-game loan spell from Sunderland in November 1976 failed to produce a Reading win, but at least he made it to the first team; Terry's month at Elm Park in 1984 amounted to just one game for the reserves. Neither were a success when they returned to manage the Club, Porterfield being sacked after 16 months in April 1991, while Bullivant lasted just eight months in 1997–98, being, statistically, Reading's least successful manager.

✪ 5 – Golden Goalies

Ideally the loan system should be of benefit to both the lending Club and the receiving side as well as the player. This is not always the case, but the loan spells of keepers **Jim Leighton** and **Tommy Wright** are the perfect example of how the system should work. Both players were out of favour with their Clubs, Manchester United and Nottingham Forest, when they were loaned to Reading. At Elm Park the two keepers hit sensational form, Leighton keeping six clean sheets in 11 games in 1991–92, while Wright is still regarded as one of Reading's best-ever loan signings during his 17-game spell in 1996. Both Jim and Tommy regained their international places with Scotland and Northern Ireland and their displays for Reading subsequently earned them permanent transfers, to Dundee and Manchester City respectively. For Leighton, his loan spell with Reading led to another honour as he was subsequently made a Member of the British Empire by the Queen for his services to Scottish football.

✪ 4 – Not Alone

Sometimes more than one player moves on loan, but in a virtually unique deal four Reading players were loaned to Division One side Bournemouth towards the end of 2007. The Royals' young stars, **Alex Pearce, James Henry, Scott Golbourne** and **Jem Karacan**, were all at the Fitness First Stadium at the same time, and frequently all played in the same team. This 'bulk borrow' proved a success as Henry, Golbourne and Karacan all netted for the Cherries during their loan spell.

Not so fortunate was goalkeeper Graham Stack during his loan spell with Leeds United. When he played in United's defeat at Burnley on 28 November 2006, he was one of six loan players in their squad that day. League rules only allow a maximum of five loan players for any one game and, as a result, Leeds were fined £2,000 for this breach.

Reading nearly breached that rule themselves, that is if it was in existence at Christmas in 1932. With a 'flu epidemic sweeping through the Club, Reading were so short of fit players that Welsh League Club Ebbw Vale offered to loan Reading their entire first team. Fortunately, the Club were able to complete their fixtures without any outside assistance.

✪ 3 – Record Breakers

Since the current system was introduced in 1969, Reading's first loan player remains the most successful. **Steve Death** made 28 loan appearances in 1969–70, winning the Club's Player of the Year trophy even though he was a West Ham player, before subsequently signing for a record fee. He went on to become one of the Club's greatest goalkeepers, making 537 first team appearances and starting a Club trend for signing loan keepers that has continued through to **Marcus Hahnemann**. Of the players who did not go on to sign permanently for Reading, Kenny Brown's two spells on loan from West Ham United in 1995 and 1996 saw him total 20 first team appearances, the highest for a Reading loan player. Remarkably, the highest Reading loan scorer was not a forward but a central-defender, **David Lee**. During an impressive month at Elm Park during February 1992 the Chelsea youngster netted five times in as many games. Or six, if you count his own-goal on his Reading debut!

✪ 2 – Eventful Time

Few players have had a more eventful loan spell than **Bryan Drysdale**. Joining Reading on loan from Bristol City in February 1977, his first game saw Reading go 3–0 down by half time in their home game against Bury, a performance that persuaded manager Charlie Hurley to resign at the interval. Two days later, new boss Maurice Evans named Bryan as team captain, a position he held in his remaining 15 Reading games.

A similar fate befell **Brian Statham** when he joined Reading on loan in March 1991. His eight-game spell saw Reading only win once, and resulted in Ian Porterfield losing his job as Reading manager. Eddie Niedzwiecki took over as caretaker boss but Brian was sent off at Brentford, the resulting suspension preventing him from playing under John Haseldon and Mark McGhee as Reading ended that season with four managers in a three-week period.

✪ 1 – Not For Sale

Clubs have borrowed players long before the current system, and back in 1921 Reading took **Sam Jennings** on loan from Middlesbrough. A regular scorer while at Elm Park, Sam was top scorer in his three seasons with the Club, scoring 46 goals in 113 first team games. The extraordinary length of his loan spell confused West Ham United, who approached Reading with a view to purchasing the free-scorer. A change in management at Reading led to the two Clubs agreeing a fee, and it was only when the Hammers tried to register Sam with the League that the error was discovered. Terms were eventually agreed with his rightful 'owners', Middlesbrough, but not before West Ham were fined for making an illegal approach for the player.

TRANSFERS

✪ 6 – All At Sea

As manager of Reading throughout World War Two, Joe Edelston had to use all his ingenuity to make signings in order to ensure that Reading could field a full team every week. But none of his signings compare with his own transfer from Hull City to Manchester City in June 1920. At the time Joe was a member of the FA touring party that was on its way to South Africa, and so the transfer was completed on the ship in the middle of the Atlantic Ocean. As such he became the only player to be transferred on the high seas.

✪ 5 – First Rung Of Success

Billy Beats was involved in Reading's history in several ways. On 27 December 1892 he scored for Burslem Port Vale in a friendly against Reading and so became the first professional footballer to score in the town. Two England caps and an FA Cup Final appearance later he had two spells at Elm Park as Club trainer and player, making 26 Southern League appearances over three seasons. While with Burslem, Billy also worked as a roofer and he was engaged in this role when Wolves tried to sign him. Wanderers were so keen to sign the powerful centre forward that when their secretary found him up a chapel roof he removed the ladder, only returning it when Billy agreed to sign for Wolves.

✪ 4 – B****y Good Signing

Early in the 1905–06 season Reading director J.R. Blandford and secretary-manager Harry Matthews travelled to Dykehead in Scotland to watch Bathgate forward **Billy McCafferty**. They were impressed with the player, but during the game some local fans accused the Reading officials of bad language and they were almost thrown out of the ground. They needed a guard for the rest of the game, but they were able to stay long enough to sign their man for £30. It proved a good signing. After 18 goals in just over a year, Billy was sold to Birmingham for £350, although this move was not a success as he only played four first team games and City complained to Reading about his 'soundness'.

✪ 3 – Just In Time

Like many Clubs, Reading's history is littered with the sale of popular players to ease financial problems, but on one occasion Reading were able to help another hard-up Club. **Terry Bell** had come to Reading's attention when he had scored two spectacular goals in Hartlepool's 2–0 victory over them in 1969. A year later he was seen as the player needed to assist Reading in their efforts to achieve promotion so the Club made Hartlepool an offer for their star forward. It proved to be an offer that United could not refuse, since it came on the day that their board was meeting to discuss entering receivership. A deal was quickly agreed which broke Hartlepool's transfer record and enabled them to keep playing.

✪ 2 – For The Record

Over the last 50 years the burden of being Reading's record signing has proved too great for many of the players involved. During that period the Club has increased its record fee 18 times, of which half have subsequently left the Club for nothing, while only three players, **Terry Hurlock** to Millwall in 1987, **Keith Curle** a year later, then **Greg Halford** after just five months with Reading in 2007, have been sold at a profit. Discounting **Leroy Lita**, who is still at Reading, only legendary keeper **Steve Death** and **Darren Caskey** can be classed as successes from all of those record signings. Perhaps the overall standard of Reading's record signings is typified by **Emerse Faé**. Signed for a Club record of £2.5 million in the summer of 2007, the Ivory Coast international's eight Premier League appearances all ended in defeat for Reading. He spent January playing in the African Cup of Nations where he caught malaria, thus restricting his appearances still further, and then was suspended by the Club for refusing to play in a reserve fixture. Not surprisingly, Faé was subsequently loaned to French Club Nice with a view to a permanent transfer.

✪ 1 – Late Payment

One of those record signings, **Craig Maskell**, nearly bankrupted Reading because they were fined for delays in paying the instalments to Huddersfield Town, increasing his price from £250,000 to over £300,000. But the delay in settling that fee was nothing compared with that involving the Club's record goalscorer **Ron Blackman**. It was not unusual for a League Club to play a non-League Club in a friendly in lieu of a transfer fee – the fee Reading 'paid' Colwyn Bay for **Bill Baggett** is recorded as £70.12.11d, this being the proceeds from a friendly between the two Clubs. A similar arrangement was made when young Blackman joined Reading from Gosport Borough in February 1947. For whatever reason the promised friendly never took place, and it was not until 28 July 1979, 32 years after his transfer, that Reading eventually played the agreed match at Privett Park

DEFEATS

Finally, most football books feature a Club's greatest victories, but not this publication!

✪ 6 – Arsenal L 0–1 16 February 1935

In the mid-1930s Arsenal could claim to be the greatest Club team in the world, and were to complete a hat-trick of First Division titles a couple of months after they visited Elm Park for a fifth-round FA Cup tie. The Gunners fielded their full-strength team, which meant that Reading faced a side containing 10 internationals, but Reading matched them man-for-man. Only bad luck and a flash of brilliance robbed Reading of a well-deserved replay at Highbury. With just 17 minutes left to play a Reading defender allowed the ball to roll out for a goal kick, only for the referee to mistakenly award the visitors a corner. This kick led to the ball falling to Cliff Bastin, who hit an unstoppable volley from the edge of the penalty area to give Arsenal a win that even they admitted they did not deserve. Reading had some consolation in the record receipts of £3,019 that the game produced. This was due in part to the fact that the game attracted the last 30,000 plus attendance in Reading, that the Club had increased prices for the tie and also because turnstile operators were instructed not to give change to anyone who did not have the correct admission money!

✪ 5 – Manchester United L 2–3 1 August 1970

Manchester United were another team that featured 10 internationals and included six from the side that had won the European Cup two years earlier. It also contained no fewer than three European Footballers of the Year in Bobby Charlton, George Best and Dennis Law. The game was part of the first Watney Cup pre-season tournament for the divisions' highest goalscorers. Not surprisingly, both sides attacked from the outset and produced an exhilarating game. Reading, again, matched their more illustrious opponents to such an extent that on the following day's *The Big Match*, Jimmy Hill described their play as 'a little piece of Brazilian style football.' United scored through Paul Edwards and two from Bobby Charlton, while strikes from **Dick Habbin** and a wonderfully crafted goal, netted by **Gordon Cumming,** kept Reading in touch up to the last minute, when a world-class save by Alec Stepney prevented **Les Chappell** from equalising. Had the game ended level it would have been decided by the country's first penalty shoot-out. As it was, United took part in that four days later in the semi-final, when George Best had the honour of netting the first such goal.

✪ 4 – Manchester United L 2–3 27 February 2007

Reading's first season in the Premier League saw the Club field a 'Cup' team in the knock-out competitions and although this brought some criticism on manager Steve Coppell from the national press these, supposedly, weakened sides still did the Club proud. Having drawn at Old Trafford, Reading went into the sixth-round draw for only the second time in their history, but within six minutes of the televised replay any chance of further progress appeared to have vanished. In that record-breaking start the visitors had taken a three-goal lead, Heinze, Saha and Solskjaer doing the damage. Gradually, Reading clawed their way back into the game and **Dave Kitson** pulled a goal back before half time. With six minutes to go, **Leroy Lita** made it 2–3 and United were rocking. With almost the last kick of the game, **Brynjar Gunnersson** sent a thunderous drive crashing against Van Der Sar's crossbar, but the ball rebounded to safety and Reading were out. Inches from extra time, United boss Sir Alex Ferguson admitted that he feared for his side's Cup future if the game had gone on for a further 30 minutes.

✪ 3 – Blackpool L 0–7 10 November 1928

Things could hardly get worse for Reading when they travelled to Blackpool in November 1928. With just six points from their first 13 Second Division games they were rooted to the bottom of the division. Ninety minutes later Reading had suffered their second 7–0 defeat of the season with Harry Hampson scoring a Club-record five of Blackpool's goals. Described by the Club as 'another staggering blow to the Club's prestige', the directors reacted by voting on manager Andrew Wylie's future, a vote he survived by five to three. Remarkably, that defeat saw an amazing turnaround of Reading's fortunes, leading to a 14-match unbeaten run which included an FA Cup win over League Champions Sheffield Wednesday that many regard as the Club's greatest victory. Of course, it might not have been that 7–0 defeat which inspired the run, as on their return from Blackpool the players were offered a free supply of Horlicks by the manufacturers.

✪ 2 – Chelsea L 2–3 7 October 1987

Drawn against First Division Chelsea in the two-leg League Cup second-round tie, Reading stormed into a 3–1 lead after the first leg at Elm Park. Even so, with Reading struggling in the Second Division, the Club were still not overconfident that they would progress in the competition, and that caution appeared to be well founded. It took Chelsea, or more precisely Gordon Durie, just 32 minutes to score the three goals needed to give them an aggregate lead. But Reading had their own 'Flash' Gordon, and **Colin Gordon** scored with a cheeky back-heel to level the aggregate score. A second goal from Colin reinstated Reading's overall lead and the team hung on quite comfortably for their 3–2 defeat, leaving the Stamford Bridge crowd to boo their 3–2 winners as the Reading players celebrated their winning defeat.

✪ 1 – Southampton L 0–7 24 October 1891

Drawn away to Southampton St Marys in the second qualifying round of the FA Cup, Reading faced a daunting task against one of the top teams in the South. So it proved as 'it was manifest to all observers that the Saints were superior to their opponents and outplayed them on every point'. Southampton ended up comfortable 7–0 winners, and so were happy to agree to Reading secretary Horace Walker's request for a £3 advance on Reading's share of the gate receipts. What the Southampton officials did not realise was that Mr Walker wanted the money to fund an appeal on the grounds that two of the winning Saints line up had not been properly registered for the game. Reading offered to replay the game, but because one of the ineligible players had scored a hat-trick in the game the FA awarded the tie to Reading, leaving the Southampton secretary to send a telegram back to his Club that simply read 'Disqualified. Pity old Saints.' Reading's success in their appeal was short-lived as they lost 8–2 at Clifton in the next round.

As a footnote, such appeals were a regular feature of the early days of the FA Cup, with one contemporary commentator stating 'protests in Cup-ties were as plentiful as blackberries in autumn'. And so they were in games between Reading and Southampton. Drawn together again two years later, Reading's winning goal in their 2–1 victory was created by **Jimmy Stewart**. A soldier at Aldershot, Stewart was serving a sentence in the glasshouse at the time of the game and Horace Walker again pulled a fast one, bribing the sergeant in charge of the cells to release

Stewart for the vital game with a bottle of whiskey. Southampton knew of this subterfuge and protested to the FA that he was not eligible to play, a protest that was turned down. That was unfortunate for Southampton but also for Reading since, as with their previous appeal, they exited the Cup in the next round with a heavy defeat, their progress in the competition being ended with the Club's record defeat, 18–0 at Preston. The prize for the cheekiest protest also belongs to Reading. During Elm Park's first season the two Clubs met again in the Cup and, on their arrival in Reading, the Southampton party were so appalled with the state of the pitch that they informed Reading they would appeal against it if they lost the tie. As it was, they secured a comfortable 4–1 victory but Reading, perversely, argued that if Southampton thought the pitch was unplayable, they could also appeal against it. 'Surprisingly', the FA did not agree with Reading's point of view!

TWELVE – IT'S A FACT

A feature of Reading's matchday programmes over recent years has been the statistics provide by Nigel 'Strap' Meek from his self-constructed *Ultimate Reading FC Database*. Nigel has turned on the database, once described as having more filters than Starbucks, to provide more strange but true facts.

SIMPLY THE BEST?

During the summer of 2005 a poll was held via the Reading FC official website to find the fans' greatest ever Reading team. The final line up, as voted for by Reading's fans, was:

Shaka Hislop

Graeme Murty	Adie Williams	Martin Hicks	Nicky Shorey
Maurice Evans	Neil Webb	Phil Parkinson	Michael Gilkes

Robin Friday   **Jimmy Quinn**

With only Evans and Friday having played for Reading before the 1980s there is an obvious modern bias, but just how good, statistically, is that team? Using the resources of Strap's *Ultimate Reading FC Database* and basing the calculation on three-points-for-a-win with a minimum of 70 League appearances, Nigel was able to calculate the following statistically-best Reading team:

George Marks

George Johnson	Adrian Viveash	Billy Wright	Dylan Kerr
Ken Bainbridge	Jack Lewis	John Salako	
Jamie Cureton	Joe McGough	Martin Butler	

With four players from the last eight successful years, three from the early 1950s, three from the 1930s and one from the 1990s, this is a far more diversified team. That statistically supreme side had an impressive aggregate record of:

Played	Won	Drew	Lost	Goals For	Goals Against
1170	626	236	308	2,182	1,428

This gave them a points average per game of 1.807 compared with only 1.52 for the fans' XI. Special mention should go to **Ken Bainbridge** who, with an average points-per-game of 1.85, is statistically Reading's best-ever player.

Since Reading joined the League in 1920, 12 players have a 100 per cent record by winning every game – **Johnny Mapson, Ben Marsden, Sam McHale, Dave Tearse, Fred Gorringe, Mark Smith, Joe Gamble, Gary Brooke, Steve Archibald** and **Horace Cooper**. Unfortunately, they only played 19 games between them! Special mention should be made of Reading's live-wire Irish winger **Stephen Hunt**, who, after a 12 minute substitute appearance, played 22 League games in 2005–06 before he finished on a losing side.

LEAGUE LOSERS

By way of contrast, a 'select' handful of players have never enjoyed a winning bonus with Reading, and from these Reading's 'worst' team can be formed:

Nick Colgan: Statistically Reading's worst keeper, Nick joined the Club on loan from Chelsea in March 1998 when the Club was already plummeting towards relegation. Five games later, he had suffered five defeats and conceded 16 goals. Despite this, Nick enjoyed a long career, winning nine caps for Eire.

Tommy McGhee: Another player whose Reading career coincided with a poor team run, the start of 1959–60 saw right back Tommy gain just one point from his eight Reading games.

Ian Porterfield: Loaned from Sheffield Wednesday in November 1976, the Sunderland legend was less successful at Elm Park, his five games producing just one draw.

Barry Butlin: An identical record to Porterfield, Barry was actually a centre forward, but he failed to score in his five-game loan spell from Nottingham Forest in January 1977. In fact he failed even to get a shot on target during his time with Reading.

Matt Lockhead: Matt had two spells with Reading in 1921 and 1922, but he was never on the winning side in either period. As well as five League defeats he also suffered an FA Cup reverse, with three of those defeats coming against Northampton Town.

John Johnstone: Reading's first six games of 1928–29 saw them earn just one point. 'Jock' played in all six games but none after that.

Emerse Faé: A disastrous season that ended in Reading being relegated from the Premier League saw the Club's record signing lose all eight League games in which he played.

Len Marlow: All five of Len's games for Reading in 1923–24 ended in defeat and also ended his League career.

Fred Gamble: Although he scored in three of his first Reading games, Fred ended with the unenviable record of no wins in his 10 Reading games in 1933–34. At least only three of those games ended in defeat, the rest being drawn.

Ian Kirkwood: Two draws are all young Scot Ian has to show from his four Reading games in the mid-1950s.

Edward Douglas: Ted 'enjoyed' a 100 per cent record in League and Cup games for Reading, his five games in 1929–30 all ending in defeat with a goal aggregate of 5–21.

So, this fictional team ended with a Reading League record of played 67, lost 53 and drew only 14. But just to prove that facts do not prove everything, consider the case of **Andy Legg**. He was a classy and versatile left-sided player who was highly thought of at all the seven League Clubs he played for, including Reading. Yet his record with Reading reveals that he lost 11 of his 12 games, scored an unlucky own-goal, and was the victim of a harsh sending off during his 10 months with the Club.

GOLDEN OLDIES VERSUS YOUNG ROYALS
The Ancients – average age 43

A. Hart: He played in goal for Reading in their very first game, against Reading Grammar School on 21 February 1872. Despite facing a school line up that featured six forwards with the protection of just two backs, the 50-year-old keeper kept a clean sheet in that historic game.

Fred Bartholomew: 'Bart' made his League debut for Reading on 15 January 1921, just days after his 36th birthday, having been with the Club as a regular in their Southern League days. He made his final League appearance towards the end of that season at the age of 36 years four months.

John Walker: Another defender from Reading's early League days, John joined the Club when he was 38 years old. He played for two seasons, and when he made his last League appearance he was 40 years and five months old. As such, he remains Reading's oldest League player.

Mick Gooding: Regarded as the fittest player at Elm Park during the 1990s despite also being the oldest, Mick made his final League appearance for Reading two weeks after his 38th birthday.

Bill Ratcliffe: The war ended many players' careers, but not Bill Ratcliffe's. Thirty-seven when he signed for Reading, Bill carried on playing for the Club, recovering from a cartilage injury, to play one week beyond his 39th birthday. Remarkably, Reading then sold him to Watford for £750 and he carried on playing for another season.

Billy Wright: Born on Christmas Day 1899, Billy carried on playing until Easter 1938, being virtually ever-present and Club captain during his first four seasons at Elm Park.

Harry Graham: Having helped Reading to the Third Division South Championship in 1925–26, a 17-year League playing career ended in March 1927 at the age of 39 years and three months, and so Harry is Reading's second oldest League player.

Johnny Brooks: Widely regarded as one of the Club's greatest-ever players, Johnny was the first town-born player to appear for England. Despite this, it is said that Johnny could never walk by a kick-about in the park without joining in. In September 1998 he played in a veterans' tournament, the last event staged at Elm Park, at the age of 66, and 49 years after he had made his first League appearance at the ground. Even then Johnny was not finished; on 19 October 2003 the Club's Supporters' Trust staged a re-enactment of the very first Reading game that had been played 131 years earlier and 71-year-old Johnny was one of several ex-Reading players to take part.

J.R. Blandford: In 1906 Reading director J.R. Blandford travelled with the reserves to Fulham. On arrival it was discovered that two players had not turned up, and so Mr Blandford and trainer Percy Caulfield made up the XI. Not surprisingly, Reading lost 3–1 but the Club avoided a fine for fielding an incomplete team. Mr Blandford was 70 at the time of the game.

Douggie Webb: In 1982 Reading travelled to Leicester City for a reserve game without a substitute. A second half injury to Greek trialist Loukas Louka meant that reserve team boss Douggie Webb came on as substitute. The former Reading player had retired through injury 15 years earlier and was aged 42 when he made his return to the game.

Substitute: After 82 goalless minutes against Plymouth Argyle on 5 February 2005, Steve Coppell decided he needed more experience in his team. As a result he replaced **Les Ferdinand**, aged 38 years and three months, with the five-month older **Martin Keown**. Later in the season, at Sunderland, both Ferdinand and Keown came on as substitutes, introducing the experience of 1,020 League games between them. It obviously worked because Reading scored two late goals to beat the League leaders.

Manager – Jimmy Wallbanks: Almost made the team as a player, making his last Reading appearance as a 37-year-old. However, his morale-boosting three-month spell as the Club's caretaker manager in 1971 at the age of 62 beats Joe Edelston, who was 57 when he left the Elm Park manager's office.

The Moderns – average age 16 years 343 days

Colin Court: Thrown in at the deep end following the unavailability of **Steve Death** and **John Turner**, youth team keeper Colin had the added disadvantage of playing in the local derby against Swindon on 20 February 1982. Despite having the misfortune of knocking a cross into his own net, it was his only mistake as Reading drew 1–1. This made Colin Reading's youngest keeper, aged 17 years and 332 days.

Adie Williams: Adie was just two months beyond his 17th birthday when he made his debut at Notts County on 22 October 1988. He was right back on his debut but played in all 11 positions before settling down to become one of Reading's greatest central-defenders.

Bobby Lenarduzzi: Most of the 'Young Royals' were born locally, with Canadian Bobby being the exception. Still on 'a working holiday' when he was one of five teenagers who played against Colchester United on 29 April 1972, he was two days short of his 17th birthday.

Neil Webb: Facing his father in the 'Golden Oldie' team, Neil rewrote the Reading record books in his youthful career at Elm Park. He was the youngest Reading player to be picked for the first team when he was unused substitute at Swindon on 21 August 1979, aged 16 years 22 days. When he did make his debut he became the Club's third-youngest player. A year later he became the Club's youngest League scorer, netting against Swindon. In 1981–82 he became Reading's youngest top scorer, and then became their youngest record transfer, joining Portsmouth for £87,500.

Peter Castle: Having obtained his headmaster's permission to play on a school day, Peter lowered the age for Reading's youngest player when he came on as substitute at Watford on 30 April 2003, just 49 days beyond his 16th birthday.

Steve Wood: Steve was a classy defender from the day he made his debut at the age of 17 years 23 days at Southend United on 25 February 1980. Along with **Neil Webb**, Steve went on to play top-flight football with Millwall and Southampton.

Melvyn Hood: Mel became the first 16-year-old, by just six days, to play for Reading when he made his League debut for the Club in the 2–1 win over Norwich City on 22 September 1956.

Steve Hetzke: 'Big 'Un' took Mel's record when he played at Darlington on 18 December 1971, aged 16 years and 169 days. Although his debut and most of his career was played in the centre of defence, Steve spent the 1978–79 season in the forward line and scored the goal against Halifax that clinched promotion.

Jerry Williams: He was another versatile youngster who began as a forward, switched to the wing and then became a very good right back. His debut, at 16 years and 339 days, could not have come in more difficult circumstances. With Reading 3–0 down at half time at home to Bury on 26 February 1977, Charlie Hurley resigned, his last act as Reading manager being to bring on Jerry as substitute. The youngster responded with a man-of-the-match display.

Adrian Cooper: Although born in Reading, eight England Schools caps earned Adrian a contract with Spurs. He failed to settle and returned to Reading in time to make his League debut against Stockport on 20 April 1974, three months beyond his 17th birthday.

Andy Proudlove: Having become the youngest player to appear for Reading Reserves, Andy then became the Club's youngest player until **Steve Hetzke** reduced his record a month later. However, at 16 years and 309 days Andy remains the Club's youngest FA Cup player when he played at Bridgewater on 20 November 1971.

Manager: As well as being one of Reading's youngest players, his membership of the five-man committee who were in charge of the game against Wolves on 18 December 1994 made Adie Williams, at the age of 23 years and four months, the League's youngest-ever manager. But 20 per cent of one game hardly counts so the youngest Royals manager is Mark McGhee, the man Adie and his committee replaced, the Scot being 34 years three months when he took charge.

─────────────── CUP OF CHEER ───────────────

SEMI SUCCESS

On 28 March 1900, Elm Park staged an FA Cup semi-final replay between Southampton and Millwall. The Saints triumphed 3–0 in what was the last time that a semi-final was contested between two non-League Clubs, with both Clubs, alongside Reading, being members of the Southern League. Although even the most avid Reading fan would admit that Elm Park hardly qualified as one of the nation's great stadiums, it still staged a semi-final before some famous grounds. Among those who followed Elm Park as the FA's ground of choice were White Hart Lane (1902), Stamford Bridge (1908), Old Trafford (1910), Hillsborough (1912) and Maine Road (1928).

RECORD REPLAYS

Reading's old ground was often used in the days when second replays were staged on neutral grounds. Strangely, those two semi-final opponents featured in two of the more memorable of those replays. In March 1900 Millwall became one of only four non-League Clubs to knock the reigning League champions out of the Cup when they beat Aston Villa 2–1. The Lions' victory was tainted by a false accusation made by their treasurer over the checking of the gate receipts, for which he had to apologise. Two years later Southampton beat FA Cup holders Spurs at Elm Park; again the score was 2–1 and, again, they were only one of four non-League Clubs to beat the Cup holders. That game, staged at the beginning of February, was played on a snow-covered pitch that Southampton's legendary full back C.B. Fry described as being 'like a skating rink'.

SEMI PARTNERS

Reading's only semi-final appearance came on 26 March 1927 when they lost 3–0 at Molineux to the eventual Cup winners, Cardiff City. One of the 15 Clubs that have reached that stage once but never progressed to the final, Reading find themselves in the company of the likes of Cambridge University, Derby Junction, Old Harrovians, local rivals Marlow and Shropshire Wanderers.

CUP TOWN

Apart from Reading Football Club, five other Clubs from the town have entered the FA Cup, although, currently, only Hellenic League Club Reading Town are keeping the professional Club company in the competition, having first entered the tournament in 1997–98. The other four Clubs are all long-forgotten, having made brief appearances in the first 20 years of the competition. Reading Hornets, later to merge with Reading Football Club, were the first of the town's Clubs to play in the FA Cup, losing 2–0 to Swifts on 4 November 1876, thus preceding their more famous rivals by a year. The Hornets' next game saw them lose 10–0 at Maidenhead and that put them off the FA Cup for good. Reading Abbey and Reading Minster both had brief runs in the 1880s, Minster writing themselves into the Cup record books, somewhat obscurely, in 1881 when they staged the only FA Cup tie ever to be played on Boxing Day. Reading South, who played their home games at Whitley Park Farm, which was close to where Reading's Madejski Stadium now stands, played six seasons, reaching the fourth round in 1885–86, albeit with the help of two walkovers.

FINAL HEROES

It seems that the way to guarantee success in an FA Cup Final is to have a goal scored by a player with a Reading connection. Reading-related players have scored in seven finals and all won winners' medals.

⊕ England international **John Plant** had a season on loan at Reading from Bury in 1898 because of the Lancashire Club's financial plight. Plant appeared to have suffered from his own financial problem since he played in boots so old that they had to be held together with tape. His financial problems were nearly worsened in October 1898 when the Reading board threatened to cut his wages unless his play improved. It clearly did improve, at least when he returned to Bury, as he subsequently scored in both of the Shakers' Cup final successes in 1900 and 1903.

❀ The next success came in 1929 when future Reading player and manager **Billy Butler** scored in Bolton's 2–0 win over Portsmouth. That game was unique in FA Cup Final history in that both sides featured a player named Billy Cook, Bolton's version later becoming one of Butler's first signings as Reading's manager.

❀ On 27 April 1935 a former Reading centre forward, **Jack Palethorpe**, gave Sheffield Wednesday an early lead against West Bromwich Albion in a final that his team won 4–2.

❀ Two of the greatest final upsets in recent years were both achieved with goals scored by players with the almost inevitable Reading connection. Second Division Sunderland beat red-hot favourites Leeds United in the 1973 final, thanks to a goal by future Reading player and manager **Ian Porterfield**. A similar shock result came 15 years later when former Reading schoolboy and midfield star **Lawrie Sanchez** headed the only goal of the game as Wimbledon's 'Crazy Gang' beat Liverpool.

❀ Only **Mark Robins**, a Reading loanee in August 1997, failed to win the FA Cup Final game in which he scored, as the game in question ended in a 3–3 draw. Even then, his Manchester United team beat Crystal Palace in the replay to eventually win the 1990 final. This was the final with the largest ever Reading representation. As well as Mark, the United side featured another future Reading loan player, **Jim Leighton**, plus **Neil Webb**, while Palace included former Reading player **Dave Madden**, future signings **John Salako** and **Alan Pardew,** while they were managed by **Steve Coppell** and coached by **Ian Branfoot**.

SPECIAL SUCCESS

On the other hand, knocking Reading out of the FA Cup is virtually certain to deny the victor Cup success. In the 121 seasons in which Reading have played in the FA Cup only five teams have beaten them on their way to winning the trophy. And on each occasion it took a special Club to get past Reading:

❀ In 1879 the **Old Etonians** scraped by Reading 1–0 in only their second season in the competition, before becoming the first amateur side to beat a professional team, Darwin, on their way to winning the trophy.

⊕ When **Spurs** won the Cup in 1901, having beaten Reading after a replay, they became, and remain, the only non-League side to win the competition since the Football League was formed in 1888. In addition, their final, played at the old Crystal Palace, attracted the highest official final attendance of 110,820.

⊕ **Cardiff City**, who beat Reading in their only semi-final appearance, went on to beat Arsenal in the 1927 final and so become the only Club to take the trophy out of England.

⊕ It took **Sunderland** a replay to beat Reading in the fourth round, but they then caused the biggest FA Cup Final shock of all time when they beat hot favourites Leeds United 1–0 in 1973.

⊕ The last team to beat Reading on the way to Cup triumph was **Manchester United** in 1996, who also became the first team to achieve the League and Cup double for a second time that year.

THE BASIC FACTS

Since Reading first entered the FA Cup in 1877 they have played a tie in every calendar year that the competition has been staged except 1879 (when Reading stood down from the competition following the death of their captain, **Henry Rogers**), 1949, 1994 and 2000. During that time they have played 134 different opponents, and of these Manchester United have proved the most frequent, with Reading having played them 12 times. After Manchester United, Reading have been drawn against Aldershot the most times, the eight ties having provided Reading with their most victories, six. They also have a 100 per cent record against Brentford and Gillingham, having drawn them both on four occasions and progressed to the next round each time. Crystal Palace have played Reading six times in the FA Cup and have not won once, while Arsenal and Upton Park have won all three FA Cup games they have played against Reading. By a strange quirk Reading and Southampton were drawn against each other on four consecutive seasons between 1893 and 1897.

BUSY TIMES

The most FA Cup games Reading have played in one season is 10, having reached this total on three occasions. In 1926–27 those 10 games took Reading to the semi-finals, while in 1900–01 they reached the quarter-finals. More unusual was Reading's 1989–90 10-match Cup run. Three games against Bristol Rovers, then four versus Welling United, led to Reading getting past Sunderland at the first attempt, before they left the competition in the fourth round at Newcastle following a replay. Three of those games went to extra time to bring the time spent in the Cup that season to 990 minutes. In both 1900–01 and 1989–90 no team, including winners Spurs and Manchester United, played more FA Cup games than Reading.

WIN SOME, LOSE SOME

Aldershot gained some revenge for those six defeats in 1945–46, the only season that saw the FA Cup played over a home and away basis. Reading were 3–1 ahead after the first leg at Elm Park, and things got even better at the Recreation Ground when Reading went in at half time with a 5–2 aggregate lead. With 20 minutes totgo they were still 6–4 ahead overall, but the Shots centre forward Harry Brooks went on to complete a five-goal personal haul to make the score on the day 7–3, with his side edging through 8–6 on aggregate. That five-goal burst was no fluke for Brooks, as he repeated it in the next round as Aldershot beat Isle of Wight side Newport 7–0. As a result, Brooks was the first player to score hat-tricks in consecutive FA Cup rounds and, not surprisingly, he is the only player to score five goals in two ties.

GOLDEN GOALIES

Other players connected to Reading to have set FA Cup records include goalkeeper **Ben Roberts**, who spent six games on loan from Charlton Athletic during Reading's 2001–02 promotion season. Five years earlier Ben, then in goal for Middlesbrough, had conceded Wembley's fastest FA Cup Final goal when Roberto di Matteo put Chelsea into the lead after only 42 seconds, having previously played in the League Cup Final against Chelsea in the same season. Ben was the eighth-youngest goalkeeper to play in a final behind **Frank Swift**, a Reading wartime guest, in fifth when he played for Manchester City in 1934, while former Reading youngster **Johnny Mapson** is the third-youngest (behind Peter Shilton and Mervyn Day) when he helped Sunderland win the trophy in 1937. It is said that both Frank and Johnny fainted as the final whistle was blown signalling their victory. Of course, Johnny's over-excitement was really due to the fact that it was his birthday the next day and so he was the oldest teenager ever to play in a Cup final!

SUPER SUB

In addition to his one start for Reading during a month's trial in March 1991, Garry Brooke also made three substitute appearances. However, the three substitute appearances he made for Tottenham Hotspur were far more memorable. In the days of only one substitute, he achieved the unique feat of coming on in three consecutive FA Cup Final appearances, in 1981 and twice in 1982.

MANAGING SUCCESS

Either side of his successful spell as manager at Elm Park, **Joe Smith** became the first person to play in a Wembley Final, for Bolton in 1923 and 1926, and then manage his Club Blackpool to success in 1953. Far less successful during his 13 days as Reading's manager in 1939, **Johnny Cochrane** was still the first manager to guide a Club to both the Scottish Cup Final, with St Mirren in 1926, and then the English Final, with Sunderland in 1937. Only Sir Alex Ferguson has matched Johnny's record since then.

THE B TEAM

Reading have played no fewer than nine different non-League Clubs whose names begin with 'B' – Barking, Barry Town, Bedford Town, Bishop Stortford, Blyth Spartans, Bognor Regis Town, Brentwood Town, Bridgewater Town and Bromley. Of those, Bishop Stortford inflicted Reading's only home defeat at the hands of a non-League Club, while the journey to Blyth was the longest Reading have faced for a competitive match.

——————— QUICK OFF THE MARK ———————

BAD START

Unfortunately for Reading, the quickest goals scored at both Elm Park and Madejski Stadium have been netted by visiting players. On 3 January 1983 Oxford United's Mick Vinter gave his side the lead after just 12 seconds to just about put the icing on the cake of a season that saw Reading relegated, knocked out of the FA Cup following their only home defeat by non-League opposition, and be threatened with a merger with Oxford United! Reading's 2004–05 season started with a home game against Brighton, kicking off at 3pm on 7 August. Thirteen seconds later Reading were a goal down, Maheta Molanga scoring from an admittedly offside-looking position. Remarkably, a minute later the score was 1–1, **Dave Kitson** equalising and setting Reading up for a 3–2 victory.

FAST STARTERS

Reading have twice scored the opening goal of a new season. The first time this happened was back on 18 August 1951 when **Les Henley** gave them the lead after only 30 seconds at Port Vale. The Club's second quick start was a little more fortunate. In the late 1970s and early 1980s the first round of the Football League Cup was staged before the League season commenced, and in 1980–81 Reading were drawn against Northampton. In those days the Cobblers shared their County Ground with Northamptonshire Cricket Club, and as a result the game had to be played on the Friday night before the rest of the round commenced. Consequently, although **Steve Hetzke**'s opening goal was not scored until midway through the first half, it was still the first of that season.

Manchester United's flying start to their FA Cup replay at Madejski Stadium on 27 February 2007 received plenty of national coverage after they scored three times in the opening five minutes and 41 seconds, but it is not the only free-scoring start involving Reading. On 30 March 2002 Reading travelled to Ashton Gate and after 14 minutes of play they were leading Bristol City 3–2.

DAVE'S EARLY DOORS

It was appropriate that Reading's equaliser against Brighton was scored by **Dave Kitson** as he always seems to make a dramatic start to his Reading seasons. The following season he scored in his first start, again against Brighton, while the opening game of 2006–07 was a bittersweet one for the big striker – within minutes of scoring Reading's very first goal in the Premier League he was the victim of a bad tackle from Middlesbrough's Chris Riggott which was to keep him out for five months. Even worse was to follow in 2007–08 as he was red carded just 34 seconds into his season, when he was dismissed for a rash tackle after coming on as substitute at Old Trafford. Some consolation for Dave is that his early dismissal does not qualify as the Premiership's fastest. That 'honour' belongs to Sheffield United's Keith Gillespie, who is recorded as being dismissed after just 10 seconds of coming on at Madejski Stadium on 20 January 2007 and immediately striking **Stephen Hunt**. As the incident took place before the game had restarted his time on the pitch should be more accurately recorded as 0 seconds.

QUICK KEV

Kitson's Premier League strike partner **Kevin Doyle** is no slouch when it comes to quick scoring either, although the young Irishman appears to specialise in away goals. On 17 February 2006 Kevin netted Reading's fastest-ever away goal when he scored after just 18 seconds at Luton. Seven months later he lowered his record by two seconds with the fastest goal in the Premiership that season, scored at Sheffield United.

SWIFT SUBS

The fastest Premiership goal from a substitute was netted by future Reading player **Shaun Goater**, when he scored for City in the Manchester derby after just nine seconds. Shaun's record has come under pressure from two Reading players in 2007–08. **Andre Bikey** scored after 20 seconds with his first touch after he came on against Chelsea in Reading's first home game of the season. On 27 October 2007 sub **Shane Long** netted the winner against Newcastle and could possibly claim to have broken Goater's record, his shot entering the net within eight seconds of the restart.

DALEY STAR

Another quick-scoring Reading substitute was the legendary athlete **Daley Thompson**. During the summer of 1994 the Olympic gold medalist and World champion joined Reading to make a documentary of him training with a professional football Club. The world's greatest athlete, Thompson proved an infectious character and was a great benefit to the Club's pre-season training so, as a reward, he was given a place on the bench for Reading's friendly at Leatherhead. Brought on at half time, Daley had not played football for many years but that did not stop him scoring with his second touch.

QUICK OFF THE MARK, MARK

The swiftest League goal scored by a Reading player came in the Third Division game against York City on 27 April 1985. The goal was scored by Mark White in 12.96 seconds, despite the fact that York had kicked-off the game. The remarkable accuracy of the timing of that goal was down to the fact that it was recorded by Derek Bradfield with a stopwatch normally used by Reading Athletics Club for timing sprints. However, Mark does not hold the record for the fastest Reading goal. That honour belongs to **Harold Cothliff**, a Torquay United winger who was a regular guest for Reading during World War Two. On 1 November 1941 Harold opened the scoring at Elm Park with the first of his two goals against West Ham, that opening strike being described in the local press as being scored 'within 10 seconds'. That goal was a small consolation for Harold, since the outbreak of World War Two affected him more than most. He was due to complete a dream transfer from Torquay United to Chelsea for a record £6,000 on 3 September 1939, but war was declared that day and the move never materialised.

RAPID RECORDS
Several Reading players have set fast-scoring records while with other Clubs:

- **Maurice Edelston** was made to wait seven years between signing for Reading and scoring his first League goal due to the war. He made up for that when he was transferred to Northampton in 1952, netting for his new Club 10 seconds into his League debut for them.

- A career-ending injury meant that **Alan Morris** never scored for Reading, but he does have the honour of scoring the fastest-ever goal at Swansea's Vetch Field when he netted against Leeds United in November 1960, again waiting just 10 seconds.

- **James Lambert** was much slower, waiting a whole 17 seconds before scoring for Oxford United against Colchester United to record the Manor Ground's quickest goal.

- Statistically, Reading's best goalscorer with 54 in just 57 League games, **Jack Palethorpe** scored what was then the quickest goal in a Wembley Cup Final. Jack netted within two minutes of the kick-off to give Sheffield Wednesday the lead in the 1935 final versus West Bromwich Albion.

- **Ronnie Dix** ended his playing career at Reading, scoring his last League goal on 16 October 1948. Over 20 years earlier, on 3 March 1928, he had scored his first League goal for Bristol Rovers against Norwich. Aged just 15 years 180 days, that strike made Ronnie the League's youngest goalscorer.

- In December 1924 future Reading forward **George James** scored four times for West Bromwich Albion against Nottingham Forest. The first of that quartet was allegedly scored after just five seconds, which would make it the fastest scored by an Albion player.

⊕ **Ted Harston** never really got a chance of a run in Reading's first team, but he made sure of a regular start when he moved to Mansfield in October 1935 by scoring a hat-trick within seven minutes on his debut at Field Mill.

DEBUT DELIGHTS

Eighty-one players have scored on their League debuts for Reading, with three of them starting off with a hat-trick. **George Johnston** and **Jimmy Liddle** both scored their trios within two months of each other in 1932, George against Northampton Town and Jimmy against Bournemouth. Remarkably, Johnston only played two more games for Reading as a forward, but Liddle was even more unlucky as he was dropped after his hat-trick. That season was a good one in which to start a playing career with Reading, as a Club-best eight goals were scored by four debutants in 1932–33. In addition to that, Jimmy and George's hat-tricks were part of a Club record seven scored that season, with **Jack Palethorpe** boosting the total with four on his own.

SUPER STARTS

Probably the most spectacular debut performance came from **Tommy Tait**. Signed with the help of a donation from Reading's Supporters' Club, the centre forward netted his hat-trick against local rivals Aldershot on 10 November 1934, and had two 'goals' disallowed. The longest delayed League debut hat-trick was scored by **Maurice Edelston** on 4 September 1946, seven years after he had signed for Reading. Of course, the war had intervened, and although Maurice had scored 107 goals in 132 Reading wartime games his League debut came at the start of 1946–47 season. Maurice's trio was scored in Reading's record 10–2 League win over Crystal Palace, with another goal coming from **Vic Barney** to make this the only game in which two Reading players have netted on their debuts.

Other Reading players have impressive scoring records in debuts that were not their first appearances for the Club. Signed in the summer of 1938, 'Tony' **MacPhee** had already played eight League games for Reading when he made his debut in the Division Three South Cup Final against Bristol City. This had been held over from the previous season, and yet MacPhee was regarded as eligible to play, much to City's regret since the free-scoring centre forward netted four times on his debut in the competition. Similarly, **Denis Allen** had played several League games for Reading before their League Cup tie against Chester on 13 September 1961. Denis scored a hat-trick on his debut in the tournament, giving him extra cause for celebration – not only did his goals secure Reading's first win in the League Cup, but he had got married earlier in the day. Matchday marriage is clearly something to be encouraged. The aforementioned Tony MacPhee was married in the morning of 25 March 1944 before scoring twice, and hitting the woodwork twice, in the afternoon. Like Denis Allen, MacPhee had extra celebrations that day since his goals inflicted a 5–1 victory over Arsenal in front of the Club's highest wartime attendance of 19,722.

FRED'S FIRST

Although not strictly a Reading debut, **Fred Bartholomew**'s first appearance at Elm Park fully warrants a mention. A well-known local amateur who worked for Huntley & Palmers, Fred was at Elm Park on Good Friday 1904 to watch a local Cup final when it was announced that one of the teams, New Inn, were a man short. Fred stepped in to make up the numbers, which he did to such good effect that he scored a hat-trick. Not surprisingly, this alerted the watching Reading Football Club officials, who soon signed him as an amateur. From that chance appearance, 'Bart' began a career that not only saw him play in every position for Reading in a 16-year playing career, but then saw him act as trainer, physio and groundsman at Elm Park, where he worked into his 70s.

FRIENDLY TRIO

Another player to score a hat-trick on his debut was another well-known local player, **Paul Stanford**. Called in to play for injury-hit Reading in a pre-season friendly against Brentford in August 1983, Paul hit a hat-trick in 14 second half minutes to turn a 2–1 deficit into an eventual 5–2 victory. This performance might have earned Paul the match ball (compensation for a signet ring he lost on the pitch), but it did not earn him a contract and he never played for Reading again, returning to play for West Reading in the Reading & District League. Scottish centre forward **John Scott** also netted a hat-trick on his Reading debut in a friendly against Oxford University in October 1921. Although he followed that up with a goal on his League debut, he was soon switched to the right wing and never repeated his early promise.

THAT'S ANDY

Another local youngster was more lucky. **Andy Alleyne** was a regular for Reading Reserves, combining a part-time playing career with his job with the Post Office, when caretaker manager **Jimmy Wallbanks** gave him his League debut against Fourth Division leaders Southport on 21 October 1972. This made Andy the first black player to appear for Reading and a reliable debut at full back was capped by a sensational goal. Early in the second half Andy launched a long ball forward from just inside his own half and it eluded everyone, ending up in the Southport net. That goal earned Reading a 1–1 draw and, by a remarkable coincidence, Southport's goal had also come from the halfway line, surely the only time that both goals in a League game have been scored from such a distance.

THE DEBUT KING

The king of debut scoring is, however, **Jamie Cureton**, who scored on every first team debut he made for Reading in various competitions. Having opened his account with a League Cup goal against Leyton Orient on 22 August 2000, he quickly followed that with a debut Division Two goal at Stoke City. FA Cup and Associate Members' Cup debut goals followed against Grays Athletic and

Hereford United in his initial season. He completed the set two seasons later when he scored both goals against Sheffield Wednesday in Reading's first win back in Division One.

SHORT STARTS

Not all debutants have such happy memories of their first games for Reading. Four players have suffered the disappointment of being sent off in their first game for the Club. **Bob Hazell** lasted only 29 minutes into his debut before being sent off against Barnsley on 8 November 1986. Rather less deserving of a dismissal was full back **John Humphrey**, who was the victim of a ridiculous sending off at Burnley on 11 December 1993. At least John's loan spell at Reading had a happy ending; not only did 10-man Reading hold on to win at Turf Moor to go top of Division Two, but they held on to win the Championship and give Humphrey a unique double since his permanent Club, Crystal Palace, also won their Championship that season. Another loan player, Leeds United's **Alan Maybury**, also went off in his first game for Reading, a home defeat to Manchester City on 27 March 1999. Finally, and as unfortunate as Humphrey 14 years earlier, **Kalifa Cisse** received two yellows during Reading's first home game of the 2007–08 season, against Chelsea.

Other unfortunate starts to their Reading careers include defender **Len Vallard**, who broke his arm on his debut against Colchester United on 12 September 1959. Of course, goalkeepers are prone to unfortunate starts and the war years threw up a couple of extreme examples. **C. Ednay** conceded seven on his debut at Coventry City on 14 September 1940, and after letting in another four a couple of weeks later his Reading career was over. On the other hand, **Peter Peters** overcame the horror of also conceding seven in an FA Cup tie at Aldershot on 24 November 1946 to end up on the winning side in his other two first team games. One keeper who was prepared for letting in a hatful was a well-known local keeper who was drafted in to face Southampton on 6 November 1943. He insisted that his real name be kept secret and played under the nom de plume of 'Smith'. This proved a wise decision as he conceded five and never played for Reading again under any name.

A rather more impressive goalkeeping start was made by **Johnny Mapson**. Recalled from a loan spell with Guildford City following the injuries to Reading's two experienced keepers, the youngster made his League debut in 1936, on that rarest of League dates, 29 February, against Newport County and saved a penalty. After one more game for Reading Johnny was sold to Sunderland for a big fee and played in their last six games to help them win the League title. A year later he became the youngest goalkeeper to win the FA Cup, helping Sunderland beat Preston North End the day before his 20th birthday. Another keeper who made an impressive start to his Reading career was the giant **Ron Butcher**. Injuries to Reading's senior keepers saw the youngster thrown in to the League side over the hectic 1937 Easter period. Playing four games in five days, Ron did not concede a goal in his first 360 minutes of play.

DEBUT DRAMA

As far as debuts against Reading are concerned, the most dramatic aftermath resulted from **John Murray**'s first start for Bury. Although he only scored once, he inspired Bury to a 5–1 home win to match their winning scoreline at Elm Park and this so upset Reading Chairman Frank Waller that he put the entire Reading playing squad up for sale. This demoralised the Club and they ended up being relegated, along with Bury. Despite the dramatic effect his debut had on Reading, 'Minty' later joined them and began to repay his part in the Gigg Lane debacle by scoring on his Reading debut.

FAMOUS BEGININGS

Several well-known players have made their debuts against Reading, with Jeff Astle for Notts County and Allan Clarke with Walsall both going on to play for England in the 1970 World Cup. Clarke also made the last of his 500-plus League appearances against Reading, a 7–0 drubbing in the last game at Elm Park in the 1970s as player-manager of Barnsley. Making his debut in that game was young Joe Joyce, although the experience did not do him too much harm as he went on to make 304 League appearances for the Oakwell Club. Probably the most famous name to begin his UK career in Reading was Peter Schmeichel. Before the great Dane became a legend at Old Trafford, he played his first game in England against Reading in a friendly for Brondby IF in 1987. Only 19 at the time, the *Reading Evening Post* reporter was astute enough to describe the unknown as giving a world-class display. Credit then to current Reading Academy coach **Nas Bashir**, as the scorer of the first UK goal against the great keeper.

MARK'S FLAG DAY

Despite suffering a series of injuries that would have finished a lesser player, left-sided defender **Mark White** still made 320 appearances for Reading between 1977 and 1988. However, he never got over the embarrassment of one of his first 'appearances' on a League ground. As a youngster in his home town of Sheffield, Mark was a ball boy at Bramall Lane and one of his duties was to return a corner flag to the Club offices at the final whistle. In one game, Mark grabbed his flag as instructed and made his way across the pitch. He was just crossing the centre of the pitch when he realised that the game was a Cup tie and that extra time was about to start. Mark had to quickly return his post to its position, much to the amusement of the 28,000 crowd!

———— FIRST TIME FOR EVERYTHING ————

MATT'S MANAGERIAL MISERY

A regular guest for Reading during World War Two, Matt Busby was so popular at the Club that when he made his last appearance for them, against Crystal Palace on 19 September 1945, he became the first and only guest to captain the Club. He was leaving to take over the management of Manchester United, having previously turned down the opportunity to become Reading's assistant manager. However, Matt's first taste of management had come a year earlier. Stationed near Sandhurst, Matt managed a Matt Busby XI that played Reading at Sandhurst's Royal Military Academy to raise funds for the 'Salute a Soldier' charity. Fortunately for Manchester United, Matt was not put off by his first game in charge as Reading won 6–1.

SINNING SAINT

Arthur Chadwick was the first person to both play for and manage Southampton, as well as being the first Saint to become a sinner by becoming their first player to be sent off. In between his two roles at The Dell, Arthur was manager at Reading, and on 26 March 1927 his old Club and his new team both made it to the semi-finals of the FA Cup. Sadly there was no happy ending as both Reading and Southampton fell at the final hurdle.

EARLY BATH

Talking of sending offs, in the summer of 1982 the Football Association announced that the so-called 'professional foul', the deliberate prevention of a goalscoring chance by illegal means, would be punished with dismissal. The first player to fall foul(!) of this ruling was Reading's **Lawrie Sanchez**, who made a brilliant one-handed diving save to prevent a certain goal for Oxford United 21 minutes into the Football League Trophy game played at Elm Park on 14 August 1982. Four days later Sanchez was able to use his goalkeeping talents legally when he went in goal at Aldershot in place of **Ron Fearon**, who had also been shown a red card for a 'professional foul.'

JOINT JOY

Jimmy Quinn and **Mick Gooding** became the first joint managers to lead their team out at Wembley when they were in charge of the Reading side that reached the play-off final on 29 May 1995. Uniquely, they also both played in that game against Bolton Wanderers.

MRS REF

On 12 March 1991 Reading's visit to Bournemouth's Dean Court was the first League game to feature a female official when Wendy Toms was the fourth official for the match. Wendy went on to become the first woman to referee a League match and the first to officiate in a Premiership game.

IF THE CAP FITS

Local Reading schoolboy **Len Grant** played in the world's first Schoolboy international when the 14-year-old appeared for England against Wales at Walsall's Hillary Street ground on 13 April 1907. Later, Len was dismayed to be ordered by the Reading schools authorities to wear his precious cap throughout the association's next game. Played on a muddy Elm Park pitch, Len complied with the strange instruction, and although he gave his usual committed performance it is reported that he was reluctant to head the ball. Despite being the town's most promising young player, Len had to wait until he was 28 to play a League game for Reading. Eighty-five years later and there is still a Grant at Reading FC as Len's great-nephew, Ron, is the Club's long-serving kit manager.

FIRST ITALIAN

There are plenty of Italian stars playing in English football but it was Reading who started the trend, back in 1913. After their successful tour of Italy in May of that year the Club were impressed by Genoa forward **Attilio Fresia**. He had scored the Italian side's two goals against Reading and subsequently played for Italy in the game that rounded off Reading's tour. The signing was delayed because Attilio had infringed the Italian FA's strict amateur rules, but he eventually signed for Reading in September 1913. Unfortunately, he struggled to adapt to the more robust English style of play and never made a Southern League appearance, subsequently being sold to Croydon Common for £10.

IN CHARGE, IN ITALY

England may have an Italian manager but almost 100 years ago a former Reading player was becoming the first true manager in Italy. As such he revolutionised the then soccer minnows, setting the country on the road to becoming regular World Cup winners. **Willie Garbutt** spent two seasons at Elm Park between 1904 and 1906 before injury cut short his career. At the age of 29 he was appointed the manager of Genoa and was responsible for the development of players like **Attilio Fresia**. He is credited with introducing to Italy such essentials as tactics, physical fitness and even hot showers! He was the first manager to pay a transfer fee in Italy, but despite these innovations one of his players said that he 'personified the archetypal old English gent.' In all he spent 15 years building Genoa into one of Italy's great Clubs, then he managed Napoli, AC Milan and Athletico Bilbao before returning to Genoa. He returned to the UK at the outset of World War Two, staying in retirement until his death in 1964. All his managerial career had been spent abroad, so it is no wonder he made the complaint early in his career that 'it's surprising you have to go abroad to teach football. In England hardly anyone will pay to hire a professional coach.'

MILLENNIUM MOMENTS

On 3 January 2000 **Martin Williams** scored a last-minute equaliser for Reading at Gillingham to become the first League player to score from a penalty in the new millennium. By coincidence, Reading's other scorer in the 2–2 draw was **Mark Nichols**, who had joined them four days earlier on loan from Chelsea to become the final transfer of the old millennium.

SECOND, SECOND SUB

Reading missed out on a Wembley 'first' by three minutes. During the Simod Cup Final on 27 March 1988, Luton became the first team to bring on a second substitute at Wembley, Marvin Johnson beating Gary Peters by three minutes to become the national stadium's first 13th man.

FRESH FIELDS

The Field family made something of a habit of recording 'firsts'. Edgar was a member of the first Reading trophy-winning side when he played in the team that beat Marlow on 27 March 1879 to become the first winners of the Berks & Bucks Cup. He subsequently won two England caps and in the second, against Scotland on 12 March 1881, he scored England's first own-goal, living up to the contemporary description that he was 'a robust full back who kicked erratically'. His brother Charles also scored a memorable first goal, although he had more reason to celebrate than his brother's historic effort. On 7 November 1877 C.G., as he was known, scored Reading's first competitive goal, against South Norwood in the FA Cup, following 'a brilliant run down and by a clever kick'. Later in life Charles was granted the freedom of the town, although it may have been awarded for his 50 years' service on Reading's council as much as that first goal.

WELSH WINNER

Another important international goal was scored by **Richard Morris**, a winger who made his name with Plymouth before joining Reading. Not only was he the first Plymouth player to win a full cap, but he also scored the winner in a 3–2 triumph over Ireland that resulted in Wales winning the 1907 Home International tournament for the first time.

HARRY STAYS ON

One player who did not achieve a first for England was **Harry Kinsell**. A full back for West Bromwich Albion at the time, and subsequently a popular full back with Reading, Harry was upset when some contemporary reports suggested that he was sent off following a scuffle during his England debut against Ireland in a wartime match in 1945. That would have made Harry the first England player to be sent off, but it was definitely not the case and he spent the rest of his life defending his honour.

FURTHER FIRSTS

Reading players that did notch up some notable firsts were:

⊕ **Harry Millar** scored in Bury's first three League games and was their top scorer in 1896–97, their first League season, having scored their first League hat-trick. Despite these successes, he was badly barracked by the Gigg Lane crowd and so was loaned to Reading in 1898–99, finishing their joint top scorer in that season.

⊕ Popular Reading player **George Getgood** was the first player to win champions medals for both the North and South sections of the Third Division. With

Southampton he won the Championship in 1921–22, and then captained Wolves to the Northern version two years later.

❀ **A.H. 'Tommy' Hooper**, an amateur guest for Reading during the war, later became the first player to score an Amateur Cup Final goal at Wembley when he scored Bromley's winner in the 1949 final.

❀ Either side of his successful managerial spell at Elm Park, **Ted Drake** won First Division Championship medals with Arsenal and then, in 1954–55, he guided Chelsea to their first League title, thus becoming the first person to win the Championship as both a player and manager.

❀ A year after leaving Reading, full back **Colin Meldrum** scored for Cambridge United against Lincoln City on 15 August 1970. Not only was it the home side's equaliser, but it was also their first goal in the Football League.

❀ Scunthorpe's new ground Glandford Park was 'christened' by former Royal **Dave Cowling**, who, in 1998, scored their first goal in their new home.

READING LEAD THE WAY

❀ Reading were the first Club to win the third level of the Football League under its three different titles, having won the Championship of Third Division South in 1925–26, the 'unified' Third Division 60 years later and then the newly renamed Division Two in 1993–94. In addition, Reading have won the Fourth Division title in 1978–79 and the Championship in 2005–06, which only leaves the Premier League to complete the set!

❀ Reading were the visitors for what was Ipswich Town's first ever FA Cup tie on 4 October 1890. Unfortunately, Reading were beaten 2–0 to set an unwanted Club record as that defeat was the Club's seventh successive FA Cup loss.

❀ On 13 January 1906 Reading became the first Club to play Hull City in the full rounds of the FA Cup, the Humberside Club having been elected to the Second Division after just one year since its formation. Thirty-five-year-old Reading made their point in respect of this apparent injustice by winning through a Billy McCaffery goal. The game was played at Hull's early ground, the Circle. Since then, Reading have played Hull at Anlaby Road, Boothferry Park and the Kingston Communications Stadium, plus both Elm Park and Madejski Stadium, a total of six different grounds.

❀ Being the first to play in a city is not enough for Reading, however. On 24 October 1891 the Club travelled to Southampton St Mary's Antelope Ground for what was not just the first FA Cup game to be played in that city, it was also the first Cup tie in Hampshire. Still in Hampshire, eight years later Reading became the first team to play a Southern League game in Portsmouth. Neither of those trips to the south coast had happy endings for Reading as both resulted in defeats. However, that was not the end of the story as far as that FA Cup tie was concerned – see 'Six of the Best' for the reason why.

❂ In 1960 Headington United changed their name to Oxford United in order to raise the then Southern League Club's profile. The first game they played under their present title was a friendly against Reading.

MULTI-NATIONALS

Reading's starting line up for their third-round FA Cup tie against Burnley on 6 January 2007 featured 11 different countries of birth/nationalities:

Adam Federici (Australian international)
Ulises de la Cruz (Ecuadorian international)
Scott Golbourne (England)
Sam Sodje (Nigerian international)
Ivar Ingimarsson (Icelandic international)
Andre Bikey (Cameroonian international)
John Oster (Welsh international)
Seol Ki-Hyeon (South Korean international)
Bobby Convey (US international)
Shane Long (Eire)
Leroy Lita (born Democratic Republic of Congo)

To prove that this was no fluke, in the next round Reading's finishing team at Birmingham also featured 11 different nationalities, with the Irish and Icelandic representatives being replaced by Kenyan-born **Curtis Osano** and **Graeme 'Jock' Murty**.

READING'S BEST

By way of contrast, Reading could obviously field several teams of players born in the town. Using those local players with the most appearances, an impressive line up can be produced:

Mike Dixon: He was a ridiculously brave goalkeeper who made 134 Reading appearances during the first half of the 1960s, having previously played alongside the likes of Martin Peters in a Schoolboy international at Wembley.

Len Grant: Len played in the very first Schoolboy international game, then waited 14 years after that match to play for Reading. In the end he made 79 appearances at full back, plus several as captain.

Ray Reeves: A true Elm Park legend, 'Bomber' was an awesome physical presence in the Reading defence of the 1950s and early 1960s. His powerful shooting meant that any free kick within 40 yards of the goal was a goalscoring chance for him.

Rod Thornhill: A versatile, if occasionally ungainly, player, 'Spider' was reliable wherever he played during his 221 Reading games.

Stan Wicks: One of the best defenders ever to play for Reading, Stan moved to Chelsea in 1954 and promptly helped them to their first Championship before a knee injury ended his career.

Sylvan Anderton: Sylvan also went to Chelsea, but not before he had established himself as one of the classiest players outside the top flight. In all he played 178 games for Reading in the 1950s.

Jimmy Wheeler: With more appearances than any Reading-born player at 453, and with more goals, 168, for Reading than anyone other than **Trevor Senior**, 'Jimmy Wee' remains one of the Club's most popular players.

Neil Webb: Probably the best Reading-born player, Neil has 26 England caps to prove it. He also scored 22 goals in 81 Reading appearances that were all made before he was 19.

Brian Leach: Brian played most of his career as a defender, but he began his career as a centre forward and had just returned to the forward line when he moved to Headington United in 1957.

Johnny Brooks: If Neil Webb is the town's best player then Johnny is the most skilful. Like Neil he played all his Reading games as a youngster before a big money move to Spurs, where he progressed to the England side in November 1956 and won three caps. As a 13-year-old he once scored 19 goals in Castle Institutes' 44–1 Reading Minor Cup victory.

Jack Deverall: One of only four Reading players to play both sides of World War Two, Jackie was a hard-shooting winger who won two England Schools caps before scoring twice in Reading's record 10–2 League victory over Crystal Palace.

Manager – Adie Williams: Part of the five-man committee that took charge of the 4–2 win over Wolves on 18 December 1994, Adie also had two permanent spells as a Reading player and only **Jimmy Wheeler** made more appearances as a Reading-born player.

Groundsman – Gordon Neate: Although 'Fred's' playing career only lasted 107 games spread over 10 injury-hit years, he is still a valuable member of the groundstaff at Madejski Stadium, 52 years after he first joined the Club.

Chairman – Roger Smee: He had two spells playing for his home-town Club, in the late 1960s and then another in the 1970s before retiring to become a successful businessman. His next return was the most important, saving the Club from the spectre of Robert Maxwell's Thames Valley Royals, and then guiding Reading FC back to the Second Division.

Of course, not everyone born in Reading has played for the Club. Over 40 players have enjoyed League careers, making almost 4,000 appearances, that have not involved playing for their home-town Club. Currently, Hayden Mullins is playing in the Premier League for West Ham United, something no town-born player has achieved for Reading to date.

So, ignoring current players, a team featuring the 'traitors' with the most League appearances for other Clubs could look like this:

George Epgrave: keeper George played 46 games either side of World War Two, mainly for Southampton.

Shaun Gale: He made 218 appearances with Portsmouth, Barnet and Exeter City.

Leigh Cooper: Brother of Reading's Adrian, Leigh was a Plymouth Argyle stalwart, playing almost 400 games in total.

David Tuttle: After a great career with Reading Schools, David made over 200 appearances, the majority with Crystal Palace and Sheffield United.

Steve Wicks: Probably the best Reading-born player not to play for the Club, he had a long career in the top flight, mainly with Chelsea and QPR as well as caps at under-21 level.

Mark Harris: Mark is another 300-plus appearance player who is best remembered for his time at Swansea City.

Les Slatter: A right winger who travelled further than most to get away from his birthplace, he played for, among others, York City and made 104 appearances in total.

Chris Weller: Chris was pacey forward with over 100 appearances for Bournemouth.

Dennis Brown: He was a constant thorn in Reading's side in the 1960s, netting 104 goals for Swindon and Aldershot.

Shaun Brooks: Son of Reading great **Johnny Brooks**, Shaun made almost 400 appearances with several Clubs and then became an advisor for the film *Mike Bassett: England Manager*.

Martin Allen: The son of Reading legend **Denis Allen**, Martin made over 300 League appearances, mainly with QPR and West Ham United. He eventually returned to his home-town Club as Alan Pardew's assistant.

Manager – Freddy Cox: Admittedly Freddy did play eight wartime games for Reading, but that was as a guest from Tottenham. No player could have been more under Reading Football Club's nose since Freddy went to Battle School, which is situated at the end of Elm Park's Norfolk Road. He went on to manage several Clubs, all of which were particularly hard to beat, especially by Reading!

IN ATTENDANCE

Before Reading moved to Madejski Stadium in 1998 they had never enjoyed a season where every home attendance was in excess of 10,000. The closest they came was in 1950–51 when Elm Park's League average was 15,996, and the lowest gate of the season was 9,378 for the final game, an afternoon kick-off against Millwall. Even so, that compares favourably with the 1984–85 season, when the highest attendance at Elm Park was just 5,423.

On the other hand, 17 crowds at Elm Park have exceeded the Madejski Stadium record attendance of 24,135 that watched Reading's game against Manchester United on 19 January 2008. Of those, only three were for League games, while Manchester United, three times, and Arsenal, twice, are not surprisingly the most frequent big attractions. Rather less obvious was the visit of Doncaster Rovers, who attracted 25,050 on 7 January 1950 for a third-round FA Cup tie, and Wrexham's 26,303 on 9 January 1957, a replay for the right to face the Busby Babes. Both of those games ended in defeat for Reading, and of those 17 big gates only four saw Reading victories – so much for the famed 'Elm Park Roar'!

MY CUP OVERFLOWETH

Reading have set the ground records at several Clubs. Of the current 91 other League grounds the 19,072 at Colchester United's Layer Road on 27 November 1948 will remain a record now that they have moved to their new Weston Homes Community Stadium, even though the FA Cup tie only lasted 35 minutes before fog caused the game to be abandoned. Also in the FA Cup, Cheltenham Town's record attendance at their Whaddon Road ground was the 8,326 that saw Reading win 2–1 on 17 November 1956. Yet another FA Cup tie set the record at Merthyr's Penydarren Park when 19,000 witnessed another Reading victory back on 14 December 1946.

A LEAGUE OF THEIR OWN

Since joining the League in 1920 Reading have played 103 different Clubs, the most recent being Newcastle United. This figure is equal to the total achieved by Oxford United, even though they entered the League (and subsequently left) 40 years after Reading. Both Clubs are some way behind the 127 different Clubs that Grimsby Town have met. Of the other 91 Clubs in the League during 2007–08 Reading still have to meet Cheltenham Town, Morecambe, Yeovil and Dagenham & Redbridge, although only Morecambe have yet to be played in any of the three main tournaments.

FREQUENT FRIENDS

Of the 103 Clubs that Reading have played in the League, Bournemouth, in their different names, have been Reading's most frequent opponents, the two Clubs meeting exactly 100 times, with Reading winning 41 times to Bournemouth's 35. Exeter City have been beaten the most times in the League by Reading, losing 31 games in Reading and 16 times away, both records. Included in those wins are a Club best 13 doubles, compared to Exeter's solitary home and away victories in one season. Bristol City have achieved the most doubles over Reading, winning home and away in nine seasons, although Reading have repaid the compliment five times.

SICK TO THE GILLS

Reading's least 'popular' opponents are Gillingham, who have inflicted the most home defeats, 12, and the most away, 24, against the Club. To make matters worse, they beat Reading on the very first League game at Elm Park in 1920 and then repeated the 2–1 scoreline when the Club designated their visit in 1971 as their centenary game. This represents a complete change of fortune from the Southern League meetings between the two Clubs when Reading gained their most victories against one Club, 26 in 40 meetings. Perhaps their change of name from New Brompton to Gillingham towards the end of their Southern League career threw Reading off the scent.

WINNERS AND LOSERS Part 1

Reading have scored the most League goals against Northampton Town, 160 in 88 games, while Southend United are the most welcome visitors, having conceded a total of 102 goals in 44 games at Elm Park. Equally welcome are Mansfield Town, who have never won in 24 League visits to Reading. Other Clubs still looking for their first away League victories in Reading are Crewe Alexandra, in 16 attempts, Halifax Town and Cambridge United both in 10. Bradford Park Avenue have lost on all five visits to Elm Park, and of the 103 Clubs Reading have faced in the League, they have beaten all of them except Manchester United and Arsenal.

WINNERS AND LOSERS Part 2

Steve Death and **Martin Hicks** both played in 193 Reading League victories, more than any other Reading player. Hicks is Reading's record appearance holder with exactly 500 League games, and this results in him having suffered more defeats (167) and played in more draws (140), than any other player. Those games also saw a total of 661 goals conceded. Strangely, the man who recommended Hicks to Reading, **Dick Spiers**, himself a former appearance record holder and a centre half, appears to be Reading's most attack-minded player, his 451 League starts seeing 724 goals scored.

GOALS, GOALS, GOALS

Reading players have scored 30 or more goals in a season on 13 occasions, with **Trevor Senior, Ron Blackman** twice and **Jimmy Quinn** netting 40 goals or more. Of those four, Senior and Quinn finished top scorer in the League, while Blackman was top of the Third Division scorers in 1951–52. Strangely, only Trevor Senior, in 1983–84 and 1985–86, and Jimmy Quinn, in 1993–94, saw their goals rewarded with promotion. Even more unusually, **Kerry Dixon**'s 32 goals in 1982–83 and **Alf Bacon**'s 30 in 1930–31 were scored in relegated sides. In 2000–01 **Jamie Cureton** scored 30 goals, plus one for Bristol Rovers, but he was almost matched by **Martin Butler**, who netted 28 times. The best two-striker total, however, belongs to Jimmy Quinn and **Stuart Lovell**, who scored 62 between them in 1993–94. In the Southern League days, the goalscoring stakes are led by **Allen Foster**, who topped Reading's scorers in all four of his seasons, ending with a total of 67 goals in that league.

HAT-TRICK HEROES

Special mention should be made of **Tony MacPhee**, who, during the 42 games of the 1940–41 wartime season, scored 45 goals. Included in his total were a Club record five hat-tricks in the season, part of a total of 16 wartime and six League hat-tricks he scored for Reading. On purely League games, **Ron Blackman** netted a career total of 11 hat-tricks for Reading, four of which were scored in 1951–52, a season's total matched by **Jack Palethorpe** in 1932–33 and **Les Chappell** in 1973–74.

STREAKY BACON

As well as scoring 30 goals in the 1930–31 relegation season, **Alf Bacon** also set a Club record by scoring in eight consecutive games from 7 February to 3 April, when he ended his run in style with a Club record six goals against Stoke City, a feat that brought his total for the run up to 16. **Trevor Senior** also scored in eight consecutive appearances in 1984–85, although he missed 11 matches between the seventh and eighth games through injury. For a while it looked as if **Dean Horrix** would match Senior's effort as he also scored in the first five games of Senior's run. Trevor also holds the Club scoring records for the FA Cup, with 18 goals, and the League Cup with 14.

TOP SCORER?

On a goals-per-game ratio, **David Lee** is the only player to average one goal for every League appearance. Admittedly his top billing is due to the fact that he only played five games during a month's loan in 1992, although he still deserves his mention as all five games were played at centre half. More relevant were the records of two 1930s centre forwards, **Frank Newton**'s 31 goals in 34 League games giving him a ratio of .912 per game, while **Jack Palethorpe** weighed in with 54 in 64 games, .844 goals per game. None can compete with **Stan Clayton**'s Reading record, though. A solitary appearance in a Boxing Day 1942 War League South match at home to Aldershot saw the Notts County guest score twice to give him a two goals a game average!

PENALTY POINTS

Few of those top scorers had the advantage of being the Club's regular penalty taker so the record for spot kicks is held by **Ray 'Bomber' Reeves**, his nickname giving a clue to his style of power over placement. It clearly worked as 'Bomber' scorer 22 times from penalties, rarely missing during his career. Jack Lewis in 1951–52 and **Darren Caskey** in 1999–00 both converted nine spot kicks in a season. With **Martin Williams** also scoring one spot kick in that second season (his success being the first League penalty of the new millennium), 1999–2000 was Reading's most profitable season from 12 yards, along with 1981–82 when **Steve Hetzke** (four), and **Neil Webb** (six) also totalled 10 penalties.

THIRTEEN – FAMILY
FORTUNES

OH BROTHER

Until **Noel Hunt** joined brother **Stephen** in August 2008, only two brothers had played for Reading in the League, **Tony** and **Barrie Wagstaff**. Despite contrasting physiques and playing styles, the slightly built Tony was a skilful playmaker who was behind most of the goals in Reading's free-scoring 1969–70 season, while younger brother Barrie was a 6ft defender, the two had very similar playing careers. Spotted playing for the Don & Dearne Boys Club, they joined Sheffield United as apprentices, graduating to the Blades First Division team before joining Reading in July 1969 for a joint fee of £17,000. Between them, the two brothers played over 400 games for Reading but, surprisingly, the defensive Barrie scored 27 goals compared to his attack-minded brother's mere seven. They also wrote themselves into Reading's record books with their goals, Barrie becoming the Club's first scoring substitute when he netted at Bournemouth on 10 January 1970, while Tony netted Reading's first goal in the Fourth Division 18 months later at Hartlepool. The two finally went their separate ways when Tony left Elm Park for Cheltenham in 1974, Barrie staying for another year before joining Rotherham United.

Two sets of brothers played for Reading in their Southern League days, although only **Herbert** and **William Smith** played for the Club at the same time. Both **Harry Turner** and his brother, **Archie**, made just two appearances each for Reading, but they had longer careers with Southampton. In particular, Archie was the only Hampshire-born player in their 1900 FA Cup Final team, and later he became the county's first England international, winning two caps.

TWIN SET

In the mid-1960s Reading featured near-identical twins **Barry** and **Brian Rusher** in their youth and reserve teams, but neither made it to the first team. However, two twins were involved in one of the strangest sendings off at Elm Park. On 25 October 1986 Oldham's Ron Futcher lashed out at Reading captain **Martin Hicks**, breaking the defender's jaw. The attack was unprovoked but was behind the referee's back so it went unpunished, although Futcher later paid an out-of-court settlement to Hicks. Reading's next home game was against Barnsley and featured Ron's identical twin brother Paul. The Barnsley player was totally confused by the hostile reception he received from the Reading fans and, clearly rattled, he ended up swiping out at **Trevor Senior**, who collapsed right in front of the referee. The unfortunate Paul Futcher was promptly shown the red card that his twin had deserved two weeks earlier!

OTHER BROTHERS

⊛ Other famous brothers, half of whom played for Reading, include **Kevin Bremner**, who had the pleasure of outscoring his Scottish international brother Des when the two opposed each other as Reading and Birmingham City met at Elm Park on Boxing Day 1986. Another Reading brother to score against his international brother was **Denis Allen**, who scored against former Spurs star Les in the game against QPR on 13 May 1966. Denis and Les were members of the famous Allen family that includes cousins Bradley and the free-scoring Clive, while Denis's son Martin was **Alan Pardew**'s assistant manager at Madejski Stadium. One player who did not get one over on a relative was legendary Reading defender **Maurice Evans**. He was out injured when Reading travelled to The Dell on Easter Monday 1960 for their game against Southampton. The Saints needed to win to clinch promotion and they did that with the only goal of the game, a powerful header scored by Brian Clifton, Maurice's cousin.

⊛ Not related to Denis or Les, **Ralph Allen**, who scored seven goals in a remarkably short Reading career in 1936, as well as 32 in 28 games for Charlton Athletic, also had a famous brother. Ralph scored 115 goals in 172 League games, while his brother, Jack, scored 148 League goals as well as netting both of Newcastle United's goals in their 1932 FA Cup Final win over Arsenal.

⊛ Long-serving **Jimmy Wallbanks** spent 50 years at Elm Park as player, trainer and even caretaker manager in 1971 and was one of five footballing brothers who played professionally. Although John and Fred never made the League sides at Portsmouth and West Ham United respectively, Harold played for Fulham and Horace with Grimsby Town and Luton Town, as well as having a short spell at Elm Park on trial in January 1939.

⊛ **Charlie Keetley** was a free-scoring player who scored 115 goals in 191 League games, although only three of them were scored for Reading during the 1935–36 season. He was one of nine brothers, all of whom played professionally, with five of them sharing 514 League goals. Particularly prolific were Frank, who once hit six goals in 21 minutes for Lincoln City, and Tom who also scored six for Doncaster Rovers. All nine Keetley brothers were born in Derby or the surrounding area, and yet only Frank went on to play for County.

⊛ On 22 October 1988 subsequent Reading loanee **Ray Wallace** made his League debut for Southampton against Sheffield United. Already in the team were his twin Rod and brother Danny, making it the first time that three brothers had played together in the League.

⊛ If nine players in a family sounds like a lot, the Raisbecks can beat that. **Billy Raisbeck** played for Reading during their 1904–05 Southern League season, while his most famous family member was the Liverpool star Alex, who was described as the Reds' first world-class player. In Billy and Alex's contemporary pen pictures, the writers constantly made reference to the fact that the Raisbeck family could field a complete team. **E. Lloyd Davies**, another Southern League player at Elm Park, was one of six footballing brothers, four of whom received international honours for Wales, with 'E' going on to win 12 caps and, as such, he remains Northampton Town's most capped player.

☻ Versatile and stylish, mid-1990s Royals midfielder **Paul Holsgrove** helped create something of a unique family record with another Berkshire Club. The son of Wolves defender John Holsgrove, Paul played for Hayes, alongside his brothers Peter and Lee. The three Holsgroves then moved to Ryman's Premier League Club Windsor & Eton, and in January 2005 they each scored for the Royalists in a 3–3 draw with Heybridge Swifts.

FAMILY FAVOURITE

Another famous footballing family at Reading was the Edelstons. Father Joe was appointed the Club's manager in April 1939 and one of his first actions in charge at Elm Park was to sign his son, Maurice, as an amateur. There were never any accusations of nepotism in this deal as Maurice became one of Reading's greatest players. Maurice's elder brother, Joe Jr, played once for the Club during the war, while completing the family connection, Joe Snr's daughter, Kathleen, acted as Club secretary for a short period at the end of the war. Both Joe and Maurice set unusual records during their playing careers. Joe was the only player to be transferred while sailing on the high seas, and Maurice's record is equally obscure; although he signed for Reading in 1939, the war meant that he had to wait seven years to make his League debut, but he made up for lost time, scoring hat-tricks in his first two League games against Crystal Palace and Southend United to become the only amateur to score consecutive League hat-tricks.

THE PERFECT PEDIGREE

However, even the Edelstons cannot compete with the pedigree of former Reading Academy scholar **Josh Webb**, now with Blue Square Premier League Club Weymouth. He is the son of **Neil Webb**, who, after making his name with Reading, went on to find fame with Nottingham Forest, Manchester United and 26 times for England, is rightly regarded as the greatest player ever born in Reading. Josh's mother is Shelly Alexander, a former presenter of the BBC2 football magazine show *Standing Room Only* and currently on the *Football Focus* production team. If that was not enough, both of Josh's grandfathers played for Reading, **Tony Alexander** making 11 appearances for Reading in the mid-1950s, while **Douggie Webb** remains one of the Club's most popular players as a free-scoring forward who holds the Club record for most goals for the reserves. But to complete the set, Josh's paternal grandmother, Joan Webb, was office manager at Elm Park during the 1970s and was often the first voice heard when phoning Elm Park during that time.

RELATIVELY SPEAKING

⊛ Another father and son duo to play for Reading were **Joe Bacuzzi** and his son **David**. Dave played 118 classy games for Reading, having signed from Manchester City in 1966, while Joe, also a right back, played two games as a wartime guest. The war was a busy time for Joe as he played 13 times for England and, in the first of those games, against Wales on 11 November 1939, he sustained an injury and was replaced by Jim Lewis, thus becoming the first England player to be substituted.

⊛ **Jimmy Mullen** also played for England, the spectacular Wolves winger making 12 full and three wartime appearances for his country as well as two for Reading as a guest. Twenty-five years later, Jimmy's namesake and nephew also played on Reading's wing, having progressed through the youth system, and had played eight League games before being sold to Rotherham United where he enjoyed a lengthy career.

⊛ As well as a short spell at Elm Park in 1991, **David Byrne** played for 23 different Clubs in three different countries. Included in that total, David played for 10 different London sides, the last of which was a four-game spell with Tottenham Hotspur. Those games were played in the Inter Toto Cup when David was asked to help out the Club by his brother-in-law, Spurs manager **Gerry Francis**.

⊛ **Billy Wright**, who played in five different positions for Reading in the 1930s, was no relation to his famous Wolves and England namesake, but he did have a famous father, who was particularly famous in Bolton. Not only did **Jockie Wright** play in the very first game at Burnden Park, he also had the honour of scoring the first FA Cup goal at Bolton's old ground.

⊛ A father with a famous son was Blackburn Rovers' **Harry McShane**, who played for Reading as a wartime guest in 1942–43. After he retired as a player, Harry stayed in the game as a highly respected scout for Manchester United, and among the players he discovered were Andy Ritchie and Nicky Butt. One player he never discovered was his son, Ian McShane, who found fame as TV's *Lovejoy* and more recently in *Deadwood*. Ian did manage to combine his two passions when he played an ageing football star in the 1979 film *Yesterday's Hero*.

In fact, so many Reading players have footballing fathers, with **Liam Rosenior,** son of Leroy, currently representing them, that a good team could be formed from the talented offspring:

Borislav Mihailov: Like his father Biser, 'Bobby' played in goal for Levski Sofia before his injury-plagued 18 months at Elm Park.

Ken Brown: Son of the West Ham United player of the same name, Ken had spells at both Norwich City and Plymouth Argyle while his father was managing the Clubs. Young Ken had two spells with Reading in 1995 and 1996, his second loan period making Reading the fourth Club he had played for at Elm Park in the previous six months, having already played against Reading for Southend United, Crystal Palace and West Ham United.

Neil Clement: Another loan player with Reading (in 1998), Neil was a gifted left-sided player who was the son of QPR and England defender Dave Clement.

Billy Wright: Billy could fill almost any position in this imaginary team, while his father, Jockie, was a goalscorer with Bolton in the 1890s.

Chris Casper: A member of the Manchester United youth team that included David Beckham and Gary Neville, Chris's father was a vital member of the highly successful Burnley side of the early 1960s.

George McLuckie: Another son of an international, Jimmy McLuckie having played once for Scotland, he ended his career at Ipswich, the Club from which Reading signed son George in 1958. In addition, Jimmy was Ipswich's first professional captain.

Stuart Beavon: A consistent and inventive midfielder for Reading throughout the 1980s, Stuart has far happier memories of Elm Park than his father Cyril, whose playing career was ended by an injury sustained in a game there while playing in the local derby for Oxford United.

Trevor Morley: A vastly experienced forward, Trevor ended his League career with Reading in 1998, his father Bill having enjoyed 12 seasons with Nottingham Forest.

David Head: Unlike Morley, David Head had a short League career, playing just 12 times for Reading in 1960 after he had been signed from Swindon Town who were managed by his father Bert. On leaving Reading, David followed his father's footsteps by becoming manager at Trowbridge Town at the age of just 23.

Wayne Wanklin: The only member of the team whose father did not play professional football, 1970s midfielder Wayne's father played in other games, being capped for Wales at Rugby Union and then playing for Hull's Rugby League side. Wayne was born while his father was with Hull and, as a Reading player, he scored the first goal of his League career in the town of his birth.

On the other hand, Reading players have fathered some fine players, so the following team could play under the name of Dads' Army:

Mike Walker: On Reading's books but never making the League side, Mike subsequently enjoyed almost 40 years in the game as a player and manager. His son, Ian, followed in his father's footsteps, making over 400 League appearances, mainly for Spurs and Leicester City. Also like his father, Ian was a full international although, unusually, while his father was capped for Wales, Ian played for England.

Joe Bacuzzi: A World War Two guest for Reading, Joe's son **David** was also a full back who played for Reading in the 1960s after spells with Arsenal and Manchester City.

Harry McShane: Harry made just one appearance as a wartime guest for Reading, having been a player with Blackburn Rovers. His football-mad son Ian never made a senior appearance for any Club, instead concentrating on an acting career in films and on television.

Johnny Petts: A big money signing from Arsenal, Johnny never really commanded a regular first team place. John moved on to Bristol Rovers, where his son Paul began his League career.

Dave Shipperley: At one point Dave was Reading's record signing, having cost £50,000 in 1979. His son, Neil, was often rumoured to be a Reading transfer target, but unlike his centre half father Neil was a striker with 120 goals to his credit in a widely travelled 15-year career.

Charlie Barley: A classy player in the 1930s, Charlie made 214 first team appearances for Reading, and like his son Derek he was previously on Arsenal's books. Derek never really made it in the League, but he did have the honour of captaining England Youth in 1949.

Wally Hinshelwood: He is the only Reading dad to produce two League footballers, sons Martin and Paul. Both played the bulk of their careers with Crystal Palace, about the only London Club their father never played for. Martin later managed Brighton, but Paul's managerial career was doomed once his nickname 'Doris' became public knowledge!

Johnny Brooks: Both father and son, Shaun, were born in Reading, with Johnny becoming the first town-born player to be capped by England. Although Shaun's career did not reach the same heights he was highly regarded at all his Clubs. As with the Petts, Shaun began his career with his father's final League team, Crystal Palace.

Denis Allen: Son Martin probably had a more illustrious career than dad Denis, playing for West Ham United in the top flight and being capped for England at under-21 level. Although he never played for Reading he had a spell as assistant manager to **Alan Pardew**.

Douggie Webb: If Johnny Brooks was one of the town of Reading's two greatest players, then Douggie Webb was the father of the other, **Neil Webb**. Douggie was a very popular player and played a major role in the development of his son to full international level.

Stuart Beavon: The only member of the 'team' to share his name with his son, Stuart Snr was a skilful midfielder, whereas his son is one of the most consistent goalscorers in non-League football. Young Stuart made his name with Didcot and was, for a time, linked with being given a chance at Reading. Like his father he scored in a Cup final, netting twice in Didcot's 2005 FA Vase Final victory.

ROYAL FAMILIES

During the summer of 2006 a new acronym came into popular use, with WAGs being used to describe the Wives And Girlfriends of England's World Cup squad in Germany. The exploits of those WAGs were hardly a credit to the squad as the partners appeared to spend most of their time shopping and partying. Back in Reading, the wives and girlfriends of the players of Reading Football Club had different plans to exploit the new-found fame of their Premiership husbands.

Organised by Amanda Hahnemann and Karen Murty, the wives of Reading's goalkeeper and captain, but involving most of their playing partners, the group formed Royal Families to raise funds for local women's charities. Setting themselves a target of £60,000, events were staged in an effort to reach this figure, including a fashion show, a race night, a dance and, bizarrely, a barbeque on New Year's Day. Not surprisingly, the players backed their partners fully, acting as models for the fashion show and offering themselves for auction as dance partners. This brought out the natural competitive nature of footballers as they strived to achieve the highest bid, a competition that came to a swift conclusion when Ibrahima 'Superman' Sonko stripped to the waist and his impressive physique immediately prompted a £700 bid!

Another player raised even more for the charity. Local firm Sarha Shoes agreed to sponsor young Irish striker **Shane Long** to the tune of £250 for each goal he scored for Reading's reserves, and £1,000 for a hat-trick. Shane really did his bit, finishing top scorer in the Premier Reserve League with 14 goals as Reading won the title at the first attempt.

All these efforts combined to shatter their £60,000 target as they ended the season having raised over £100,000 and were rewarded by a visit from another of Berkshire's royal families when Sophie, Countess of Wessex, visited Madejski Stadium to congratulate the players' partners on their efforts.

FOURTEEN – ASSORTED BISCUITS AND ROYAL REGALIA

THANKS, ADOLF

Reading have Adolf Hitler to thank for the signing of their legendary footballing policeman **Bill Amor**. On the day he was to have a trial for Plymouth Argyle, Bill was called up by the Royal Marines. He served throughout the war, and after he was discharged he joined the police and was transferred to Reading. It did not take the local Club long to spot the pacey winger and he was soon in Reading's first team.

MIST SIGNING

Similarly, Reading can thank the weather for setting in motion another transfer. Inside forward **Cyril Dean** was a member of the Aston Villa team travelling to Aldershot when their journey was delayed in Reading due to thick fog. One of Villa's directors took the opportunity to meet up with an old friend, Reading director T.W. Stone, and during their conversation Cyril's name came up as a potential signing. Reading manager **Billy Butler** followed up this tip once the visibility had cleared, and a couple of months later, in January 1937, Cyril became a Reading player.

ROYAL SUPPORTER

Fifty years before Reading changed their nickname to the Royals, they almost had a genuine royal supporter. Travelling back from an away game at Northampton, the players discovered that they were sharing the train with the Prince of Wales, later to become King Edward VII. With his benefit game coming up shortly, centre forward **Joe Bailey** plucked up the courage to approach the royal party and sold the prince a ticket for the game, although it does not appear that he went to the match. Another royal patron of the Royals was Major Ronald Ferguson, father of Sarah, the (then) Duchess of York, who bought an Elm Park season ticket in 1996 for one of his grandsons.

ON THE SPOT Part One

Stuart Beavon was one of Reading's regular penalty takers during the 1980s and his total of 15 successful spot kicks is only exceeded by Ray Reeves. His most important kick was in the 1988 Simod Cup Final at Wembley when he scored to put Reading into the lead against Luton Town, but that was not Stuart's only success at the national stadium. During 1974, ITV held a competition for young penalty takers, with the winners taking part in a shootout before the League Cup Final. Stuart made it through to the final where he scored an impressive five out of six against Gordon Banks.

ON THE SPOT Part Two

Injury curtailed **Derick Williams**'s Reading career, forcing him to retire at the age of only 21. However, he had still enjoyed at least one moment of glory. Playing for England under-18s in a 1983 international tournament held in Yugoslavia, Derick helped his country reach the final to face the home nation. With the scores still level after extra time, the resulting shoot-out reached 10–10. Derick then saved the Yugoslavian keeper's spot kick before successfully converting his penalty to win the tournament for England.

UNDER THE HAMMER

After Reading moved to Madejski Stadium in 1998 an auction of Elm Park's fixtures and fittings was held prior to the old ground's demolition. As well as professional bidders, over 400 fans put in offers for a lasting memory of what, for many, was their spiritual home. A wide range of items were snapped up, and while the turnstiles went to a variety of sporting venues at least one ended up in the living room of a former Supporters' Club Chairman, who converted it into a bar. The floodlights went to Basingstoke Town, the directors' box to St Albans City and the dugouts stayed locally with Reading Cricket and Hockey Club. There was even a buyer for the clock that had been positioned on the roof of the South Bank terracing, even though someone had stolen the hands before the auction. However, there was no joy for 70 per cent of fans who took part in a pre-auction survey regarding the most sought after item from Elm Park. The most unlikely poll winner was a sign from the Southbank toilets, known affectionately as 'The Black Hole of Calcutta', that read 'The Toilets Have Been Renovated For Your Comfort', but unfortunately it did not survive the fans' pillaging that took place after the final League game at Elm Park.

ALL SIGNED UP

Builders working on Reading public house the Eldon Arms made a strange discovery: a contract between Reading Football Club and **Arthur Hadley**. Dating from 11 September 1896, the 100-year-old document revealed the simplicity of such arrangements in those days. Containing just four clauses, it stated:

- Arthur would be paid 15/- (75p) a week up to 30 April 1897. As a result he would not be paid during the closed season.
- He was instructed 'to devote yourself to football only.'
- To play only for Reading Football Club.
- And to 'obey the executive committee', a reference to the fact that although the Club had turned professional, it was not to be a limited company with directors until another year.

All of this proved satisfactory to Arthur because he stayed at Elm Park for three years, quite a long time in those days, scoring seven Southern League goals in 33 appearances.

ANCIENT STRIP

Another Arthur also left a legacy. A defender for Reading between 1907 and 1909, **Arthur Hallworth** stayed in the area after his playing days were over and lived the rest of his life at Hare Hatch, a village between Reading and Maidenhead. When he died in August 1977, aged 95, a perfect set of Reading Football Club's playing kit was found in his possessions. The kit had been taken home because in those days players were responsible for washing their own strip.

ONE WIN

On 19 August 1970, Third Division Reading travelled to Newport County's Somerton Park for a League Cup tie and suffered a shock 2–1 defeat at the hands of the Fourth Division Club. As the season progressed the size of the shock grew as County failed to beat any of their Fourth Division rivals. It was not until the following January that they finally secured a second victory, having drawn four and lost 23 games during that period.

MEMORABLE WIN

By way of contrast, Reading's victory over Liverpool on 8 December 2007 was a notable event in many ways. Not only was it the Club's first win over a 'Big Four' Club, but the visitors were the most expensive side that Reading had ever beaten. The Reds starting XI was conservatively valued at £50 million, with another £20 million on the bench, while Reading's starting line up cost under £3 million. More remarkably, that Reading starting XI consisted entirely of players who had graduated from the Club's Championship side of 2005–06. Not only was the game Liverpool's first defeat of the season, but their two previous away defeats had been against Besiktas and AC Milan in the European Champions League. In addition, it was the first time they had conceded more than two goals in a League game for over a year, the first time that their record signing, £26 million Fernando Torres, had started and lost and the first time since October 2005 that Steven Gerrard had scored and finished up on the losing side.

WEAKENED SIDE?

Liverpool boss Rafa Benitez is one of many Premier League managers who rotates his squad, yet Reading boss **Steve Coppell** came in for some unwarranted criticism from the national press for his decision to field a 'Cup' team for knockout competitions. The Reading boss was criticised for his team selection against Spurs in the third round of the 2007–08 FA Cup, but the facts put a different complexion on the dispute. Although the team that faced Spurs at White Hart Lane admittedly contained 'only' six full internationals compared to the seven for the previous week's League encounter, the 'Cup' side boasted 169 caps, 50 per cent more than the League side.

In addition, the 'Cup' side was the most expensive ever fielded by Reading, costing over £8 million, double that of the 'stronger' side. More importantly, the 'weaker' team secured a well-deserved draw whereas the 'strong' team suffered defeat at the hands of Spurs' basically unchanged side. The press have also chosen to ignore the fact that in the two years since Reading had joined the Premier League only two of the top-flight Clubs have not been knocked out of one of the Cup competitions by a team lower than them in the League, one was Spurs, the other Reading.

SAME SIDE

On the other hand, Reading were unchanged for the first 12 games of their 1929–30 season. Manager **Andrew Wylie** named the same side week in, week out, although, in reality, it was actually selected by the board of directors. The fixed first team was: **Lance Richardson, Percy Thorpe, Bill Pickering, Syd Chandler, Alf Messer, Charlie Barley, Harry Goodwin, Frank Kennedy, George James, Johnny Hunter** and **Bob Oswald**. Surprisingly, the team remained unchanged despite the fact that they failed to win any of their last seven games in that run.

PRESS GANG

The local press have occasionally been in trouble with Reading Football Club. In December 1932 the Club complained that goalkeeper **Richard Mellors** had 'suffered from unjustifiable and unkind press criticism from the *Reading Standard*.' The Club appeared to have a case seeing that the keeper had kept a clean sheet during the game in question. A year earlier, comments made about Reading forward **Frank Eaton** led to legal action, although this was withdrawn when an apology was issued. Unfortunately, these disputes led to the Club banning the editor of the *Sports' Chronicle*, Mr H.H. Sirrett, from the ground, even though he had been responsible for the formation of the Supporters' Club. A stranger ban occurred in the late 1920s when press photographers were not allowed in on match days, the directors fearing that action pictures in the newspapers would lead to reduced attendances. Another local reporter to feel the wrath of the Reading board was the *Evening Post*'s Clive 'the Hound' Baskerville who was temporarily banned from Elm Park at the start of the 1997–98 for reporting derogatory comments made by former Reading manager **Jimmy Quinn**.

On the other hand, the *Reading Standard* headed a campaign to raise funds for the hard-up Club in 1924. Their campaign was led by the following statement in praise of the sport:

'There is no fun to compare with a good game of football. No amusement known provides the thrills, excitement and often hearty laughter that football yields. Win or lose, this applies. Football is the cheapest fun the worker gets.'

GIANT-KILLERS AT LAST

Despite their successes under **Steve Coppell**, Reading do not have a great record in the FA Cup. With just one semi-final appearance to date, the Club had good reason to celebrate their 2–1 victory over Gillingham on 28 November 1978. With the Gills one division higher than Fourth Division Reading, that first-round win was the first time that they had beaten a Club from a higher division since they overcame eventual League champions Sheffield Wednesday back on 26 January 1929, a run of almost 50 years.

OFF PAT

Signed by Reading from Southampton, **Pat Earles** scored the very first goal in the long-defunct Tennants Caledonian Cup when the Saints played Manchester City. The game went to a penalty shoot-out that must be unique as all 22 players, including Pat, were successful with their kicks. With the score at 11–11 the game was decided in the Saints' favour by the toss of a coin. Pat has an unusual place in Reading's history: despite being a religious man and a model professional he was still selected as the first Reading player to undergo a random drugs test back in 1979.

STING IN THE TAIL

The end of that Caledonian Cup game was almost as eventful as the FA Cup tie that took place at Elm Park on 21 December 1970. For 87 uneventful minutes Reading and Shrewsbury Town rarely raised an exciting moment between them, then **Dick Habbin** opened the scoring to give Reading the lead. This was too much for one Shrewsbury player and, almost immediately, Roberts was sent off. Undeterred, Shrewsbury pressed for an equaliser and Harkin hit the bar when he should have scored. Berated by teammate Woods for his miss, the two exchanged words, and then punches, in the Reading penalty area. All was resolved, and seconds later Harkin did get the ball into Reading's net, only for it to be disallowed for offside. A goal, a sending off, the woodwork struck, a fight and a disallowed goal, all in three mad minutes.

SHORT STAYS

One of the shortest careers in football history is credited to **Mark Bowen**. The former Welsh international joined Reading on trial on 7 December 1999, his 36th birthday, and made his debut the following day in the Club's victory over Leyton Orient in the Auto Windscreens Shield. Despite this, Mark was unable to agree terms with Reading and left the Club the following day.

However, Mark is a Reading stalwart compared with **Eric Nixon**. A goalkeeping injury crisis in early 1996 led Reading to take Eric Nixon on loan from Tranmere Rovers. It was poetic justice that Reading gave the experienced keeper his return to first team football since his last game for Tranmere had been in the play-off semi-final defeat 18 months earlier against Reading. Eric completed the appropriate documentation just a minute before the 6pm deadline on 9 January, playing just one game for the Club in the tie at Leeds United later that evening. After the final whistle, Eric showered and changed, said his goodbyes and his Reading career was over after just four hours!

CONSTANT KEEPERS

During that 1995–96 season Reading suffered a seemingly endless goalkeeping injury crisis that saw seven different keepers used. Regular keepers **Bobby Mihailov**, **Simon Sheppard** and **Nicky Hammond** were all injured (Hammond with chicken pox!) during the season, occasionally at the same time, resulting in the Club loaning former England keeper **Chris Woods** and **Steve Sutton**, as well as **Eric Nixon**. Player-manager and striker **Jimmy Quinn** also played a half in goal after Sheppard broke his arm against West Bromwich Albion, and he was the only one of the seven not to concede a goal that season.

ALL RIGHT

However, that variety of goalkeepers was nothing compared to the changes **Steve Coppell** was forced to make to the right side of his midfield during the 2007–08 season. With long-term injuries to the Club's two regular 'number sevens' **Glen Little** and **John Oster**, Reading tried a wide variety of players to fill the problem position. Initial incumbent **Seol Ki-Hyeon** was exchanged for Fulham's **Liam Rosenior**, and although the new man was usually a right back he was used in the more forward position for a while. Left wingers **Stephen Hunt** and **Bobby Convey** were tried on the opposite flank, as were strikers **Kevin Doyle**, **Shane Long**, **Dave Kitson** and **Simon Cox**. Midfielders **Emerse Faé**, **John Halls**, **Brynjar Gunnarsson** and **Marek Matejovsky** all had a spell on the right wing, while youngsters **James Henry** and **Jimmy Kebe** both found themselves on the flank before **Glen Little** ended his 12-month injury nightmare. That is a total of 16, and it could even be 17 because, in an attempt to force a late equaliser at Everton, goalkeeper **Marcus Hahnemann** joined the forwards for an injury-time attack and found himself out on the right wing for a brief moment!

SHATTERING SHOTS

Powerhouse forward **Percy Freeman** possessed one of the most awesome shots of any Reading player, although it was not always as accurate as Reading fans would have wished. One blockbuster ruptured the spleen of an unfortunate Chester City defender, another put the Club's electronic scoreboard out of action, while one wayward effort soared completely out of Elm Park and brought down a line of washing in a nearby garden. **Frank McPherson** was another hard-shooting Reading forward who caused damage to the area surrounding Elm Park in the early 1930s. One of his wayward shots flew out of the ground, smashed through a window of a house behind the Town End goal and damaged a gas fitting on the opposite wall. Another damaging shot came from York City's Charlie Twissell. During a drab game at Elm Park on 24 October 1959, in which the main feature was the wayward shooting of both sets of forwards, the visitors' centre forward 'excelled' all others by shooting so high over the Reading bar that his shot smashed a floodlight, sending a shower of glass down on an unfortunate policeman sitting below the light.

Even more embarrassing was the fate that befell one anonymous player in 1936. Reading's innovative young manager, **Billy Butler**, was one of the first to realise the benefits of using players to enhance the community spirit in the town and would visit a variety of Clubs and societies with his players. On one such occasion, in February 1937, he took a few first team players to visit the South Oxfordshire Church Lads Brigade to give a demonstration of their training methods and ball skills. This good idea backfired when one of the Reading stars miscontrolled the ball, sending it crashing through a window.

MAURICE MISSES MATT

Maurice Evans was one of the greatest talent spotters when it came to goalscorers. The man who brought **Kerry Dixon** and **Trevor Senior** from obscurity to become Elm Park legends later discovered John Aldridge and Dean Saunders while in charge at Oxford United. But he did miss out on one star. He passed on a youngster who played a trial game and had the misfortune to be part of a United team played off the pitch by a rampant Reading youth side, who ended up comfortable 4–2 winners. Unfortunately for Maurice and Oxford, the outplayed young forward was Matthew Le Tissier!

WAR BREAK

There are many stories regarding unofficial Christmas truces during World War One when British and German troops met up in no man's land. Former Reading player **Herbert Smart** wrote of the first Christmas of the war while he was serving in France with the Royal Field Artillery, telling how the German troops had a Christmas tree decorated with Chinese lanterns. During the truce he met up with a German soldier who had been a waiter in London and exchanged cigarettes and cigars. Herbert was not fooled by the friendly nature of the opposing forces, writing home to say 'Fancy a German shaking your flapper as though he was trying to smash your fingers, and then a few days later trying to plug you! I hardly know what to think but I fancy they are working up a big scheme. But our chaps are prepared.'

CHEAP TICKETS

Over 90 years later, and with British soldiers facing similar threats in Iraq and Afghanistan, Reading Football Club announced that they would offer reduced admission to their Premier League home games to troops who had served in those conflicts, but this was not a new decision. During World War Two Reading had allowed any member of the armed forces in uniform half-price admission to Elm Park. Even then, this was not the first time the Club had attempted to be benevolent. During the Depression of the 1930s Reading wanted to allow the unemployed half-price admission, but the Football League refused to sanction the Club's generosity. Despite this setback the Football Club, in conjunction with the fledgling Supporters' Club, arranged for Depression-hit supporters to gain admission to Elm Park by 'payment' of 20 Summit cigarette coupons.

GETTING SHIRTY

That was not the only time that an innocent Reading act caused the Football League to take exception. In 1984 the local Reading radio station, *Radio 210*, agreed to sponsor the Club's shirts, but the Football League objected on the grounds that the only numbers allowed on shirts were players' numbers. Surprisingly, even in these days of large squads, no one has yet to claim a number as high as 210 (although future Royal **Les Ferdinand** asked if he could wear 99 at Newcastle when he discovered that Alan Shearer had already commandeered the number-nine shirt!).

ONE-MAN SHOW

'Sir Les' may have been purely a number nine, albeit a very good one, but for total versatility Southern League star **Fred Milnes** takes some beating. An amateur throughout his long playing career, Fred played for a number of professional Clubs, including, in 1906–07, Reading. However, he was always sure of a game with the Pilgrims, mainly because he was the founder, manager, secretary and captain of the Club! A select amateur Club, Fred arranged two groundbreaking Pilgrims tours of North America either side of his time at Reading. The first in 1905 nearly led to soccer ousting American football as the major sport in the States. Concerned at the growing number of deaths and serious injuries being sustained by 'gridiron' players, Fred was asked to meet President Theodore Roosevelt, who was conducting a campaign against 'gridiron', and he hoped that the Pilgrims' tour would help promote soccer as an alternative. Despite some early successes, a game in St Louis attracting 28,000 fans and another being the first football match to be played under lights in the US, soccer is now reliant on David Beckham as its latest crusader.

GREAT GARY

If there was an award for Reading's most successful player it would surely go to **Gary Peters**. Signed by Reading in 1975, in his first season Gary played a major role in Reading's first promotion in 50 years, and three years later he missed just one game as Reading won the Fourth Division title in some style. He moved away from Reading in 1979 but his success continued, winning promotion with Fulham and then Wimbledon, winning consecutive promotions in his two seasons with the latter, before returning to Elm Park 10 years after he first joined. Expecting to play a fringe role, Gary was soon back in the first team and was a regular in the squad that returned Reading to the Second Division after a 60-year wait. Gary finally left Reading in 1988, having played in the Simod Cup-winning team of that year. Now a successful manager, Gary guided Preston to promotion in 1995–96 and took unfancied Shrewsbury Town to the play-off finals in 2006–07.

PENALTY POINTS

The only Club that Gary failed to win promotion with as a player was Aldershot, but at least he faired better than another player with Reading's historic local rivals.

In August 1974 former Reading forward **John Sainty** moved from Bournemouth to Aldershot, but after his League debut for the Shots it was discovered that the documentation had not been properly registered and so they were penalised with a point deduction. That lost point almost proved disastrous as Aldershot toyed with relegation all season, eventually staying up only by goal difference. Another Reading connection with a points deduction concerned the Club's 1930s manager **Joe Smith**. As captain and top scorer of three-times FA Cup winners Bolton Wanderers, Joe Smith was one of the most famous players in the country, so it was big news when he moved to Stockport County in March 1927. His first appearance attracted a crowd of over 22,500 to Edgely Park for his debut against Stoke City. Just before kick-off the Club received a telegram from the Football League stating 'Don't play Smith. Registration not in order', and that Joe's transfer had not been completed in time for him to play. Stockport's Chairman, Ernest Barlow, decided to ignore the warning, putting the telegram in his pocket, preferring to play Joe and face the wrath of the Football League rather than disappoint their biggest crowd for years. He was rewarded with a £200 fine and a two-point deduction, the latter penalty being particularly galling as County only drew the game.

TALES OF THE ORIENT

Reading's favourite opponents, certainly during World War Two, were Clapton Orient. During the hostilities, Orient were one of the weaker sides and consequently were on the wrong end of some big defeats. Reading put nine past them on one occasion, two eights, a six and a five, while Reading's centre forward **Tony MacPhee** took full advantage, netting 17 goals against them during that period. That 9–0 Reading win, on 29 March 1941, was obviously a disappointment for the visitors but also for Reading because they were six up after only 20 minutes. Orient must have been even more disappointed after the match at Elm Park on 30 October 1943 because they were 2–0 up after 20 minutes, only to end up losing 8–2. Travelling from East London during wartime restrictions was clearly a problem, and on another occasion they only had one player present at Elm Park by kick-off time but still managed to make a team up in time to suffer another defeat. Three years later they were forced to borrow two Reading players, but near the end of the war they did notch up a rare win over Reading, beating their visitors 2–1 thanks in part to the fact that Reading had three goals disallowed. Once the League restarted in 1946 Orient tried to confuse Reading by changing their name to Leyton Orient, but it did not work as the O's took eight games before they secured a win over Reading under their new name.

LONG WAIT

When Reading played Chelsea at Madejski Stadium on 14 October 2006, it was the first time the two Clubs had met in the League for over 76 years, the longest gap between any of Reading's 103 opponents. Until their elevation to the Premier

League in 2006, Reading had also gone 75 years since they met Tottenham Hotspur and Everton in the League, that gap being the longest Everton had experienced against any League Club.

HAPPY CAMPER

The prize for the most determined Reading player must go to **Bryan Carnaby**. On returning from a spell in South Africa in 1971, Bryan wrote to all 92 League Clubs for a trial but only four replied. One was Reading, and although he was offered a trial he probably did not realise that it would stretch over eight months and that he would have to impress three different managers during that period. In the end Charlie Hurley decided that the dynamic midfielder was worth a permanent contract. His faith was immediately repaid when Bryan scored within 12 minutes of his League debut and then subsequently scored one of the goals that clinched promotion for Reading on 21 April 1976. After his playing career was over Bryan trained as a physiotherapist and returned to Elm Park in that role in 1980–81. As his previous employment had been at a holiday camp, Bryan is probably the only person to be signed by a League Club from Butlins!

THWARTED BY THROW

From as early as 1907 Reading had campaigned for a change in the laws of the game regarding a foul throw. The Club maintained that penalising an illegal throw with a free kick was disproportionate punishment and that the free kick should be replaced with a throw-in to the opposing side. It seems a small point, but on 13 December 1924 it proved an important one. Playing a fifth qualifying round game against Darlington at Elm Park, Reading's **Dai Evans** took a foul throw. The resulting free kick was caught by the swirling wind and the flight of the ball deceived Reading keeper **Joe Duckworth**, ending up in the back of the net for what proved to be the only goal of the game. Knocked out of the FA Cup by the very punishment they had campaigned against, further salt was rubbed into Reading's wound when the following summer it was agreed that a foul throw should, as suggested by Reading, only be punished by a throw to the opposition.

THE MISSING INTERNATIONAL

According to the record books, Reading have supplied England with three international defenders, **Johnny Holt** and **Herbert Smith** at the start of the 20th century and **Nicky Shorey** 100 years later. But Reading fans believe that the total should be four. On 6 March 1875 **Edgar Brownlow Haygarth** played at right back for England against Scotland at The Oval and gave what was described as a hardworking display on a muddy pitch. Despite this, 'EB' was not selected again for England. Haygarth was, and still is, described as being a Swifts player but that must be a matter of some dispute. In those early days players were not tied to one Club and the best players, of whom Haygarth certainly was one, would play for whichever team had the most attractive fixture on any particular weekend. He certainly played for the Swifts at the start of 1875 but subsequently appeared for Reading, including a game against Southall the Saturday before the international, and one contemporary report referred to him as 'the Reading captain.' One reason for this perceived slight against Reading might be that, at that time, Reading were not members of the FA whereas Swifts were. Even if Haygarth is not currently recognised as the Club's first international, he still has an unparalleled position in Reading's history. Not only did he play in the Club's very first game, back in 1872, but later in that year, on 20 November, he had the honour of netting Reading's very first goal, against Windsor Home Park (at least he would have 'netted' if goalnets had been in use in those days!).

Haygarth was not the only England international with disputed 'heritage'. Arthur Reed's playing career was ended by a knee injury suffered during only his third game for Reading in 1922, but he had already caused some controversy over his selection for England a year earlier. Selected while still an amateur with Tufnell Park, he was transferred to Queen's Park Rangers before the game against Belgium, causing no end of confusion in various record books.

SIGN OF THE TIMES

Edgar Brownlow has another claim to fame in that he was a member of Berkshire's first team, at a time when such representative games were regarded as very important fixtures. He was the only Reading player in the side that faced Buckinghamshire on 23 January 1873, whereas Maidenhead supplied three players and Windsor five, giving an indication of the comparative strengths of local Clubs back then.

Another indication of the changing fortunes of Clubs over the years arises from the formation of the Southern League. When the initial vote was taken, the still amateur Reading Club received a sizeable 22 votes but lower than Chatham and Luton with 26. Millwall, a driving force behind the new league, obtained 25 votes, while it is doubtful which of the other two Clubs receiving 24 votes would cause modern Reading fans more anguish – Marlow or Swindon Town! Behind Reading in the votes tally was Woolwich Arsenal with 19, while failing to be elected into the new league with just one vote was Tottenham Hotspur, who, nine years later, won the FA Cup.

DOUBLE DEATHS

Two Reading players have the probably unwanted distinction as having died twice. **Harry Kinsell** was shown as having died in 1990 but that was definitely not the case as the 1950s Reading full back survived until August 2000 when he finally passed away, aged 79. Reading winger **Freddy Briggs**, who played at Elm Park as far back as 1938, was recorded by the usually reliable *Association of Football Statisticians* as having died in 1985. Far from being upset by his alleged demise, the sprightly Briggs took great pleasure in showing friends the news of his passing, right up to his actual death at the good age of 91, 14 years after it was first reported.

TAKING THE MICK

Other unwanted distinctions involve disciplinary records. **Mick Tait**, the 1980s Reading hard man, was the first player to have been sent off with four different League Clubs, having been dismissed at Oxford United, Hull City, Portsmouth and Reading. His dismissal while with Oxford also set a then record when, early in his career, he was one of three United players to be sent off against Plymouth. In total 'Iron Mike' was dismissed nine times in the League, a total 'bettered' by only two other players. Despite the many suspensions that Mick served he carried on playing until he was over 40, and with 760 League appearances to his credit he is 11th in the League's all-time appearance table.

THAT'S ANDY

Mick's nine dismissals are almost matched by tough but usually fair Australian defender **Andy Bernal**, who saw red eight times as a Reading player in the 1990s. In his defence, Andy's physical strength often worked against him, resulting in dismissals for challenges on players not as strong as the Aussie. Also, one of his reds was later rescinded, leaving him with 'only' seven Reading dismissals.

SEEING RED

On 11 February 1996, local 'celebrity supporter' Uri Geller attempted to demonstrate his psychic powers with a half time trick involving the entire Elm Park grandstand displaying either large red or yellow cards. Later, in the second half, those red cards were waving again at Derby County's Paul Williams, and the psychic powers seemed to work on the referee, who sent the visiting captain off for what the linesman described as 'a two-footed Cantona-style kick.' It certainly looked to be nothing of the sort, even the 'victim' Scott Taylor did not seem to realise that he was the recipient of such an assault. Derby felt hard done by and requested a copy of a video of the incident to help their appeal. Unfortunately, when local TV station Meridian's video arrived it turned out not to be of the Reading versus Derby game but a Phil Collins concert.

OLD LES

Les Ferdinand only had a few months as a Reading player for the final 12 games of his illustrious career, but he still set two Club records. They both came in the same match, at home to Coventry City on 16 February 2005. Eight minutes into the game he scored the 170th goal of his career and so overtook **Jimmy Quinn** as Reading's oldest League goalscorer. Minutes later Les acquired a less-wanted record, becoming the oldest of the Club's players to be cautioned in a League game.

TOOTHLESS REF

One referee who caused problems of a different nature was Jack Plummer. A longstanding helper in the Club's early days, he was a member of the Special Effects Committee as well as acting linesman for the Club, prior to the introduction of neutral officials. He also refereed for Reading Amateurs, a Club that came into being when Reading adopted professionalism in 1895. During one game he was asked to look after two players' false teeth. Unfortunately, Jack had to rush off straight after the game to go to the theatre and forgot about returning the teeth. Eventually, they were discovered in the Clubhouse wrapped in newspaper, but that was not until Sunday lunchtime, which was too late for one of the toothless players as he was also the local vicar!

SHORT-TIME REF

Another Reading referee to get into trouble was **Horace Walker**. Originally a Reading player, Horace later acted as secretary and treasurer of the Club until they entered the Southern League in 1894. Horace refereed Elm Park's first game, which was abandoned following a thunderstorm, and was one of the country's top officials. In February 1904 he was in charge of the Aston Villa versus Spurs FA Cup tie that had to be abandoned after 20 minutes play because fans rioted. As a result, Spurs were fined £300 by the FA. Another game abandoned by Mr Walker lasted rather longer. The 1900–01 test match between Southern League Second Division champions Brentford and bottom of the top flight Swindon was played at Elm Park, but after 107 goalless minutes the game was called off due to failing light. In the end it did not matter as Bristol City's election into the Football League meant that both Clubs played the next season in the top flight.

A GOOD JUDGE OF A PLAYER

It was not always referees who cautioned footballers in Reading. On 17 March 1928 two Reading schoolboys played in a trial match at Elm Park, and after scoring twice **Johnny Howlett** was picked to play for England against Scotland. While practising for his big match, Johnny was arrested and charged for playing football in Wantage Road, a street adjoining Elm Park. Fortunately, the magistrate was sympathetic, and he not only dismissed the case but also wished the Reading youngster good luck for the international and gave him 2/6d.

REGULAR SCORER

Reading had a double reason for signing Millwall's **Kevin Bremner** in August 1985. Not only was the all-action forward to play a vital role in that season's successes, but his playing for Reading also stopped him scoring against the Club. During 1982–83, 'Mad Max', as he was known to the fans, had scored against Reading for three different Clubs, Wrexham, Plymouth Argyle and Millwall, his efforts virtually relegating Reading single-handedly that season.

RON'S BENEFIT

Until the 1960s, loyal players would be awarded a benefit match, usually a normal League game rather than a specifically arranged testimonial game. On Easter Monday 1952 Reading's game against Southend United was designated for the benefit of four of the Club's all-time great players, **Les Henley, Ron Moyse, Maurice Edelston** and **Ron Blackman**. For Blackman it turned out to be a benefit in more ways than one. He netted a first half hat-trick before adding another two after the break to become the only player ever to score five League goals in a game against Southend. In addition to that, Ron's third goal was his 100th in the League.

STRANGE START
Reading manager **Ian Porterfield** had a strange start to his career at Elm Park. Appointed on 14 November 1989, his first four games in charge were all against Bristol Clubs and after 10 weeks at Reading his team had played 20 times, seven games in the League and 13 in Cup competitions. The end of his Reading career was equally unusual in that he was replaced by two different caretaker managers before **Mark McGhee** was appointed, meaning that the Club had four managers in the final three weeks of the season.

——————— JUST THE JOB ———————

AT THE BAR
At one time, a retiring footballer's ambitions fell into two categories, to stay in the game on the coaching or managerial side or become a publican. One Reading player achieved both. When Reading sacked **Harry Marshall** just before Christmas in 1920 they handed over the job to the Club's longest serving player, captain **Jack Smith**. This promotion earned Jack an extra £1 a week for his additional responsibilities and he carried on as player-manager until the end of that season before retiring as a player to concentrate on his managerial role. However, Jack obviously found that the role of running a League Club still left him with some spare time so he combined this job with the running of a local pub. In May 1922 he decided that he preferred the licensing trade to football and quit the football Club.

FILLING IN
Reading were to appoint a second **Jack Smith** as their manager, Jack number two being in charge at Elm Park from 1952 to 1955, but he almost never had a footballing career at all. Jack's ambition was to be a dentist, but having completed the lengthy study process he fell ill just prior to his final exam and was persuaded to turn his attention to a rather different career, in football. It proved a blessing in disguise as Jack enjoyed a 25-year career as a player and a manager, the highlight of which was being capped for Wales. Jack could have received international honours a couple of years earlier as he was picked to play for England in 1942, only to discover a few days before his debut that he was born in the Principality.

CRAZY KEEPER
They say that goalkeepers are crazy, and at least one Reading keeper should know. **Dr C.J.H. Burnham** played for Reading in the two seasons leading up to World

War One, but after the hostilities ceased he became one of the most respected physicians in the country, holding the Chair of Philosophy at Edinburgh University and being the surgeon adviser to the Ministry of Pensions.

COWBOY STOPPER

Another keeper who faced a difficult career decision was **Lance Richardson**. Released by Manchester United in 1929, Lance was offered a position in his family's business, but he chose to join Reading instead. When he did finally quit the game Lance joined his family on their Argentinean ranch, working as a 'gaucho', a South American cowboy.

ON THE AIR

Widely regarded as one of Reading's greatest players, inside forward **Maurice Edelston** played most of the 1940s as an amateur, not turning professional until 1947 when he had been with the Club for eight years. Even then Maurice combined his playing career with that of teaching classics at the local Blue Coat School and running, in partnership with playing colleague Gordon Brice, his own sports outfitters in the town. When his playing days were over Maurice used the spare time to become one of BBC's leading sports commentators, having been introduced to the airways by legendary cricket commentator and Reading supporter John Arlott. Specialising in broadcasting on tennis and, of course, football, Maurice was BBC radio's summariser during the 1966 World Cup, including the final. His school teaching duties resulted in him being accorded a unique honour for a footballer as he is surely the only League player to have a library named after him.

READING'S ODD JOB XI

Rab Bernard: Rab became a publican, nothing unusual in that, except that Reading's Southern League keeper was a teetotaller!

Willie Henderson: Willie was another Southern League defender who had three different spells at Elm Park. When he eventually tore himself away from Berkshire he emigrated to Colorado where he became a salt miner.

Jeff Gulliver: Always smartly turned out, Jeff became a hairdressing equipment salesman after his 1950s spell as left back at Reading.

Alec Christie: A member of Reading's very first League team, back in 1920, Alec had previously been a decoder in the Navy.

Roger Russell: Only one appearance in seven years during the 1950s before Roger became an orderly at Broadmoor Mental Hospital where one of his duties was to escort the Kray twins to their mother's funeral.

Andy Bernal: A tough defender in the 1990s, Andy had to use more subtle skills, and fluency in Spanish, as part of David Beckham's support team during his spell with Real Madrid.

Jimmy Lofthouse: A star winger either side of World War One, Jimmy was, appropriately for a 'pint-sized player', also a glass blower by trade.

Jack Cross: Often shown in 1950s programmes as 'Jack Cross BSc', he combined his time at Elm Park with working at the Atomic Energy Research Establishment at nearby Harwell.

Tony MacPhee: A prolific goalscorer throughout the 1940s, Tony trained as an Organ Stop Maker and his precision skills were put to good use during World War Two when he worked in a local aircraft factory.

Dick Allman: Another goalscorer, this time from the Southern League days, Dick was an earthenware printer.

Gary Donnellan: Gary was an early 1980s winger who became a button salesman.

Manager – Roy Bentley: The former England centre forward and popular Reading manager in the 1960s spent part of the war years working at Bristol Zoo as a giraffe keeper.

SUPER SUBS

FIRST SUBS

❂ The first substitute to appear in a Reading game came on during the final match of the Club's May 1913 tour of Italy, when the Italian national squad made a change during Reading's 2–0 victory. However, that was not the first time that the question of substitutions had been raised during a Reading game. As far back as 22 March 1873, during Reading's first 'full' season, Marlow turned up with only nine of their first team present at kick-off, so they made the numbers up with two 'colts'. When the original choices arrived, Reading refused Marlow's request to exchange the players, but the weakened visitors still held out for a goalless draw.

❂ The Club must have also wished that they refused permission for Southampton to use a substitute in the end-of-season Hospital Charity Cup 'friendly' in May 1921. Almost immediately after Elm Park's first substitute had taken the pitch, the anonymous Saint turned sinner, performing a terrible tackle on Reading's **Harold Weston**. Not only did this end Weston's participation in the game, but it also sparked a mini riot and a spell of rough play that culminated in both sides being 'sent off' for a while to cool down.

❀ Reading's first substitute took the field during a wartime friendly against Fulham on 14 October 1939. Early in the match at Elm Park, Reading keeper **George Gale** was injured and had to leave the pitch for treatment. Initially, defender **Jimmy Wallbanks** took over in goal, perhaps because he was once described as 'a dapper little stopper'! However, at half time it became apparent that Gale could not take any further part in the game and Fulham agreed that **Walter Lawrence** could take over in goal.

❀ When the Football League finally allowed substitutes, **Ralph Norton** became Reading's first 12th man, coming on after 52 minutes for the injured **Peter Shreeves** during the first game of the 1965–66 season, at home to Watford. During that season substitutes were only allowed to replace an injured player, although this was not always strictly adhered to, substituted players suddenly developing limps as they were exchanged. Not at Reading, of course, since **Roy Bentley** only used his substitute three more times that season.

❀ The following season tactical substitutes were permitted, with Reading's first such switch seeing **Mick Travers** replacing **John Chapman** at Torquay United, again in the first game of the season.

❀ In 1987–88 the number of substitutes allowed was doubled, and although **Mark White** and **Francis Joseph** shared the League honours when **Ian Branfoot** made a double substitution at Leeds United on 22 August 1987, that was not the first time Reading had used 13 players. The 1970–71 pre-season tournament for the division's top scorers, The Watney Cup, permitted two substitutes, so when **Malcolm Swain** came on late in the game against Manchester United he became Reading's first 13th man.

❀ The current three-substitute limit was introduced for the 1996–97 season and Reading's first 14th man was **Jimmy Quinn** when he came on in the final minute of the game against Oxford United on 8 September. As both teams had used all permitted subs, and the fourth official was used due to an injury to one of the original officials, that was the first time 32 players and officials had taken part in a League game.

SCORING OFF THE BENCH

But back to **Jimmy Quinn**. Not only does he hold the Reading record with seven goals as a substitute, but he was also only the third player to make 100 League appearances as a substitute. On the other hand, Reading's all-time appearance holder, **Martin Hicks**, only made one substitute appearance in his 500 League games for Reading, but at least he made it count, scoring Reading's consolation in a 2–1 reverse at Lincoln City on 17 April 1981.

No Reading substitute has scored a hat-trick, but former Royals loan player **Paul Moody** has achieved the feat twice. In Fulham's final game of 1998–99 Paul came on and scored a hat-trick in just 13 minutes, in what was to be his last game for the Cottagers. Three years earlier he had scored a trio for Oxford United after coming off the bench, that hat-trick taking him only 12 minutes to complete. Maybe Reading did not use Paul properly during his spell on loan from Southampton in December 1992 as all six of his games for the Club saw him in the starting XI!

THE SIXTH SUB

With none of Reading's superstitious players wanting to wear the number-13 shirt for the 2001–02 season, Reading's Supporters' Club approached the football Club for the number to be allocated to the fans. With the Football League's approval, the request was ratified, and since then the squad list has included '13 – Reading Fans'. The supporters even have their own pen picture among the players' details, reading in 2002:

'RFC Fans
Position: Everywhere
Born: 1871
Birthplace: Reading
Height: Huge
Weight: Massive
Appearances: Countless
Goals: Thousands

Ever-present throughout the successful 2001–02 season – and indeed the Club's 131 year history! A versatile player who is equally adept in a fiercely defensive role or a creative attacking position, the number 13 was rewarded with a new one-year contract after showing his (and her) worth throughout last season with a series of inspiring performances both home and away. Is expected to be on top form again this season after a prolonged summer break and is not available for transfer at any price.'

Since the introduction of 'Number 13' Reading have named six substitutes at home games, the Madejski Stadium announcer listing five players and 'Reading fans everywhere.'

STRANGE SUBS

Non-playing captains are a feature of some sports but not football, unless you were at the Sealand Stadium on 27 April 1974. The last Reading game for which **John Hulme** was selected was the final game of the 1973–74 season, at Chester, and the game saw him named as substitute. Despite this, he still acted as Reading's captain and apart from tossing the coin before kick-off he took no part in the match.

Reading can probably also claim to be the only Club to have 'substituted' a manager during a game. At home to Bury on 26 February 1977, Reading were 3–0 down at half time and manager **Charlie Hurley** had seen enough. He symbolically substituted the Club's captain for 16-year-old **Jerry Williams** before leaving the dressing room to hand in his resignation and quit the Club, leaving coach Maurice Evans in charge.

SUBBED SUBS

Since two substitutes were allowed in 1987, 10 Reading substitutes have 'achieved' a unique feat by being substituted themselves. The first subbed sub was **Aaron Pietro Giamettei**, who despite that exotic name was born in Reading. On as a sub at Bradford on 18 April 1992, Aaron was replaced after just another 21 minutes. That was to be the end of his League career that had lasted a total of 54 minutes. Of the other nine only **Robert Fleck** and **Glen Little**, who was replaced after coming on twice in 2005–06, stayed on the pitch more than 30 minutes while **Michael Meaker** and **Jim McIntyre** only managed five minutes each before injury resulted in their removal. Only one subbed sub was for tactical reasons, **Tony Rougier** coming on at Cambridge United on 7 April 2001 but then being replaced by **Nicky Forster**, Reading's most used sub, by **Alan Pardew** to change things again.

FANS' CHOICE

Managers regularly make tactical substitutions, but on one occasion the change was made by the Reading fans. A goal down at home to Oldham Athletic on 21 March 1995, and their play-off hopes fading, Reading's joint managers, **Jimmy Quinn** and **Mick Gooding**, decided to change things up front, their plan being to replace **Stuart Lovell** with **Lee Nogan**. When the Elm Park crowd saw that local hero Lovell was the player about to make way, they howled their protest with such feeling that the managers changed their minds and Nogan came on for Quinn instead. And there was a happy ending for all concerned. First Nogan put Reading level and then, in the very last minute, Lovell was still present to score the winner.

CHANGED CHANGE

Another changed change took place at Elm Park on 20 October 1979. Visitors Exeter City were 2–0 down on the hour so their manager decided to change things round. He signalled to replace their number six, Dick Forbes, but, prior to the days of electronic boards, the number was held upside down and so centre forward number nine Keith Bowker slowly trudged off. It was only the disapproving jeers of protest from the Exeter fans, who, quite rightly, could not understand why their leading scorer was being taken off, that the error was spotted and the correct player was replaced. Again the sub did the business, scoring a late goal, but it was not enough as Reading held on to win 2–1.

READING RELEGATION RIGGED

Some 20 years after the event, the satirical magazine *When Saturday Comes* suggested that a travesty of justice had led to Reading's relegation in 1971. The article reported that in the closing seconds of their game at Tranmere Rovers, Reading netted a winner with the last kick of the game. Unfortunately, the previous drab, goalless 89 minutes and 59 seconds had persuaded the few reporters to leave and so miss the goal. The next day's papers recorded the game as a goalless draw and the League tables reflected just one point for Reading instead of two. The mistake went unnoticed until the summer when the League spotted the discrepancy, but by this time Reading had been relegated. That extra point won at Prenton Park would have saved Reading from relegation, but the League decided to keep quiet about the error and Reading remained relegated. The only action taken was that the League instructed all referees to restart games with a kick-off, even if, as Reading had done, the goal had been netted in the final second. Fans reading the article were initially incensed until they looked at the date of the magazine – 1 April!

AND FINALLY – WE SHOULD NOT BE HERE

This book should never have been written, Madejski Stadium should not have been built, in fact Reading Football Club should not even be in existence. Formed 137 years ago and the oldest League Club south of the River Trent, Reading should not have made it beyond its first 30 years. In 1910 the Club was on the brink. Deep in debt, relegated to the Second Division of the Southern League and with the players picking the team in lieu of a pay cut, the directors called a meeting in the town to raise funds to save the Club. Usually these meetings saved the day but this one produced a mere 12/6d, and at a second meeting a decision was made to wind the Club up. Fortunately, Reading had a resourceful manager in **Harry Matthews** and he somehow kept the Club going. Despite this, the winding up of Reading Football Club was never rescinded, possibly because Mr Matthews 'forgot' to minute the original decision!